J. H. PLUMB

# THE GROWTH OF POLITICAL STABILITY IN ENGLAND 1675–1725

PENGUIN BOOKS

Penguin Books Ltd, Harmondsworth, Middlesex, England
Penguin Books Australia Ltd, Ringwood, Victoria, Australia

—

First published by Macmillan 1967
Published in Peregrine Books 1969]

—

—

Made and printed in Great Britain by
Cox & Wyman Ltd
London, Reading and Fakenham
Set in Monotype Garamond

# CONTENTS

FOR

NEIL McKENDRICK

# PREFACE

THE greatest honour that can befall an English historian is to be invited by the University of Oxford to give the Ford Lectures, and I am very much indebted to the Electors for inviting me to give them in 1965. The version here printed is almost identical with the lectures that I delivered in the Michaelmas Term. In one or two places they have been slightly extended, and they have been pruned of a few slips, noticed by my old pupil and colleague, Professor J. P. Kenyon, who read the typescript. This is not the only debt I owe Professor Kenyon. Over the years I have greatly profited from his insight and knowledge of late seventeenth-century England. Indeed, the lectures owe a great deal not only to him but to many other of my research students who have deepened my knowledge and understanding of the Augustan Age. In particular I am grateful to Neil McKendrick, who has read and commented on each chapter at every stage.

I am also indebted, as ever, to many owners of private collections, as well as to many librarians and archivists. My principal obligations are to the Duke of Portland, the Marquess of Cholmondeley, Earl Winterton, Earl Stanhope, the Earl of Yarborough, Lord Braye, Lord Walpole and Sir George Howard, and to the librarians and archivists of the British Museum, Bodley's, the Leicester Museum, the Lincoln Record Office, and the Herts. Record Office, and, particularly, to Miss Coates of the National Register of Archives.

I also wish to thank Dr Aubrey Newman for reading the proofs, and my secretary, Mrs Pendred, who has struggled with handwriting that is even worse than Robert Harley's. For the errors that have survived their eagle eyes, I am entirely responsible.

My days at Oxford were eased by the warm hospitality that

7

was showered upon me. No one could have been given a kinder or more generous welcome, but I shall always remember with gratitude the generosity of the Warden and Fellows of Wadham College, who put a room at my disposal for the term.

J.H.P.

# ABBREVIATIONS

| | |
|---|---|
| Add. MSS. | Additional Manuscripts, British Museum |
| *Cal. S. P. Dom.* | *Calendar of State Papers Domestic* |
| *Cal. Treas. Bks.* | *Calendar of Treasury Books* |
| C(H) MSS. | Cholmondeley (Houghton) Manuscripts |
| *DNB* | *The Dictionary of National Biography* |
| *Ec. Hist. R.* | *Economic History Review* |
| *EHR* | *English Historical Review* |
| HMC | Historical Manuscripts Commission |
| *JHC* | *The Journals of the House of Commons* |
| *T. R. Hist. S.* | *The Transactions of the Royal Historical Society* |
| *VCH* | *The Victoria County History* |

# A NOTE ON DATES

All dates given are in Old Style, except that I treat the year as beginning on 1 January.

# INTRODUCTION

IN delivering these lectures I had two intentions: one was to attempt to clear up some of the confusion that has been growing in the political history of late seventeenth-century England, the second to reintroduce something that has proliferated in economic, but been at a severe discount in political history – namely a concept, in this case the growth of political stability.

The political historians who grew to maturity before the First World War – Stubbs, Lecky, Freeman, Maitland, Trevelyan, and many others – had no fear of concepts. They discovered in English history the growth of liberty, the development of freedom, of representative government, of a two-party system, of the Cabinet and Prime-Ministership. They traced them happily backwards and forwards in time, casting only a sideways glance at social structure or even at ideology in its precise chronological and social setting. Times have changed. Most of these concepts of political history have been dismissed under the convenient umbrella of Whig interpretation, and the greatest English political historian between the two world wars, Sir Lewis Namier, was preoccupied with the study of a very limited and precise political situation: the structure of the House of Commons in 1761. Political opinion, the political nation outside the House of Commons, the ideology of Whig oligarchy or that of provincial Toryism scarcely interested him. His demolition of the two-party system as a concept for interpreting the political events following the succession of George III was so shattering that not only was that particular concept blown sky-high, but others went with it. Concepts, as methods of interpreting political history, became totally unfashionable. Political historians turned to biographical methods, administrative history, or sheer narrative; social history claimed others, and the history of ideas more. Confusion was general, but the period from 1675 to

1725 fared worst. This was due to both the inherent difficulty of the period and to Dr Keith Feiling.

Feiling, in a profoundly important book, *A History of the Tory Party, 1640–1714* (Oxford, 1924), had laid bare one of its major problems – the strange transition by which the party of Shaftesbury became the party of Harley and Bolingbroke. He clearly delineated the confusions and complexities of William III's reign and stressed the growing dichotomy of party after 1694, and its far clearer definition in the reign of Queen Anne. Unfortunately, in a subsequent volume, he trespassed, as we all tend to do, beyond the confines of his own highly specialized territory and wandered into the reign of George III. He had the folly to call 1760 a watershed in party development. The result was disaster, for Namier not only blasted that view but so lowered Feiling's reputation that young scholars, particularly R. R. Walcott, fascinated by Namier's methods, rushed in to demolish the exceptionally valuable analysis that Feiling had put forward for the earlier period. In 1956, Professor Walcott published his *English Politics in the Early Eighteenth Century,* in which he insisted that the structure of politics of this period was similar to that in the 1760s. His book has been widely used and widely quoted, with the result that confusion now prevails.[1] Although there is much in Walcott's book of value, at least for the expert scholar, it is basically very unsound. Walcott all too frequently mistook genealogy for political history, and creates factions out of family relationships without even considering the political actions, ideas, or attitudes of the men in question; his case-histories are badly chosen, and at times untypical. His failure to consider his analysis in the total structure of politics is little less than disastrous. Also, his narrow chronological limits bred myopia. Two simple but profoundly important facts eluded him. One was that the late seventeenth century witnessed the growth of a large political nation with voting rights. Secondly, more general elections, and more contests at these elections, took place be-

---

1. For example, Archibald A. Foord, *His Majesty's Opposition,* Oxford, 1964, 24 ff., accepts Walcott's thesis quite uncritically. For my own earlier criticism of Walcott, see my review of his book in *EHR,* 1957, lxxii, 126–9.

tween 1689 and 1715 than for the rest of the eighteenth century. Indeed, more general elections took place between 1688 and 1714 than at any other comparable period in the history of Parliament, excluding medieval times. In the seventeenth century a political nation was in ferment, locked in a war for power, with ample opportunities for battle, and whatever their personal ambitions or intentions, politicians had to try to dominate a majority of that active, voting political nation. This could only be done by the attitudes, ideas, and organization of party. Hence the huge output of political party literature, the parade of Dr Sacheverell through the provinces, the concern of men in Norfolk for the fate of the Kentish petitioners, and so on – all these and many more are facts of politics of a higher importance than the relationship of the Earl of Nottingham to Sir Roger Mostyn, which looms so large in Professor Walcott's vision.

There was a need, therefore, to get back to, and build on, the work done by Feiling, as well as to clear away many of the current misconceptions of this period. Also, Feiling was only concerned, in detail, with the Tory party, yet the Whig party was transformed just as dramatically during these years. It divorced itself completely from radical ideology, keeping merely the shibboleth of religious toleration, and became the party not of the freeholder, the yeoman, the artisan, but of aristocracy, high finance, and aggressive commercial expansion. Nor was Feiling interested in the effect of war on English politics, although the effect was profound. The vast wars of William III and Marlborough, and their cost, called into being an executive far larger than England had ever known; an executive, moreover, that was inextricably entwined in the legislature. And the growth of a large executive is as important to the political history of this period as the existence of a large electorate. Both have as yet scarcely been studied.

In the course of six lectures, it proved difficult to deal as thoroughly or as comprehensively as one would wish with so complex a period. Some may cavil at the little attention given both to religious attitudes in politics or to the ideological and historical content of party, but both of these subjects have been, or are being, explored.[2] They were not immediately germane to my major intention, which was to deal with both the broad structure of politics and, more precisely, the development of political stability, a factor that gives this period more than a local English, or even a purely professional, interest.

Political stability is a comparatively rare phenomenon in the history of human society. When achieved, it has seldom lasted. But perhaps one should define political stability: by this I mean the acceptance by society of its political institutions, and of those classes of men or officials who control them. Conspiracy, plot, revolution, and civil war, which have marked the history of most societies of Western Europe in modern times, are obviously the expression of acute political instability. Its momentum will depend on the degree of support that they achieve, and the frequency with which they are repeated. One of the many ironies of history is that political instability in Europe before the Industrial Revolution went hand in hand with exceptional social stability. For the majority of the population knew only an unchanging world in which the patterns of belief, of work, of family life and social habits changed with glacier-like slowness. Wild political conflicts and instability had curiously little effect on this immobility of social habit. But industry, and particularly scientific industry, requires a politically stable world in which to operate with anything like efficiency; so perhaps, as the political world becomes more adamantine in its structure, society itself will be subject to quicker and more violent change. Man's need for action and variety may find its sustenance in quickly changing social habits rather than in the shock and drama of political action.

Whether that be so or not, lasting political stability itself is not a common political phenomenon until recent times; it is certainly far rarer than revolution. It has, however, been much less

2. See G. V. Bennett, 'King William III and the Episcopate', in *Essays in Modern English Church History*, ed. G. V. Bennett and J. D. Walsh, 1965, 104–31. Dr Bennett's forthcoming life of Francis Atterbury will illuminate the relations between religion and politics in this period. For ideology, the article of Quentin Skinner, cited in Chapter One, is of first importance.

studied. There is a general folk-belief, derived largely from Burke and the nineteenth-century historians, that political stability is of slow, coral-like growth; the result of time, circumstances, prudence, experience, wisdom, slowly building up over the centuries. Nothing is, I think, farther from the truth. True, there are, of course, deep social causes of which contemporaries are usually unaware making for the *possibility* of political stability. But stability becomes actual through the actions and decisions of men, as does revolution. Political stability, when it comes, often happens to a society quite quickly, as suddenly as water becomes ice. After all, Mexico had experienced generations of constant political turbulence, but within a decade, the 1930s, achieved stability. Russia, too, had been in turmoil for more than half a century, when it seemed suddenly to acquire political equipoise in the fifties. France experienced frequent political catastrophes and experiments throughout the nineteenth and twentieth centuries, but now appears to have found stability under the leadership of de Gaulle. Such political stabilities have yet to be tested by time, and they may not last. But whatever has brought about such sudden political stability merits inquiry. Stability, like revolution, is a part of social and political change to which Western Europe has been extremely prone this last five hundred years. It seemed to me that a classic example of the process existed in English history. The contrast between political society in eighteenth- and seventeenth-century England is vivid and dramatic. In the seventeenth century men killed, tortured, and executed each other for political beliefs; they sacked towns and brutalized the countryside. They were subjected to conspiracy, plot, and invasion. This uncertain political world lasted until 1715, and then began rapidly to vanish. By comparison, the political structure of eighteenth-century England possesses adamantine strength and profound inertia.[3] In these

3. This, of course, was true only of England, not of Scotland – at least the Highlands – nor of Ireland, nor of the American colonies. Nor did the existence of strong movements for reform in any way imperil the political stability of England in the last three decades of the eighteenth century. There was no powerful demand for the abolition of classes or political institutions, only their adaptation to changing circumstances.

lectures I have tried to analyse the cause for this profound change in the hope that other scholars will probe farther, not only into this particular case-history, but also into other times and other places. We are more than dimly aware of the causation of revolutions; some of the greatest historical minds of many generations have subjected them to fruitful analysis.[4] There is as great a need, if not greater, to study how societies come to accept a pattern of political authority and the institutions that are required for its translation into government. In England, as I hope to show, there were three major factors: single-party government; the legislature firmly under executive control; and a sense of common identity in those who wielded economic, social, and political power.

4. This is particularly true of the English Revolution, which in the last two or three decades has occupied some of our finest scholars, whereas the second half of the seventeenth century has attracted but few.

# CHAPTER ONE

# THE BACKGROUND TO POLITICS IN 1688

By 1688 conspiracy and rebellion, treason and plot, were a part of the history and experience of at least three generations of Englishmen. Indeed, for centuries the country had scarcely been free from turbulence for more than a decade at a time. How to achieve political stability had haunted men of affairs since the death of Cecil. James I, Charles I, Cromwell, Charles II, and James II all failed, and, as we shall see, William III did little better. Neither monarch nor minister was able to create a system of control by which the social, economic, and political life of the nation could be given coherence and order. The necessities of state only occasionally secured a precarious precedence over local needs and private will. Policies were frequently adumbrated both by those concerned with the need for strong government and by those intent on preserving their liberties. For both parties success was usually fragmentary and often transient. Few in 1688 believed that the liberties of the gentry had been firmly secured, and William III himself viewed his own prospects with disquiet.[1] And many who were responsible for his coming were soon hankering after the Stuarts, drawn reluctantly towards those principles of strong government that they seemed to embody – principles that were heightened by the political chaos that followed the Revolution when ministers and ministries, from left, right and centre, toppled and changed

---

1. H. C. Foxcroft, *The Life and Letters of Sir George Saville, Bart., First Marquis of Halifax*, 1898, ii, 203; 'Said [William III] that at the best, they would have a Duke of Venice; In that perhaps hee was not so much mistaken. Said hee did not come over to establish a Commonwealth. Said hee was sure of one thing; hee would not stay in England if K. James came again.'

like a kaleidoscope tossed by a gale. By 1700 England seemed to have escaped the danger of arbitrary government only to succumb to political anarchy. Yet in 1722, England was to survive the most violent financial crisis of its history with throne and Whig party undamaged. In the years immediately following, Walpole enjoyed majorities in the House of Commons that scarcely varied from session to session, majorities that had been unknown in Parliament since the Restoration. Indeed, by the middle 1720s the English political system had begun to assume the air not only of stability but also of historical inevitability; it had become a child of Time and of Providence, an object of veneration, the Burkeian fantasy, and a halo of glory was forming about those muddled, incoherent events of 1688, events that had so very nearly spelt anarchy and ruin to the English nation.

How the political chaos of the late seventeenth century was transformed into the adamantine stability of eighteenth-century oligarchy is an exceptionally complex process that I propose to investigate at greater length in subsequent chapters. In this first chapter, I wish to draw attention to certain long-term factors that were driving English society to a closer-knit political and constitutional structure. Nevertheless, as we shall see, these forces were also encountering many obstacles, many intractable political, constitutional, and even personal situations that frustrated their development. There was no certainty by 1700 that the factors for stability would triumph; indeed, it seemed as if they might fail. Even as late as that date, if looked as if England's development might run counter to the experience of the rest of Western Europe. In contrast to England, the growth of political stability had been a marked feature of seventeenth-century Europe from the Baltic to the Mediterranean – a fact that many contemporary Englishmen understood and deplored.

In seventeenth-century England perhaps the most powerful factor making for social stability, without which political stability would always be an illusion, was the increase in population, erratic though it might be in time and place, combined with the growing diversification of its economic life.[2] In the

2. The question of the seventeenth-century population of England is a highly debatable topic, and will probably remain so, owing to shortage of

1730s Bolingbroke came to regard these years as an age of commercial revolution – a phrase, indeed, that he himself used. From the middle of the century there had been a dramatic growth in trade to America and the Indies; consumption of sugar, tea, coffee, and tobacco soared; new textiles from the East ravished the ladies of fashion and angered the defenders of English woollens, who prophesied the ruin of English economy in such wanton addiction to luxury. The port of London itself handled ever-increasing quantities of trans-oceanic goods for the European market. This constantly growing trade caught the public imagination, and it received more attention perhaps than it deserved from statesmen and administrators who were concerned with its true value to the nation, whether we made a real profit or merely lost gold. And it became entangled in their strategic concepts, for this trade added further dimensions to foreign policy, cutting across traditional dynastic, religious, and European patterns of power. Furthermore, commerce on such a scale required ever-greater conglomerations of capital and more sophisticated financial methods, which involved both the Crown and those very rich men on whom all monarchs had to rely. The more complex trade is, the more involved its financial structure, the greater is the necessity for political stability, a fact well appreciated by the Directors of the Bank of England in 1710 who begged Queen Anne not to part with Godolphin. Good Whigs they might be, and prone therefore to nightmares engendered by Tory financial policy, but they also wished to maintain a Treasurer who had shown his capacity to raise money and control the Commons.

Foreign trade hallucinated the imagination and bemused so many minds that its importance has been overrated. The old patterns of trade – European and domestic – were still the country's life-blood, particularly the latter.

---

statistical data. For what there is, see D. V. Glass and D. E. C. Eversley, *Population in History*, 1965, particularly the following essays: Glass, 'Two Papers on Gregory King'; T. H. Hollingsworth, 'A Demographic Study of the British Ducal Families'; Eversley, 'A Survey of Population in an Area of Worcestershire from 1660 to 1850 on the Basis of Parish Registers'.

Far more influential, however, but less noticed was the steady growth of the home market and the gradual obliteration of local economic isolation. The development of inland navigation, through the canalization and control of rivers, had brought some of the most fertile and productive regions of England within easy and cheap reach of London and the great outports. By 1695 the Great Ouse was navigable by barge to Bedford; this, together with the great drains recently cut to reclaim the Fens, brought the whole of this rapidly developing agricultural area within easy reach of London and the Continent.[3] Yet the growth of river navigation was not easily secured, and often it was impeded rather than helped by England's political system: the Cheshire M.P.s, for example, held up the Weaver navigation from 1699 to 1720.[4] It was only in the 1720s that river navigation Bills secured easy passages through the House of Commons. River schemes and canal ventures met far fewer obstacles in France, where the government took an active interest in their promotion.[5] Cheap water transport, no matter how slowly it was being achieved, led to a greater diversification of economic enterprise among the gentry. It also brought great wealth to the merchant patricians who dominated the seaports and inland towns, not only economically but politically. Men seeking wealth may eye rapid political and social change with far greater tolerance than those who already possess it; these usually covet security. Sir John Turner, merchant, surrendered up the charter of King's Lynn to James II on his knees; with an equal humility he welcomed William III, married his son into the Walpole family, and became a good Whig. His influence – social, financial, political – in King's Lynn was worth as much to him as the Vicar of Bray's benefice. His barges worked the Ouse as far as Bedford and Cambridge; his ships, or rather ships in which he

3. T. S. Willan, *The Navigation of the Great Ouse between St Ives and Bedford in the Seventeenth Century*, Beds. Hist. Rec. Soc. Publ., Streatley, 1946, xxiv.

4. Willan, *The Navigation of the River Weaver in the Eighteenth Century*, Chetham Soc., Manchester, 1951, 3rd ser., 1–21.

5. Willan, *River Navigation in England, 1600–1750*, Oxford, 1936, 14–16, 31, 34–6. There were exceptions; the Harley–Foley group was able to secure a Wye Navigation Bill in 1696, but this was in a session when their Parliamentary influence was particularly strong.

possessed shares, traded from Portugal to the Baltic. To such men as he perturbations of state were an anathema; he would give his consent to any form of government – arbitrary or limited – that seemed to offer good government, ordered finances, and protection of trade. Stability was all his desire.[6]

And, of course, the diversification and strengthening of economic activities touched the active, enterprising gentry as much as it did the merchants. There had been a steady increase in the tempo of agrarian experiment and estate management throughout the seventeenth century. Indeed, the beginnings of the agrarian revolution must be brought forward into the seventeenth century. Much that was regarded by Lord Ernle or Sir John Clapham as new in the eighteenth century – the growing of root crops, the introduction of clover and new grasses, systematic rotation, and beneficial leases – was well established in East Anglia and probably elsewhere by the reign of Charles II.[7] The opening of the rivers, and the consequent growth of coastal traffic, further stimulated agricultural production, helping to create metropolitan markets in cheese, butter, and beer as well as wheat, barley, meat, leather, and root crops. By the 1690s Nottingham ale was on sale widely in London, and by the reign of Queen Anne, Thomas Bass was shipping his beer down the Trent from Burton.[8] This increased local activity created affluence, and affluence expressed itself in the market towns and seaports, as it did with the nobility, in conspicuous building. The centre of King's Lynn with its great merchant houses and splendid

6. J. H. Plumb, *Walpole*, 1956, i, 26; H. L. Bradfer-Lawrence, 'The Merchants of Lynn', in *A Supplement to Blomefield's Norfolk*, ed. C. Ingleby, 1926–9.

7. Plumb, *Studies in Social History*, 1955, 184–7, and 'Sir Robert Walpole and Norfolk Husbandry', *Ec. Hist. R.*, 1952, v, 86–89; E. Kerridge, 'Turnip Husbandry in High Suffolk', ibid., 1956, viii, 390–2; G. E. Fussell, 'Low Countries' Influences on English Farming', *EHR*, 1959, lxxiv, 611–22. For an excellent discussion of agrarian development in seventeenth-century England, see Charles Wilson, *England's Apprenticeship, 1603–1763*, 1965, 141.

8. Wolterton MSS., Account Book of Col. Robert Walpole, fo. 3b. Bottled whisky was already on sale in London, too, at 3*s*. a bottle: ibid., fo. 9b. For Bass, see C(H) MSS., Correspondence.

Custom House was rebuilt between 1660 and 1690. Leicester, an overgrown, walled village of gardens, orchards, and closes with scattered timber-and-mud houses, was being rebuilt in brick in the 1690s; by the 1730s it was filled to overflowing. Stamford, one of the loveliest of English towns, owes much of its beauty to the architectural renaissance that it enjoyed at this time.[9] Indeed, by 1770 there was scarcely a town in the land that had not been almost entirely rebuilt and often doubled in size in the previous hundred years. This rebuilding of English provincial towns on a patrician scale between 1670 and 1770 is everywhere visible, but as yet it has not been studied in the context of economic and social history. Its connexion with the growth of political stability is twofold. Growing prosperity in a wider economic context was creating in so many towns a nucleus of rich men, deeply rooted locally but with nation-wide economic links, who, by the nature of their social standing, were ripe material for oligarchy. Of course, such groups of men were to be found in Norwich, Bristol, Exeter from time out of mind. Naturally, the new ports fertilized by the Atlantic trade were developing in the same way; Liverpool had its tightly locked nexus of rich merchants – the Johnsons, Norrises, Claytons, Clevelands, and Houghtons[10] – and so had Glasgow. Such mercantile élites were, however, now appearing in more unlikely places – Wigan, Derby, Bridport, and Great Yarmouth. And these men of new wealth, whatever their social origins, had far less difficulty in capturing social and political power in their little towns than they would have had in a more complex and industrially advanced society.[11] In the late

9. For King's Lynn and the work of its alderman-architect Henry Bell, see Sacheverell Sitwell, *British Architects and Craftsmen*, 4th ed., 1948, 104. For Leicester, *The Journal of Celia Fiennes*, ed. G. C. Morris, 2nd ed., 1949, 163. In Celia Fiennes's day the new brick-and-stone houses in the Newarke had been built and the Castle refaced; from this time on the pace quickened: *VCH Leics.* 1958, iv. For Stamford, A. Rogers, *The Making of Stamford*, Leicester, 1965, 72–3, 89. The revival of Stamford was due to the Welland being made navigable (*c.* 1673) and the development of the stage-coach along the Great North Road in the reign of Charles II.

10. *The Norris Papers*, ed. T. Heywood, Chetham Soc., Manchester, 1846.

11. Wilson, *England's Apprenticeship, 1603–1763*, 179.

eighteenth and early nineteenth centuries it proved far more difficult for the new industrialists to unseat the established élites. Of course, as we shall see, there were sharp divisions of opinion between them; but after 1714 they dovetailed neatly enough into an oligarchical system.

As important as the growth of new wealth is the effect of this increased economic activity on the gentry. It provided them with innumerable new outlets for economic enterprise – clay-pits, timber sales, gravel, minerals if they had them – as well as a readier market for surplus agrarian production, and for the thrifty, prosperous gentleman of small estate there were far more opportunities, through his attorney, for profitable short-term investment than there had ever been for his father or grandfather. Richard Baxter related how Thomas Foley (true, no gentleman, merely the son of a nailer, Goodman Foley, but soon to flourish as the founder of one of the leading county families of the West Midlands) 'did partly for himself and partly out of charity take to use the monies of many honest, mean people that knew not else how to live or to use it'.[12] As with Foley, so with the squires. They, too, found it easier to raise small sums locally to tide them over their own moments of difficulty, those tem-porary disasters of agrarian life – bad harvest, cattle disease, failure of tenants, a plethora of daughters. In his early youth, harassed by debts due to his heavy family commitments as well as his own and his wife's extravagance, Robert Walpole had little difficulty in raising considerable sums in King's Lynn not only from his rich relations, the great merchant family of Turner, but also from humble women such as Mistress Peatfoote, Mistress Wardell, and Mrs Buckenham.[13] By such small threads the landed gentleman was being increasingly stitched into the new

12. Richard Baxter, *The Catechizing of Families,* 1683, 231.
13. Plumb, *Walpole,* i, 107–8. His father, too, had borrowed various sums from local figures – minor gentry or yeomen – e.g. £300 at 5 per cent from William Ruding in 1690, two separate sums of £100 from Edward Garrett of Westacre (on which he paid only 4½ per cent interest), and £500 from Captain Forster, also at 5 per cent. On his father's death, Walpole consolidated these debts by borrowing £1,000 from a Mr Robinson. All these transactions were carried through by the Walpoles' attorney, Charles Turner of King's Lynn: C(H) MSS., Vouchers.

economic fabric of society; trade, speculation, a venture ceased, at least, to be alien to them. A country gentleman might wish men totally engaged in trading activities to remain in that subordinate role to which he thought they had been ordained by God, but it grew increasingly difficult not to recognize a mutual self-interest with them. And perhaps it is not surprising that Toryism in its most anti-metropolitan form was strongest between 1689 and 1715 in those regions – the South-West, the North-West, and the Welsh Marches – that were economically the most backward, and were least touched by the growth of trade, population, and agriculture. A richer, more affluent commercial society grows by its very nature more complex and so creates the preconditions for stability. Furthermore, this growing complexity of economic activity of the possessing classes was calling into being a new professionalism that further strengthened the process. Because the older universities decayed rapidly after the Restoration it would be wrong to think that the great drive towards increased education had died by the end of the century. Far from it, and the incipient professional classes – the estate agents, farm managers, surveyors, attorneys, etc. – were already numerous throughout provincial society, and more often than not acted as bulwarks between the landed gentry and their ignorance or folly. For every estate that was cheated and swindled by an avaricious attorney there were dozens that were protected and improved by excellent advice.[14] And in the final analysis it was the prosperity and security of the landed gentry that was the first necessity if England was to achieve political stability.

Social and legal processes were also aiding the gentry and

14. Robert Robson, *The Attorney in the Eighteenth Century*, Cambridge, 1959, 73, 84–86. Charles Turner, attorney of King's Lynn, did a great deal of business for both Sir Robert Walpole and his father, including the holding of their manorial courts. He displayed near-genius in his handling of Sir Robert's debts during his early years. His letters are in the C(H) MSS., Correspondence. For the growth of the professions at this time, see E. Hughes, 'The Professions in the Eighteenth Century', *Durham University Journal*, 1952, N.S., xiv, 46–55, and 'The Eighteenth-Century Estate Agent', in *Essays in Honour of J. E. Todd*, ed. H. A. Cronne, T. W. Moody, and D. B. Quinn, 1949.

bringing greater security to their estates. Professor Habakkuk has demonstrated how the development of instruments for long-term mortgage enabled gentlemen both to survive the natural disasters of agrarian life or to undertake improvements that would otherwise have been beyond their means, and how the widespread use of stricter marriage settlements gave greater protection to estates from generation to generation; also, estates tended to grow in size and this in itself provided greater security from the follies of heirs and the disasters of time.[15] Indeed, the growing stability of the landed class is reflected in the steady shrinkage of the land market between 1714 and 1770.[16] A stable gentry obviously encouraged social cohesion and with it the acceptance of established political institutions, so long as they did not act inimically to their interests.

However, these economic, social, and legal factors that were aiding the growth of political stability were very slow to develop. They were adopted by the wary and the prudent, of whom there is no finer example than Sir Robert Walpole's father, who not only took careful account of every screw of buttons that he bought and never purchased a suit of clothes, but also introduced new agrarian techniques on his farms and manipulated mortgages and marriage settlements with great dexterity.[17] There were, however, many gentlemen who were unwary and imprudent, who felt that to be gentlemen they needed to be prodigal, and many of them soon ended up in the hands of the scriveners. Many, too, were badly hit by the sharp depressions of the late seventeenth century, when the correspondence of gentry is full of lamentation about uncollected rent.[18] Yet these factors were constantly building and strengthening pyramids of power

15. H. J. Habakkuk, 'Marriage Settlements in the Eighteenth Century', *T. R. Hist. S.*, 1950, 4th ser., xxxii, 15–30; Mary E. Finch, *The Wealth of Five Northamptonshire Families*, Northants. Rec. Soc., Oxford, 1956.

16. Habakkuk, 'The English Land Market in the Eighteenth Century', in *Britain and the Netherlands*, ed. J. S. Bromley and E. H. Kossmann, 1960, 157.

17. Plumb, *Men and Places*, 1961, 126–8.

18. D. C. Coleman, 'London Scriveners and the Estate Market in the Later Seventeenth Century', *Ec. Hist. R.*, 1951, iv, 221–30; Plumb, *Walpole*, i, 16.

that were bound to secure, sooner or later, a more stable society, even if they were as yet very little connected with the *form* that political stability might take; certainly, there was a drift towards the formation of urban and rural oligarchies, but that was as true of Europe as of England – as compatible with stable absolutism as with stable Parliamentary monarchy. In England, however, the political events of the last half of the seventeenth century were largely at cross-purposes with this general drift; every event seemed to be part of a conspiracy to impose political anarchy rather than political stability – a situation that had baffled thinking men ever since the beginning of the century.

The crux of the problem lay in the difficulty of securing a balanced relationship between these concentrations of local power, whether rural or urban, with the monarchy. In consequence, most practical men of affairs felt a sneaking sympathy for the régime of Louis XIV and Colbert, whose government seemed not only much more stable than their own but more efficient. William Blathwayt, Samuel Pepys, Sir Leoline Jenkins, all wished to see a strengthening of royal authority combined with the technical efficiency that was such a marked aspect – at least in their eyes – of French government. Blathwayt, indeed, as Secretary to the Committee for the Plantations, seized every opportunity to extend the King's authority and to suppress all tendencies towards local individualism. Like Charles D'Avenant, he greatly admired Louis XIV's colonial administration.[19] Perhaps more important than their attitude to authority, however, was their concern for systematic efficiency.[20] We in

19. Charles D'Avenant, *Works*, ed. C. Whitworth, 1771, ii, 32. Naturally, the suspicious country interests not only sensed this Francophilia among courtiers but inflated it into nightmare proportions. After all, one of the main charges against Clarendon was that he intended to introduce arbitrary government on the French model.

20. As soon as William Blathwayt became Secretary at War, he wrote at once to Lord Preston, minister to France, begging to be sent anything in print or in manuscript bearing on the organization of the French Army. He himself made many abstracts of French ordinances. See Gertrude Ann Jacobsen, *William Blathwayt*, Yale, 1932, 223–4. Many of Charles II's ministers had great admiration for Louis's military administration: ibid., 212. For Blathwayt's attitude to the plantations, ibid., 99–100. Of course,

Cambridge have heard a great deal about revolutions in government, but in many ways the developments in administrative efficiency between 1660 and 1715 were (as will be shown below) far more fundamental in moulding both the nature of our constitution and our politics than the schemes of Thomas Cromwell.[21] What Blathwayt, Pepys, and the rest brought to government was a rational approach to their needs as administrators. Pepys wanted systematic knowledge of stores, personnel, state of readiness of ships at Chatham, Portsmouth, and elsewhere, and he set about creating an administrative machinery that he hoped would make these facts readily available. For such men, decisions could only rest on knowledge and mastery of facts; and this could only be achieved by systematic arrangement of communications and by a constant demand for accurate statistics. It is not surprising that both Pepys and Blathwayt should be friends of William Petty and great admirers of his approach to government, or that William Lowndes should make use of Gregory King at the Treasury, or that Petty himself should have been a great admirer of Thomas Hobbes.[22] Many of Charles II's civil servants were drawn into membership of the Royal Society by a sense of their intellectual compatibility with the practitioners of natural philosophy. Both believed that the practical problems of life were best approached through knowledge. Of course, it led them all at times into absurdities, to the pursuit of chimeras, and the statistical approach to the problems of government remained crude, as did the attempt at greater administrative efficiency.[23] But this widespread attitude among

not all politicians were so impressed by the latest developments in France. John Locke's detailed observations of French methods convinced Shaftesbury of the weakness of France's administrative machinery. See John Lough, *John Locke's Travels in France, 1675–9*, Cambridge, 1953.

21. S. B. Baxter, *The Development of the Treasury, 1660–1702*, 1957; A. Bryant *Samuel Pepys*, vol. iii: *The Saviour of the Navy*, Cambridge, 1938; G. N. Clark, *Guide to English Commercial Statistics, 1696–1782*, 1938; J. P. Kenyon, *Robert Spencer, Earl of Sunderland, 1641–1702*, 1958, 90–91.

22. Quentin Skinner, 'History and Ideology in the English Revolution', *Historical Journal*, Cambridge, 1965, viii, 171 n. 129.

23. Of course, what seems wildly incompatible, on an intellectual plane, today, did not seem so to men of the seventeenth century. Shaftesbury, the

royal officials that sound government required a deeper knowledge of political arithmetic, a more intellectual and systematic approach to administration, steadily strengthened the sinews of the State. Throughout the 1670s and 1680s, the core of the government was growing both stronger and more efficient in spite of the wild conflicts of political life. One of the most dangerous aspects of the Revolution of 1688 was that it came near to destroying one of the most efficient systems of government that England had enjoyed since the Tudors. Fortunately, the disasters of war, and the continuation in office of men such as Bridgeman, Lowndes, and Blathwayt, re-established the effectiveness of the central administration, indeed improved on it. And by 1714, Britain probably enjoyed the most efficient government machine in Europe. But that is a complex subject. What I would stress here, in this brief survey of these long-term factors that were creating conditions more favourable than not to political stability, is that there was a far stronger intellectual consciousness of the needs of government in men who wielded social and political power than there had been earlier in the century; William Petty, William Lowndes, Charles D'Avenant, Henry Martin, and the rest were seeking the foundations of good government not in the arrangements and limitations of political power but in the practical arts of administrative efficiency, rooted in practical knowledge. And the growth of a powerful and efficient executive was to prove, perhaps, more important in the development of political stability than the resolution of the arguments between Whig and Tory, or that crushing of the electorate which is a marked feature of politics between 1689 and 1729.

These necessities of state for more informed government, and for greater control of resources, were naturally most readily felt in those departments, apart from the Treasury, that dealt with the Army and Navy. And, of course, they were intensi-

---

friend of Locke, who prided himself on his rationalism, had an unshakeable belief in the power of the stars to influence human destiny. 'He had the dotage of astrology in him to a high degree: he told me, that a Dutch doctor had from the stars foretold him the whole series of his life': Gilbert Burnet, *History of My Own Time*, Oxford, 1833, 1, 175–6.

fied by war. Charles II's wars, however, were intermittent and of short duration, and posited more problems for efficiency and administration than they solved. In marked contrast, the long, complex wars of Louis XIV helped to strengthen the central-ization of his monarchy; Charles II's wars merely aroused the combatant jealousies of his legislature without doing much more than exciting the ambitions of his executive for greater control and effectiveness. In this William III and Queen Anne were luckier; their wars lasted for most of their reigns, and in spite of much hostility from Parliament, the executive steadily streng-thened, until it began to win back the initiative in the House of Commons.

Nevertheless, the forces making for political stability were not aided in Britain, as they were in France and elsewhere, by either the personalities of its monarchs, the image that monarchy evoked, or even by its philosophical advocates. And as for religion, which should have been the major prop of an efficient monarchy, it nearly destroyed it.

Whatever charm Charles II may have possessed, he certainly lacked, in strong contrast to Louis XIV, single-minded dedi-cation to the business of government. It was the unbuttoned ease, the air of summer relaxation that he brought to the monarchy, rather than his sexual licence, that undermined the awe and respect of his courtiers, servants, and supporters and provided so much grist to his enemies and to those who wished to belittle the monarchy. Can one think of Henry VIII, or even James I, sexually driven as they were, pursuing their lusts in the stews of Covent Garden? Would any other king have merely sent into temporary exile a courtier who had handed him verses as obscenely libellous as those given to him by Rochester?[24]

24. *Poems on Affairs of State, 1660–78*, ed. George de Forest Lord, Yale, 1963, i, 424. After considerable obscenity the poem ends:
'I hate all monarchs with the thrones they sit on
From the hector of France to the cully of Britain'.
From Rochester's attacks on Charles II to Pope's on George II one finds a flood of trenchant, bitter, sometimes obscene and sometimes witty verse purporting to expose every imaginable weakness and folly in the reigning monarch: ibid., xxix–xxx.

And the behaviour of Charles II's close associates was not only wanton, obstreperous, and lewd, but also exhibitionist.[25] Charles II's Court, after the Restoration, resembled in tone and manner his Court in exile. It lacked confidence, a sense of grandeur, all belief in its own inevitable destiny. The King and his courtiers were haunted by the thought that they might be back in Brussels, Cologne, Paris, or Strasbourg. This and the air of deceit, the lack of candour about his religion, and the monstrous web of suspicion that his prevarications inevitably created, prevented that sense of identity between monarch and men of affairs that was an essential feature of centralizing monarchy. And monarchy, which elsewhere was a natural focus of absolutist sentiment, was far less effective in Britain. Charles II made both passive obedience and divine right incongruous and uncomfortable; James II made them unpatriotic.

Another unlucky blow of fate for those who preferred strong monarchy as a route to political stability was the fact of Thomas Hobbes. His bleak arguments for a central overriding authority in the State were based on a materialism that repelled the natural supporters of monarchical power in the Church as well as many of the aristocracy and gentry. He brought to the concepts of absolutism the rank smell of atheism; and the upshot of *Leviathan* was to divide intellectual life. The hatred of Hobbesian views is well illustrated by the case of Daniel Scargill, a young Fellow of Corpus Christi College, Cambridge, who was expelled in 1669 for having 'gloried to be an Hobbist and an atheist'.[26] Of course, other writers on politics held similar views to Hobbes and he possessed some admirers, if more detractors, but his attitudes were too intellectual.[27] What Charles II needed was a Burke, a master of emotional rhetoric; as an apologist of absolutist government Hobbes may be regarded as a disaster to his cause. Louis XIV was far better served by Bossuet who, although

25. The brawls, pranks, and follies of Charles II's boon companions may be found in J. H. Wilson, *The Court Wits of the Restoration*, Princeton, 1948.

26. James L. Axtell, 'The Mechanics of Opposition: Restoration Cambridge *v.* Daniel Scargill', *Bulletin of the Institute of Historical Research*, 1965, xxxviii, 102–11.

27. Skinner, *Hist. J.*, viii, 171–3; S. I. Mintz, *The Hunting of Leviathan*, Cambridge, 1962, *passim*.

intellectually inferior to Hobbes, possessed greater stature as a man if not as a writer. Ill served by philosophers – how extraordinarily dingy to have to fall back on the antiquated Filmer – Charles II and James II at least did better with historians, and in the context of history had the best of the argument.[28] So much so indeed, that the Revolution of 1688 led to one of the great falsifications of English history, for Brady's discoveries were useless for the Whig oligarchy. And it is hard not to convict William Petyt, whose views on the Anglo-Saxon origins of Parliament supplanted Brady's, not only of error, but also of deceit. Yet brilliant as the intellectual life of England was at the time of Charles II and James II, it remained, except in polemic theology and satirical poetry, largely disengaged from *authority*; at no time was it systematically organized by or for the State, either to explain, support, or adorn it. Undoubtedly, the materials for a coherent ideology for the support of a strong, centralizing monarchy existed in philosophy, history, and theology. There were men of great literary talent who could have been used in its service.[29] But neither the Court nor the government supported these elements in society. Neither Charles II nor James II or their servants consciously attempted to exploit the arts of their time for the glorification of monarchy. One has only to compare St James's with the Louvre, let alone Versailles or Fontainebleau. Again there is no sense of grandeur; no attempt to marmorealize the monarchy.

In many ways its own worst enemy, the monarchy was not much better served by those institutions that proved the bulwark

28. See J. G. A. Pocock, *The Ancient Constitution and the Feudal Law*, Cambridge, 1957, and 'Robert Brady, 1621–1700', *Cambridge Historical Journal*, 1951, x, 186–204.

29. John Dryden was, but he was exceptional and not entirely reliable. After all he was beaten up in Rose Alley on 18 December 1679, probably by the Duchess of Portsmouth's brother-in-law, in consequence of his satirical references to her. There never existed in England that close contact between the Court and the arts that is such a marked feature of French life at this time. And although Sir Christopher Wren was employed by a succession of monarchs, he was only permitted to patch or add to Hampton Court, never to build a palace. Lack of funds is not a sufficient argument; the monarchy was suffering from a crisis of confidence.

of absolutism elsewhere. The armed forces were too small, too incoherently officered from a Court point of view, to offer much aid. It is true that in James II's short reign he attempted to rectify this, introducing where possible professionally trained officers. He suppressed the militia and expanded the Army, but time proved too short and he was overwhelmed by events.[30] The judicature in the hands of a Scroggs or Jeffreys was reasonably reliable and, of course, was used with deliberate political intent. There is a sharp change in the royal attitude to the judges after 1668, that vital year of decision in which Charles II must have decided to move more determinedly along the path towards arbitrary government. From 1660 to 1668 judges had been granted their office *quamdiu se bene gesserint*; with the appointment of Judge Wilde to the Common Pleas on 16 April 1668 their tenures were *durante bene placito* and the words meant what they said, for Charles II removed many judges. Nevertheless, the Civil War and commotions of the seventeenth century had strengthened rather than weakened the protection given to liberties and freeholds through the triumph of the common law, no matter how inimical they might be to the necessities of the State; and they proved difficult obstacles to royal authority, as James II was to discover.[31] Juries too, proved hard to circumvent. After all, it was the Grand Jury of London who allowed Shaftesbury to die in his bed. Yet it could be argued that the judicature, bent on interpreting the law of treason to the last iota of advantage to the Crown, was the strongest weapon at the service of arbitrary government, although the Church also provided considerable support. The cult of Charles I as King

30. The militia proved to be extremely unreliable from the monarch's point of view in the reign of Charles II. On occasion it refused to act against Dissenters, and hundreds of militiamen deserted to Monmouth as soon as they had a chance: J. R. Western, *The English Militia in the Eighteenth Century*, 1965, 49, 54.

31. A. F. Havighurst, 'The Judiciary and Politics in the Reign of Charles II', *Law Quarterly Review*, 1950, lxvi, 62, 229: '. . . by the end of 1683, after no less than eleven judges had been arbitrarily removed in the course of eight years, the King had a judiciary just about to his liking': ibid., 247; and 'James II and the Twelve Men in Scarlet', ibid, 1953, lxix, 522 ff.

and Martyr had taken quite powerful roots, and fear of Presbyterianism closed the eyes of most clergy to the dangers to their own Church of a powerful Roman Catholic monarchy – most but not all. Even men as accommodating as Tenison were at times subjected to sharp nightmares when Rome loomed over them, threateningly near, a phantom that they dispelled by a well-directed blow at transubstantiation or the Virgin Mary.[32] But fears of Rome leered like gremlins in the superstructure of the State, frightening and troubling men who should have been whole-heartedly for monarchy at its most authoritative. So the long-term forces making for political stability had not the full support of those institutions of government that, in the context of the seventeenth century, were most natural to it. And, of course, in every European country, even indeed where absolutism was most consistently developed, as in France, there were still many factors as well as many institutions making for incoherence and instability. In those England was richly endowed. The two most important institutions were Parliament and local government; far less important but not inconsiderable were two problems – Ireland and Scotland – and an enigma – the City of London. To these must be added the strong individualism created by chartered rights, liberties, and freeholds, all centuries old, and sanctified by law as well as time; nor must the turbulence natural to an agrarian society in which grinding poverty was the lot of most men be forgotten. Finally, there was a tradition of conspiracy, riot, plot, and revolt among the ruling class that stretched back to the Normans. By 1688, violence in politics was an Englishman's birthright.

The key to political instability was Parliament, a medieval institution launched by the Tudors into a world for which it was unfitted. The need to identify the authority of the ruling class with the acts of the Reformation arose out of the Tudors' own lack of a trained professional class of royal officials, capable of controlling and ordering provincial England.[33] So long as

32. Edward Carpenter, *Thomas Tenison*, 1948, 38 ff.

33. See John P. Dawson, *A History of Lay Judges*, Harvard, 1960, 134–45. The powers of the Tudor monarchy always remained very modest. Domestic peace was rare, violence common. 'The English

the Crown, the gentry, and the merchants were involved in social revolution, religious crisis, and external danger, the relationship with Parliament, although often strained, worked. No permanent system of control of the Commons was devised; clientage and the creation of boroughs strengthened the Crown's influence but did not establish it, nor did it give any permanent security to the monarchy. Already in Elizabeth I's reign the Commons were managed with difficulty, and their capacity for intransigence, obstinacy, and violent criticism was frequently and amply demonstrated. After 1601, they were fundamentally out of hand – difficult to screw money from and a hotbed of criticism; no one could manage them for long, neither James I, Charles I, Cromwell, nor Charles II.[34] Before the legislature, the executive was often impotent. Of course, attempts were made to control it: through managed elections – Charles I and Oliver Cromwell both tried that, but to no avail – or through exploitation of loyalty, well warmed with pension and place, and kept steady by a patriotic foreign policy; that too had been tried. Danby, who saw the possibilities of this approach more realistically than any other seventeenth-century politician, also failed. The Popish Plot and the Exclusion crisis blew his party to smithereens, and like so many others he finished in the Tower.[35]

Because of its inability to control Parliament, the monarchy was starved of its necessary supplies in the pursuit of profit and power

---

monarchy emerged from the Wars of the Roses under firm, strong guidance, but inherently it was a ramshackle structure ... a generation later even the reforming schemes of Henry VIII's minister, Thomas Cromwell, failed to obliterate its inherited weaknesses. By continental standards it was one of the shallow little backwaters of monarchy': J. R. Lander, *The Wars of the Roses*, 1965, 33. A. L. Rowse gives a vivid picture of the turbulence of Elizabethan England in *The Expansion of Elizabethan England*, 1955.

34. J. E. Neale, *Elizabeth and her Parliaments, 1584–1601*, 1957, 376–422; W. B. Mitchell, *The Rise of the Revolutionary Party in the English House of Commons*, New York, 1957; H. R. Trevor-Roper, 'Oliver Cromwell and His Parliaments', in *Essays Presented to Sir Lewis Namier*, ed. R. Pares and A. J. P. Taylor, 1956, 1–48. For Charles II, see below, Chapter Two.

35. Andrew Browning, *Thomas Osborne, Earl of Danby and Duke of Leeds, 1632–1712*, Glasgow, 1951, 3 vols.

throughout the seventeenth century. The Scots in Ripon and the Dutch in the Medway were both results of the failure of the executive to exercise reasonable control over the legislature, or get money without it. An unbridled legislature, combined with an empty exchequer, is half-way to political anarchy.

The deep sense of independence, with its attendant suspicion of the Court, that ran through the Commons, was based on the position of the gentry and provincial merchants in local government. The extent of social, political, and judicial power in their hands was formidable; and behind this power lay the sanction of arms, for in the last resort they controlled the militia. As Sir Henry Capel told his fellow squires in the Commons in 1673, 'Our security is the militia: that will defend us and never conquer us'.[36] Local royal officials, apart from the Lord-Lieutenants, had become nonentities, and the gentry, as Justices, bore the whole weight of administration. But their power was more extensive than this; they were very largely their own judges and, as Dawson has shown, judicial investigations and decisions that were properly a matter for Chancery were often delegated to them.[37] Of course, they were subject to supervision: first Star Chamber, then Judges on Assize, could belabour them for incompetence, punish them for tyranny, and exhort them on behalf of the

36. Grey, *Debates*, 1763, i, 218. He moved to vote Charles II's small standing army a 'grievance'. He was strongly supported in this debate. After all, the militia was a natural prop of the Whig gentry, a fact realized by Charles II who purged it in the hope of bringing it under the control of the loyal gentry. Whether or not the Tory militia officers could have got their rank and file to fight except against foreigners is doubtful: Western, *The English Militia in the Eighteenth Century*, 58–61. James II sensibly ignored the militia. Hence the clause in the Bill of Rights 'That the subjects which are protestants may have arms for their defence suitable to their conditions and as allowed by law'.

37. Dawson, *A History of Lay Judges*, 167–71. They were still settling their own vendettas, under the cover of the law, in the early eighteenth century. Sir Thomas Cave successfully arraigned William Barsby, Under-Sheriff of Leicestershire, for denying him votes in the Leicestershire election in 1715. Two of Cave's friends, Sir George Beaumont and Edmund Morris, were appointed by the judges to be arbitrators. They awarded £250 to Cave, who hounded Barsby for the money: Leicester Museum, Braye MSS., nos. 2982–7.

Crown. But only Cromwell and Charles II attempted to reduce their power; both failed. By 1688 the gentry were as deeply entrenched in their neighbourhoods as the baronage of Henry III. And they possessed a like intractable nature: both felt that, if the need arose, they had the right to rebel. The power of the seventeenth-century gentry was sanctioned by violence – riding out against their enemies, hamstringing their neighbour's dogs, beating their farmers' sons, or shooting down their riotous labourers. They played ducks and drakes with the law when it suited them, breaking with impunity what they were supposed to maintain. At Wigtown in 1708 the magistrates were involved with a large gang of smugglers who attacked and wounded the customs officers and seized a large cargo of brandy. Robert Walpole, a J.P. of Norfolk, had smugglers call regularly at his back door at Houghton and even used an Admiralty barge to run his wine up the Thames. He held government office at the time. Justices frequently closed ale-houses for no other reason than that it drove custom to the one they owned themselves. Their quarrels, usually about rights of property, were frequent and bloody.[38] A sea of turbulence washed about the gentry's lives, and they deeply resented any threat to the freedoms that they felt belonged to them as gentlemen. Since the days of the Tudors no government, royal or republican, had got to terms with them. Like Charles I or Charles II, Cromwell had failed absolutely to take the gentry into his control, and so made Restoration inevitable. Charles II's failure nearly toppled his throne. James II's was more complete; they chased him out of his kingdom. To bring the independent country gentry into some ordered relationship with government, or to diminish their role in it, became an absolute necessity if political stability was ever to be achieved. The Bill of Rights, however, underscored their liberties and privileges no less heavily than Magna Carta had

38. C(H) MSS., John Wrott to Robert Walpole, 1 May 1701; Max Beloff, *Public Order and Popular Disturbances, 1660-1714*, Oxford, 1938, 92–106; P. W. J. Riley, *The English Ministers and Scotland, 1707-27*, 1964, 136; Plumb, *Walpole*, i, 121–2, 166; and Baxter, *The Development of the Treasury*, 107. It was estimated that 12,000 inns were closed between 1689 and 1696.

done for John's barons. Magna Carta, indeed, played the part of Moses' tablets of stone in the political beliefs of the gentry. On 11 December 1667, L. C. J. Keeling was bitterly attacked in the Commons for calling Magna Carta 'Magna Farta', which was 'thought to be tending to arbitrary government in the judicature'.[39] And in many ways the Bill of Rights makes more sense if seen in a medieval context of charters than as the corner-stone of the modern constitution. Parliament and the structure of local government were the key problems for centralizing monarchy, but there were others, less powerful but equally intractable, or so it seemed.

Firstly, there was Ireland and Scotland. Only Cromwell, backed by a well-trained professional army, had crushed them into subservience. And once he and his army had gone, the Irish erupted again, creating problems of law and order that necessi-tated a highly professional standing army that Parliament would not tolerate and Charles II could not afford. The Revolution of 1688 made things worse, not better, and opened a fresh era of civil war and rebellion. It seemed unlikely that Scotland or Ireland could be brought to heel without strong monarchy backed by force. And if they were not brought to heel, what government in England could ever feel secure? Cromwell's ruthless policy might solve a crisis, but it could never breed the security requisite for stability. Charles II and James II had succeeded in reducing both the Scottish and Irish Parliaments to complete subservience.[40] Charles II, prompted by Lauderdale, had allowed his mind to drift to the possibility of a Parliamentary

39. Grey, *Debates*, i, 62–63, 67; also Faith Thompson, *Magna Carta, its Role in the Making of the English Constitution*, Minneapolis, 1948. This, it seems, was not the first time that Magna Carta had been so abused. '. . . and when they, with all humility, mentioned the law and Magna Charta, Cromwell told them, their *magna farta* should not control his actions': Edward Hyde, Earl of Clarendon, *History of the Great Rebellion*, ed. W. Dunn Macray, Oxford, 1888, vi, 93. I owe this reference to Professor H. R. Trevor-Roper.

40. 'Never was King soe absolute as you are in poor old Scotland' (Lauderdale to Charles II, 16 November, 1669): *The Lauderdale Papers*, ed. Osmund Airy, 1885, ii, 164.

Union with Scotland.[41] After 1688, however, the Scottish Parliament became far more independent, asserting its rights about trade and succession so emphatically that Scotland became one of the major problems of William's and Anne's ministers.[42] The political systems of both countries had to be firmly dovetailed into the English, if Britain was to be secure. Between 1705 and 1725 this was achieved, permanently for Scotland but for Ireland only for a generation or so; but in 1688 this was not foreseeable.

And there was the enigma nearer at hand: the City of London had long been divided in itself; many of the great merchants who dominated the aldermanic bench were drawn to authoritative and patriarchal concepts of society, and a monarchy *à la française* would have held no terrors for them – indeed, many would have welcomed both Louis XIV and Colbert. The great trading companies – East India, Levant, Africa – depended upon royal charter for their monopolies, and these they wished to preserve against the growing threats of interlopers. Edward Backwell, Sir John Fleet, and others distrusted the Whigs as much as they loved the monarchy. And there were Presbyterians as well as High Anglicans who had no wish to venture on radical courses. Throughout the Civil War and the Commonwealth the City magnates had shown a great suspicion of radicalism among the City's lower middle class. Some of their colleagues,

41. Lauderdale realized that a dependent and solid block of Scottish voters would be to the Crown's advantage. It would also have consolidated his own immensely strong position both in Scotland and England. The Commons realized the former, his colleagues the latter; support for the scheme proved lukewarm at Court: Maurice Lee, Jr, *The Cabal*, University of Illinois, 1965, 50–67.

42. Riley, *The English Ministers and Scotland, 1707–27*, 10–12; also R. S. Rait, *The Parliaments of Scotland*, Glasgow, 1924, 386. The crucial factor was the abolition by the Claim of Right of the committee of the Scottish Parliament called the Lords of the Articles, who prior to 1689 had prepared all legislation for Parliament. William III quickly realized his mistake, attempted to retain the committee, but failed. Ministerial influence in the Scottish Parliament was also seriously reduced in the 1690s. By 1703 the relations between Scotland and England had reached crisis-point and the possibility of an invasion of Scotland by English forces had occurred to Godolphin.

however, were less happy about the *status quo* and they looked with longing at the power and security of their Dutch cousins in Amsterdam. Also, the lesser merchants, who played a conspicuous, if not a dominant, role in the Common Council, were as suspicious of the monarchy as they were of some of their own aldermen. They had helped to purge the City government time and time again in order to support first Parliament, then the Army, and finally Cromwell.[43] Throughout the Commonwealth their power had grown and the Restoration did not deprive them of their political voice; indeed, the City was more democratic in 1660 than it had been in 1640 or was to be in 1730. Nor were the smaller merchants without leaders – Papillon, Ward, Pilkington – who all suffered severely for their opposition to the surrender of London's charter in 1681, and were as convinced of the iniquity of French absolutism as Colonel Birch, Sir John Maynard, or John Wildman. At critical times for the government the anti-royalist forces in the City were able to sway decisions. The monarchy never achieved control of the City. It protected Shaftesbury, and the savage persecution of Ward, Papillon, and Pilkington is a measure of Charles II's fury.[44] Political control, however, was not the only problem with regard to London that remained unsolved. The financial relations between the monarchy and the City, or rather between the central government and the City, for it was equally true of Cromwell, had never found a satisfactory basis. Without the financial resources of the City no government could hope to survive, but the relationship was ambivalent, subject to suspicion and extortion, and totally unsatisfactory.

As well as finance, there remained also the question of policy: men of business, great or small, were aware that government policy deeply influenced their prosperity; they wanted a sound monetary policy, although what it should be baffled them, and naturally they wished to pursue an aggressive economic policy in relation to the world's trade, although here again the situation

43. Valerie Pearl, *London and the Outbreak of the Puritan Revolution,* Oxford, 1961, 274–5, 283. There is a great need for a study, such as Miss Pearl's, of London at the time of the Exclusion crisis.

44. D. Ogg, *England in the Reign of Charles II,* Oxford, 1934, ii, 636–8.

was not simple, some merchants still fearing the Dutch more than the French. But in pursuing profit and power Cromwell had proved more reliable than the Stuarts, for Charles II's addiction to the French troubled many merchants as much in their pockets as in their consciences. In order to achieve political stability, London needed to be tamed, neutralized, or wooed. Although it played less part in the Revolution of 1688 than in any other upheaval of the seventeenth century, the implacable hostility towards the Stuarts of the majority of those Londoners who exercised political and social power in the City had been a major factor in their repeated defeats, and indeed rendered easy the accession of William and Mary. But even so, the City continued to present grave difficulties to any government, because like so many institutions in England's political life it was basically inimical to direct control, whether Whig or Tory or a mixture of both. Xenophobic, greedy, unsophisticated, and obstinate, the politically-minded citizens of London could be as suspicious of authority as the squires of Wales.

These institutions, therefore, presented the major obstacles to the growth of political stability, and their relationship with the central governemnt had to be solved *politically* before Walpole was able to enjoy and the Pelhams inherit the years of political peace that are the hall-mark of eighteenth-century politics – at least up to 1765. There were also minor problems, but difficult ones – the question of Dissent, for example. Charles II had failed to establish a truly national Church either by comprehension or repression, and his own policy of toleration had proved unacceptable to his subjects. His solution was forced on the gentry by the events of 1688, but the nature of the religious toleration that was granted became first-rate tinder for political passion, and the problem of Dissent was no less acute, no less divisive after the Revolution than before; only the Catholic question had been solved by James II's flight and William III's accession.

Less obvious, and more difficult of solution, was the whole question of freeholds and liberties, a matter that James II had made worse by his attacks on the universities, the Army, and the Navy. A university fellowship, a commission in the Army or Navy, a benefice in the Church were considered to be free-holds, to be property. The whole experience of the seventeenth century had added limpet-like strength to men's attachment to such possessions. And England was littered with them, myriad marks of status, of possession, of profit: stewards of hundreds, precentors of cathedrals, beadles of corporations. Usually these offices were held for life and they all enjoyed standing and status within the community they adorned; most of them carried a vote. Such freeholds bred independence, truculence, a willing-ness to fight and litigate that bordered on neurosis, and yet when they conglomerated, as in the universities, the cathedral cities, and the Parliamentary boroughs, they could build up into formidable heaps of political influence. Difficult to discipline, secure in their self-importance, their holders, with the gentry, became the leaders of political opinion outside London and the great towns, an opinion that proved easy to influence – through newspapers, pamphlets, and ballads – but hard to manage. Yet if Britain was ever to enjoy political peace, it was necessary to harmonize their interests with those of the national government; or, at least, to give them that sense of security of which the policy of the Stuarts, and indeed of Cromwell, had deprived them.

Such men, simply because they possessed vested interests, were potentially manageable. These men, with the landowners and merchants, great or small, were the men of property for whom John Locke wrote his 'Two Treatises', the necessary nerves and sinews of the State.

The perturbations of politics in seventeenth-century England, however, had called into being a wider political nation than this, and one far less easy to control. Inflation in the sixteenth and early seventeenth centuries had reduced, almost to triviality, the property qualification – a 40s. freehold – of voters in the county electorates, which brought the Parliamentary franchise not to hundreds but to thousands of small farmers, shopkeepers, craftsmen, and owners of modest freeholdings. At the same time the growth of the population, although slow, had increased the number of men qualified. The same is true of the boroughs with wide franchises – Bristol, Norwich, Hull, Coventry, Nottingham, Exeter, and the rest. Often two to three thousand men now possessed a vote. This would have been of little consequence had their betters lived in harmony, for elections could have been managed without consulting them, as, indeed, at times they were. But throughout the seventeenth century the gentry were deeply divided on a plethora of issues, as were the merchants and professional men of the large corporate towns. Naturally, they tried to use the electorate as a weapon in their battles. The consequence was a huge outburst of contested elections the like of which Parliament had never known. During 1690 nearly four thousand voters polled in Norfolk and the number steadily rose, reaching about six thousand by 1710. Norfolk was contested at almost every general election from 1679 to the death of William III. Essex differed little from Norfolk; the number of voters was somewhat fewer – about four thousand – but they went to the poll seven times in twelve years in William III's reign. Many other counties had similar electorates and similar experiences. In the large towns there was a similar increase; this increase in votes is very marked between 1689 and 1715, and is a measure both of party strife and of political awareness.[45] After all this was a time when, according to the demographers, the population was static. If one remembers the comparative smallness of the population at this time, extracts from this the women and children and, of course, the labouring poor whom no one considered

45. Plumb, 'Elections to the House of Commons in the Reign of William III' (unpublished Ph.D. thesis, Camb. Univ. Lib.), 64. The numbers voting in Norfolk for a few selected contests between 1689 and 1715 are as follows:

| 1689 | Sir William Cooke, Bt. | W. | 1,995 |
| | Sir Henry Hobart, Bt. | W. | 1,798 |
| | Sir Jacob Astley, Bt. | T. | 1,670 |
| | Sir Roger Potts, Bt. | T. | 1,153 |
| 1698 | Sir William Cooke, Bt. | W. | 3,107 |
| | Sir Jacob Astley, Bt. | T. | 2,960 |
| | Sir Henry Hobart, Bt. | W. | 2,244 |
| | Lord Paston | T. | 1,987 |
| 1710 | Sir John Wodehouse, Bt. | T. | 3,216 |
| | Sir Jacob Astley, Bt. | T. | 3,200 |
| | Ashe Windham | W. | 2,783 |
| | Robert Walpole | W. | 2,397 |

worthy of political rights, then the number taking part in politics at election times in these constituencies is very impressive. The total number of voters is very difficult to estimate, but a conservative figure for William III's reign would be about 200,000 – perhaps one-thirtieth of the entire population. An electorate, therefore, for the first time in English history, had come into being. This new political nation proved very mettlesome, very contrary, very fickle in its moods; above all it helped to give substance to parties and give them added power. As Charles II and James II realized, until this electorate was reduced, subjected, or prevented from voting, there was no hope whatsoever that England would achieve political stability. The battle to control this new electorate is a vital issue in this period, to which I shall return again and again. It called into being new methods of propaganda and electioneering; it was subjected to vicious attacks by the Crown and to subtler forms of corruption and manipulation by the aristocracy and gentry. Its subjection was a prime necessity either for arbitrary government or rule by oligarchy.

In addition, some would add, as a final factor in the creation of political instability – tradition. The fact that Englishmen had for centuries rebelled against kings and ministers, conspired and plotted against them, risen often in riot and violence, had so conditioned them to a life of political instability that change might prove almost impossible. Traditions are quickly bred and quickly destroyed and they snap suddenly in a world of rapid social change. Historians too often think of rapid social change as creating conditions of turbulence; but societies can move as quickly into stability as into revolution, and between 1688 and 1725 Britain did just that. And traditions changed just as rapidly: by 1730 Englishmen were congratulating themselves on their tolerance, on their capacity for political compromise, on the preservation of their liberties. In 1688, however, it seemed as if the forces of political instability had won, for the Revolution had been undertaken by those forces in society that were thoroughly opposed to strong executive government. For the Revolution of 1688 was a monument raised by the gentry to its own intractable sense of independence.

CHAPTER TWO

# PARLIAMENT PRESERVED

THE House of Commons was the bugbear of politics. Reformed or unreformed, no one could manage it. James I fumed, spluttered, and roared at it – all to no avail. He considered its reform very seriously but was too wise to attempt it. Charles I did better by ruling without it for eleven years; but for the crass folly of his Scottish policy, he might have dispensed with it for good. Back at Westminster, Parliament soon showed its mettle; after a brief honeymoon of comparative unanimity, the Members were quickly at loggerheads with each other; within a few years they were quarrelling with the Army as bitterly as they had formerly with the Crown. Purged to the point of ridicule, their intransigence remained. And Cromwell did little better with Parliaments of his own devising. Like their predecessors, they were full of squires, and squires detested governments.[1] Naturally, the Restoration brought a short period of harmony, although this is perhaps somewhat illusory. Reports of the Commons' deliberations at this time are scarce, but we know that in 1660 Lord Wharton had a well-drilled regiment of Presbyterians in opposition; they were organized by counties, each company headed by an experienced Parliamentarian. It would have been surprising if they had held their peace.[2] Within six years what harmony there may have been had broken down and discord reigned in its place. By 1670 the Commons had the bit between their teeth, and it was not long before they were hell-bound for chaos.

Yet viewed from the back-benches, or the country houses of Wales or East Anglia, or even from the taverns of London, it was not the truculence of Parliament that men feared but its

1. Trevor-Roper, 'Oliver Cromwell and His Parliaments', in *Essays Presented to Sir Lewis Namier*, ed. Pares and Taylor, 1–48.
2. G. F. Trevallyn Jones, 'The Composition and Leadership of the Presbyterian Party in the Convention', *EHR*, 1964, lxxix, 307–54.

weakness. Its life to them seemed to be far too precarious and desperately in need of stronger protection. So greater control of Parliament by the executive or greater independence from it became the crux of politics. The battle for Parliamentary independence was fought at many levels, and, to the nervous squirearchy, the executive seemed to possess the heavier armament. The Crown's prerogative rights in relation to Parliament were formidable. In 1660 Charles II could prorogue and dissolve Parliament at will. He could summon it wherever he wished, and he could veto its Acts. A few years later his powers were increased. In 1664, very early in the Parliamentary session, the Triennial Bill of 1641, which had been regarded as the keystone of Parliament's independence, was repealed. Once again the monarchy could rule without Parliament so long as it had the money to do so. Charles II was cock-a-hoop at his success, achieved before the laggard country gentlemen had reached Westminster. He boasted that he had shown the world that England was a monarchy again. The opposition, which had constantly grown with each Parliamentary stage of the repeal, thought differently: for them it was 'farewell Magna Carta'.[3] Furthermore, these prerogative rights of the Crown, whether age-old or reasserted, were justified by the growing sophistication of historical studies. As academic supporters of Charles II foraged among the historical records in the Tower of London, they discovered the origins of Parliament to lie not in the Anglo-Saxon forests but in the grace of the Plantagenets. Parliament, they loudly proclaimed, did not exist of *right*, but of *grace*. To the opposition this smacked not of history but of arbitrary government.

Against the constitutional powers of the monarchy Parliament had, however, one supreme weapon – money. It was quite impossible for Charles II to exist without Parliamentary aid,

3. Caroline Robbins, 'The Repeal of the Triennial Act in 1664', *Huntington Library Quarterly*, San Marino, Calif., 1949, xii, 121–40. A Declaratory Act was passed in its stead that required the King to hold a Parliament every three years, but there was no sanctions clause and both Charles II (March 1684) and James II (November 1688) ignored this provision: J. P. Kenyon, *The Stuart Constitution,* Cambridge, 1966, 361.

so long as wars and rumours of wars abounded; so Parliament had to be called, or kept in being, and his prerogatives were merely of tactical value to him. Strategically, they were of little importance, unless he were to make himself financially solvent – a most unlikely prospect. Over the long term the control of Parliament could be achieved in three ways: by building up a Court party powerful enough to dominate the Commons among those elected; by making certain of obtaining a Court-tied majority through electoral management; or by a mixture of both methods.

A great deal of attention has been paid to the organization of the Court party; less to that of the opposition.[4] Naturally, places, pensions, and honours were used by the Court, but so was skilful persuasion and management. The latter was probably on a geographical basis. A reliable county leader, usually a dependable place-holder, would have his lists of sympathizers. Often Members of Parliament for a particular county had a favourite tavern; for instance, the Herefordshire Members met at the Blue Posts in Chancery Lane, the Cornishmen at the Fountain in the Strand, the men of Lancashire at the Swan, Billingsgate.[5] Doubtless there were professional groups, too, of lawyers and merchants. The formal organization of the Court party remained very rudimentary. Even with a liberal use of money, promises, and regal attention, such methods proved unsatisfactory. They were partly vitiated by the factional strife at Court: Clarendon was always hated; the antipathies of the Cabal were far stronger than their sympathies; Danby, who came nearest to success, was never popular with the pro-French group or with the young 'chits'. Yet, combined with the use of

4. Browning, 'Parties and Party Organisation in the Reign of Charles II', *T. R. Hist. S.*, 1948, 4th ser., xxx, 21–36; E. S. de Beer, 'Members of the Court Party in the House of Commons, 1670–8', *Bulletin of the Institute of Historical Research*, 1934, xi, 1–23.

5. C. H. Collins Baker and Muriel I. Baker, *The Life and Circumstances of James Brydges, First Duke of Chandos*, Oxford 1949, 41. These meetings of Members from a particular county were to have a long history. '. . . dined with Lord Derby amongst our Lancashire members at the Swan, Billingsgate, all full of interest for members' (Thos. Johnson to Richard Morris, 24 March 1701): Liverpool Public Library, Norris MSS.

royal prerogative, this method helped Charles II stumble along. Both he and the Court realized that the problem of Parliamentary management went deeper than this. Clarendon looked back wistfully, if perhaps mistakenly, to Cromwell's reforms; so, oddly enough, did those who opposed him.[6]

The heart of the problem was, of course, the electorate. The anti-Court interest was as fully aware of this as the Court, and to protect the electorate, and if possible extend it, was one of their major concerns, just as it was the Court's to try to control it and diminish it. In this struggle, however, the opposition had considerable success.

The growth of the electorate in the seventeenth century has never been remarked upon and little attention has been given to the struggle that it provoked. Yet without a realization that the electorate grew very rapidly, the politics of the later seventeenth and early eighteenth centuries lose their meaning. It is because historians such as Walcott have largely ignored the constituencies that the history of party is in the sorry mess that it is. A big, politically conscious electorate that could sway power first one way and then another is a unique feature of English politics from 1660 to 1715 and, of course, is the reason for the vast proliferation of political propaganda of this period. So, as we shall see, when Charles II and James II came to remodel the corporations, it was but the last act of a long battle. The struggle to control the electorate involved far more than Parliament and the Court. It touched the entire political nation; on its resolution depended the pattern of power in the counties, cities,

6. For Clarendon's organization of the Commons and also that of Arlington of the Cabal, see *English Historical Documents, 1660–1714*, ed. Andrew Browning, 1953, 229–36; also Lee, *The Cabal*. For Danby, see Browning, *Thomas Osborne, Earl of Danby*, i, 191–7, 206–7; iii, 71–120. Professor Browning printed in these pages various working lists of Danby and his helper, Wiseman. They need to be treated with the utmost caution, as more frequently than not they are the over-sanguine hopes for a session and contain names such as Sir Henry Capel, who was consistently in opposition. They need a far greater critical apparatus than has at present been provided for them. Nevertheless, they give a good idea of the Court's methods and the unwearying attention required to keep even a modest number of M.P.s loyal to the Court. Also in these lists there is no hypocrisy about the value of pension, place, or honours.

and boroughs. So long as there were two groups of men fighting for the control of the franchise in the Parliamentary boroughs, there could be little hope of political stability, nor could there if the franchise favoured those elements among the country gentry who were becoming increasingly dissatisfied, possibly through growing economic difficulties, with Charles II's government at the turn of the 1660s.[7]

During the Tudor Parliaments the nature of the electorate was not an issue of great importance; indeed, the methods of election varied very widely, but the voice of the commonalty was rarely heard, and when heard, disliked. In 1489 the right of Leicester's citizens either to vote in a Parliamentary election or to express themselves on local assessments was expressly forbidden by Act of Parliament, and the right of election restricted to the corporation who, although capable of an occasional flicker of independence, more often than not docilely accepted the nominations of the Chancellor of the Duchy of Lancaster.[8] Contests in the old-established boroughs were rare, even though conflict between patrons did occur. Frequently, boroughs, great and small, were content to evade the payment of wages by allowing the nomination to be taken over by the local gentry. And the number of Elizabethans who ever voted at a Parliamentary election must have been quite small.[9]

7. Kenyon, *The Stuart Constitution*, 387.

8. Mary Bateson, *Records of the Borough of Leicester*, 1905, iii, 359. The corporation's bravest act was to refuse to elect Thomas Beaumont in 1597 on the grounds that being an encloser himself, he was unlikely to redress that evil when practised by others: ibid., 337. Northampton's franchises were likewise restricted.

9. J. E. Neale, *The Elizabethan House of Commons*, 1949, 140–61. For quarrels between the Earls of Huntingdon and Leicester Corporation, ibid., 171–6. See also Plumb, 'Political History, 1530–1885', *VCH Leics.*, 1954, ii, 106–7. In 1593 Charles Dymock, the uncle of Sir Edward Dymock, was made freeman of Lincoln with a view to representing them in Parliament on condition that he did not ask for wages: HMC, Lincoln MSS., 74. In 1620, the governing body at Nottingham voted 17 to 6 to invite 'two foreigners' to represent them, on the grounds that 'the greater part of this company do hold it convenient that two foreigners be chosen for the time to serve in this Parliament for the easing of the town's charge': *The Records of Nottingham*, ed. W. H. Stevenson, 1900,

But once the Commons had secured the right to judge controverted elections, the question of franchise acquired a new importance which increased as borough after borough drew away from the direct tutelage of its courtier patron and became a battleground between Court and country or between rival factions among the gentry. There is a marked change in the attitude towards the nature of the Parliamentary franchise after 1620, particularly among those lawyers who were critical of the Crown. It is John Hampden who is in the forefront of the struggle to secure the revival of ancient boroughs, and when they were revived, he demanded the widest possible franchise for them. And it is he, and his friends, such as Eliot and Hakewill, who are constantly pressing for the widest possible interpretation of the franchise in every controverted election, and controverted elections cease to be rare; indeed, they became very numerous after 1620. Time and time again the Commons decided on the widest possible construction of the right to vote. In 1624, at Cirencester, there was a dispute about the nature of the franchise, and the Committee of Privileges came, according to Serjeant Glanville, to the following decision, which was accepted by the House and reluctantly by the Crown:

there being no certain custom nor prescription who should be the electors and who not, we must have recourse to common right which, to this purpose, was held to be, that more than the freeholders only ought to have voices in the election; namely all men, inhabitants, householders, resiants within the borough, . . . [and] that the agreement of competitors, or any others, cannot alter the law, or make an election by freeholders only, lawful; where the same ought to have been by all the inhabitants, householders and resiants.[10]

---

iv, 373. There were five candidates in 1621, nine in 1623 (including the lawyer John Selden). In 1625, the corporation reverted to townsmen, but the cost presumably proved too burdensome, for on 20 November 1627 they again decided, with only two dissentients, that 'two gentlemen of the country [i.e. Nottinghamshire] shall be chosen for easing the town's charges' and they settled on a Cavendish and a Pierrepoint: ibid., iv, 387; v, 129 (ed. W. T. Baker). There are many other examples of corporations turning to the gentry at this time; they were, of course, encouraged to do so by the gentry themselves.

10. John Glanville, *Reports*, 1775, 107–8. During the 1623–4 Parlia-

In the same years the Commons, when considering the case of Chippenham, decided that even a royal charter could not deprive a freeman of the vote had he exercised it in previous elections; indeed, their resolution of this occasion is exceptionally radical, for it defined 'the general liberty of the realm, that favoureth all means tending to make the election of burgesses to be with the utmost indifference; which, by common presumption, is when the same are made by the greatest number of voices that reasonably may be had, whereby there will be less danger of packing or indiscreet proceedings'.[11] These decisions secured a large electorate in about thirty-five Parliamentary boroughs, and an electorate that constantly grew with the growing urban population of the seventeenth century. The group in the House of Commons, led by Eliot and Hampden, finally persuaded the Commons Committee for Elections to accept a resolution that 'the election of burgesses in all boroughs did of common right belong to the commoners and that nothing could take it away from them but a prescription and a constant usage beyond all memory to the contrary'.[12] In borough after borough a struggle begins to shape between those who demand a wide franchise and those who wish to see it limited to a few rich men of power; sometimes the leaders of the movement for a wider franchise are the gentry of the county, sometimes they are leaders of the Puritan movement within the boroughs, who were backed in the Commons by Eliot, Hampden, Hakewill, and Pym. It is clear that the struggle was helping to polarize that division within the governing class that was to lead to the Civil War, and in 1640 petitions about controverted elections rain on the House of Commons; time and time again the question is one of franchise, and time and time again the decision goes in favour of

---

ment, the Committee of Privileges several times insisted that a royal charter could not alter the Parliamentary franchise established by custom. This collection, in which the rights of freeholders to vote were constantly reiterated, was edited and published at the beginning of the first movement for Parliamentary reform. Interest in the rights of freeholders had been made a matter of public and historical debate through John Wilkes and the Middlesex election: ibid., lxxxv-lxxxvii, 66-7, 191-2.

11. John Glanville, op cit., 55.
12. *JHC*, xvii, 143.

the wide rather than the narrow franchise.[13] As we shall see, all opposition from the reign of James I to Queen Anne wanted to extend the franchise, and most ministries wanted to restrict it.

Irritated by the behaviour of Parliament, both the Levellers and the Army grandees developed strong views on the necessity of Parliamentary reform, which embraced both the franchise and the distribution of seats. Naturally, the Levellers demanded a greater increase in the electorate than anyone else: all but servants (in the seventeenth-century sense) and those in receipt of alms were to be given the vote. A few extremists even talked of universal suffrage. But the Levellers, like James I, wished to see a drop in the number of representatives, as did the grandees, who of course demanded a far higher property qualification for voters; yet even their proposals envisaged a considerable increase in the electorate. The most singular aspect, however, of the reforms carried through by the *Instrument of Government* and the *Humble Petition of Advice* was not only the sharp reduction in the number of M.P.s, but also in the proportion between members for counties and boroughs. Urban representation was drastically reduced and about three-quarters of the Commonwealth Parliaments were composed of county Members. No wonder they proved intractable. It is important to stress, however, that elections to these Parliaments involved more of the nation than ever before, and it should be remembered that a taste of political power, no matter how brief, was given to yeomen, craftsmen, and men of the middling sort. The decision of Richard Cromwell to call a Parliament according to the ancient constitution was of momentous importance.[14] The sharp in-

13. A few examples must suffice. During the Long Parliament the following boroughs were granted a wide franchise by the decision of the House of Commons: Honiton and Ashburton (revived in 1640), Great Bedwin, Cambridge, East Grinstead, King's Lynn, Leicester, Mitchell, Northampton, Reading, Tewkesbury.

14. For a full discussion of the changes made in Parliamentary representation during the Commonwealth, see Vernon F. Snow, 'Parliamentary Re-apportionment Proposals in the Puritan Revolution', *EHR*, 1959, lxxiv, 409–92. The full returns of Richard Cromwell's Parliament do not exist, and there may have been some minor differences between it and the Parliamentary franchise of 1640. For example, Wisbech returned John

crease in the number of M.P.s was bound to make the problem
of control more difficult, and the diminution in county membership and the restoration of the beggarly sea boroughs did not, of
course, work to the advantage of the Protector. Many of them
were firmly in the hands of the gentry.[15] Yet the independence of
Parliament still seemed to many men in politics to be linked with
the necessity for a wider franchise. The old constitution might
protect their interests, but they realized also the necessity to
strengthen them, and as soon as they had a fresh chance they set
about doing so.

The Convention Parliament of 1660, again elected in accord-
ance with the ancient formula of 1640, still favoured wide rather
than narrow electorates in the cities and boroughs. It confirmed
large franchises in twelve cases before it was dissolved.[16] The
Cavalier Parliament of 1661, taking its cue from the Court,
behaved quite differently and put the process in reverse. Unless
presented with evidence that was impossible to ignore, the
Commons Committee for Elections plumped for a narrow
franchise in all controverted elections.[17] The danger had been

Thurlow in 1658; in 1640 Wisbech had not been enfranchised, but then
every Parliament from 1601 to 1640 had witnessed new or revived representation and the franchise was not as fixed in 1660 as it was by 1689.
In essentials, however, Richard Cromwell's Parliament was based on the
old franchise.

15. The major result of the elections for Richard Cromwell was an
immediate conflict between the country gentlemen who dominated this
Parliament and the Army leaders.

16. *JHC*, viii, 40, 21 May 1660. 'The Mayor of Chichester was this day
called to the bar of the House: and kneeling there, Mr Speaker did let
him know that the House had evidence of the return by him made for the
city of Chichester and they looked upon his carriage as wilful contempt,
having refused to admit the voice of the commonalty to make election.'
The Commons decided for a wide franchise for Tavistock, Ludgershall,
Great Yarmouth, Heydon, Great Bedwin, Higham Ferrers, Plymouth,
Chichester, Northampton, St Ives, Clitheroe, and Helston. Several
returns were still undecided at the dissolution: ibid., 12, 33, 35, 42, 55, 59,
70–71, 90, 177.

17. In 1661 the following boroughs were declared closed: New Wind-
sor, Lincoln, Truro, Tavistock, Clitheroe, Ludlow, Bewdley, and
Sudbury: ibid., 292, 357, 373, 414–15. However, two boroughs, St
Albans and St Ives, retained their enlarged electorates: ibid., 336, 351.

realized by Clarendon. Indeed, before the elections of 1661, the Secretary of State had written to the corporations advising that the franchise should be limited whenever possible to the mayor, aldermen, and common councillors, usually newly appointed royalists.[18]

Further proof of the Court's fear of large electorates can be seen from the nature of the charter granted by Charles II to Newark in 1673 by which the borough was enfranchised. The right to vote in Parliamentary elections was kept firmly in the hands of the mayor and corporation. Newark's charter was, however, another tactical move in the battle to control the composition of the Commons, a kite flown to see if Charles II might emulate Elizabeth I or James I by the creation of new Parliamentary boroughs and so secure, if need be, an increased base for the Court party. The kite, however, flew badly. The Commons argued so vehemently against Newark's elevation – indeed, they prevented its Members sitting for three years – that this method was dropped, and no further attempt was made to strengthen the Parliamentary influence of the Court's supporters in this way.[19]

18. *Cal. S. P. Dom.*, 1660–61, 582, 7 May 1661: '... that there be a proviso for elections for Parliament to be made by the Common Council only.' The Court had ample opportunity to appreciate the radicalism of large electorates. In March 1661 the London electorate, the largest ever assembled in the opinion of several witnesses, disregarded the preferences of their Recorder and aldermen and elected two Presbyterians and two Independents, known enemies to the episcopacy: ibid., 536–42.

19. Grey, *Debates,* ii, 368–71; iii, 180–93; iv, 297–304. Both Sir Thomas Lee and Henry Powle bitterly attacked the limitation of the franchise. Many thought the chief danger to be the making of boroughs while Parliament was sitting. Sir Anthony Irby expressed this frankly: 'If, the Parliament sitting, boroughs be made, they may be so many new members sent as we are already, and what will be the consequence of that?' And Sir Thomas Meres thought that, if they accepted Newark, they would soon have two Members from the Royal Society. The fact that the opposition to the Crown, led by Eliot, Hampden, and Pym, had been ardent for the revival of enfranchisement of boroughs had, of course, conveniently passed into limbo. There was no opposition to the enfranchisement of Durham, both city and county, in 1675, partly because it rectified an obvious anomaly, and in both cases the franchise was a wide one. When the enfranchisement of the Palatinate of Durham had been proposed in the

The move to secure a larger electorate naturally received great impetus during the Exclusion Parliaments. Contested elections were more numerous than ever before, and petitions poured into the Committee for Elections, twenty-eight being received on 19 March 1679; more followed, and fifty were before the House before it was two months old. And the decisions were, naturally enough, in favour of a wide franchise, frequently notwithstanding that the memory of men ran to the contrary. Aldborough in Yorkshire, a tight little burgage borough with thirteen voters, was declared an open borough, the vote belonging to all inhabitants, and the loyal Tory Member, Sir John Reresby, thrown out. The country party used its historians as well as its majority. The Keeper of the Records, Lawrence Halstead, was brought before the Committee to testify on New Windsor and the Commons devoted an entire morning to discussing the case; the decision of the 1661 Parliament to close it was once more reversed in the hope, of course, of destroying the royal or 'castle' influence.[20] The Whigs were naturally aware that the Court party possessed many loyal agents in the boroughs who were being used to refuse the claim of their inhabitants to participate in the voting, and on 19 March 1679 the Commons ordered 'That it be an instruction to the Committee for Elections, that they do examine and made a special report of all miscarriages and undo practises in Sheriffs, Mayors, Bailiffs and other officers concerned in returning members elected to serve in Parliament', an order that was reiterated on 17 May of the same year.[21] But as the exclusionists wrested the initiative

---

reign of James I, two Members for Barnard Castle had been suggested; this was dropped in 1675. Even James II promptly refused the petition of Saffron Walden to be represented in Parliament: *Cal. S. P. Dom.*, 1685 (Feb.–Dec.), 154.

20. *JHC*, ix, 568–71, 622; (Aldborough) 585–6: For Aldborough, see also *Memoirs of Sir John Reresby*, ed. Andrew Browning, Glasgow, 1936, 169–70, 178, 180–81; Sir Thomas Lawson Tancred, Bt, *Records of a Yorkshire Manor*, 1937, 202–13. The time devoted to New Windsor was a deliberate tactic to demonstrate the attitude of the House in its opposition to royal influence and to show where the power lay.

21. Ibid., ix, 571. The Whigs' difficulty was, of course, that they had been so thoroughly purged from local office that many strategic positions

from the supporters of the Court in the counties and boroughs, the tune of the Commons changed, and on 25 March 1681 grateful thanks were offered to many cities and boroughs who had elected their Members 'according to the ancient constitution of election of members to serve in Parliament'. Here 'ancient constitution' meant the popular franchise.[22]

The number of voters in the county constituencies and also in the large boroughs had become so large by the end of the century that it forced candidates and their supporters to develop new, or to extend old, techniques of political persuasion. The 1690s witnessed the development of the poll-book. The first books were handed about in manuscript, but later they were printed, often handsomely bound, and of course sold at the booksellers. They provided a basis for canvassing and for exerting every possible form of political pressure on voters.[23] Large constituencies such as Yorkshire developed specific areas for canvassing and local committees to exploit them, as well as subscriptions to pay for this activity. The political dining-club is a further development of this age, for the Green Ribbon Club had many provincial counterparts. Such clubs were useful in tying a particular tavern to the party interest, and so could become a distributing centre for pamphlets and ballads either printed or passed around in manuscript, a development that

---

for elections were held by Tories; it availed the Tories little, for often the overwhelming appearance of Whig voters led them to decline the election. See J. R. Jones, *The First Whigs*, Oxford, 1961, 162–3, and 'Restoration Election Petitions', *Durham University Journal*, 1961, N.S., xxii, 49–57.

22. *JHC*, ix, 708.

23. Polling-lists had been made earlier in the seventeenth century at the time of an election; for example, a series of lists exists for Scarborough and Reading as early as the reigns of James I and Charles I, but the poll-books are quite different. Usually they were written up after the election from the voting-lists and were made for the specific purpose of studying the way electors had voted. The most comprehensive list of printed poll-books is the 'Draft Register of Poll Books' in the possession of the History of Parliament Trust. For Queen Anne's reign, see the invaluable, and as yet unpublished, Ph.D. thesis of W. A. Speck, 'The Organization of the House of Commons, 1702–14', Bodleian, Oxford, ii, 445–8. The poll-books have been greatly neglected as a source of party politics – Walcott ignores them.

led to the violent controversy about press licensing.[24] Coffee-houses also became headquarters and propaganda centres, hence the fierce denunciation accorded them by the supporters of the government; an abortive attempt to suppress them was made by Charles II in 1675[25]. Again, the introduction of a reasonably efficient postal service with cross-posts aided the dissemination of propaganda, but this was soon to strengthen the government as much as the opposition.[26] Nor was it long before the government was using customs and excise officers as their local political agents. The use of the clergy for the seamier side of politics was of course a fact of life long before Charles II was at loggerheads with his Parliaments, but there was no lightening of that load. Such an efflorescence of techniques of political pressure would be sufficient evidence in itself of a large and politically aware electorate, but such figures as we have for a little later in the century are even more eloquent. Persuasion by either side had become a necessity. And that fact should be pondered. Elections could, and did, go either way, for between the dedicated Whigs and Tories was the mass of voters,

24. J. G. Muddiman, *The King's Journalist, 1659–1689*, 1923, 124–30. Censorship was imposed in 1662 with the Printers and Printing Act which, lapsing in 1679, was not reimposed by the Exclusion Parliament. Royal authority over printing was re-established by Royal Proclamation in March 1680, which was promptly ignored: Peter Fraser, *The Intelligence of the Secretaries of State*, Cambridge, 1956, 114–32.

25. Browning, *Thomas Osborne, Earl of Danby*, i, 194–5. On 29 December 1675 a Proclamation was issued suppressing all coffee-houses. This caused so violent an outcry that the Court was forced into a partial retreat, and a new Proclamation was issued on 8 January 1676 permitting coffee-houses to remain open until midsummer, so long as they entered into recognizances not to allow scandalous newspapers, books, libels, etc., or to permit persons giving utterance to false rumours, etc. This period was extended each half-year in order to give the Court power to supervise coffee-houses. It availed little. The Court's Proclamations caused considerable indignation. Danby also considered acting against those book-sellers whose shops had become centres for the distribution of Parliamentary news: ibid., iii, 2–3; also Fraser, *The Intelligence of the Secretaries of State*, 117–20.

26. The Penny Post, significantly enough, was set up in April 1680, J. G. Muddiman believed, in order to aid Oates and injure James, Duke of York: Muddiman, *The King's Journalist, 1659–1689*, 221.

who could be swayed by events, by their fears and hopes.

It has often been argued that voting for the counties, being open, was unfree. As Namier wrote, 'as the voting was open and recorded in poll books, people in dependent positions could seldom exercise a free choice',[27] a sentiment echoed by Walcott: 'the freeholder was often a tenant of some other land and amenable to pressure from the landlord. Add to this, open polling, treating and free transport to distant polls, and it becomes obvious how easily elections could be managed by the leading families.'[28] But this, as so often in Walcott's work, superimposes the mid-eighteenth-century pattern, which is itself open to question, on the quite different political structure of the period

27. Sir Lewis Namier, *The Structure of Politics at the Accession of George III*, 2nd ed., 1957, 65.

28. R. R. Walcott, *English Politics in the Early Eighteenth Century*, Oxford, 1956, 10. Walcott implies that the frequent contests in the counties in this period were due to quarrels among the great landowners and squires. 'The local grandees, of course, often fell out amongst themselves, especially where the independent country squires were at loggerheads with the peer – usually some great noble with Court and London connexions – who tended to dominate the county.' This begs the question. Lords Denbigh, Guernsey, Ferrers, Crewe, and twenty-three leading gentlemen of Leicestershire did not press Sir Thomas Cave to stand for Leicestershire in 1714 because they disliked the Duke of Rutland and his influence, but because they were Tories, as was Cave, and Rutland was a Whig. The vast correspondence about this election in the Braye MSS. at Leicester Museum amply illustrates the virulence of party feeling, and this can be confirmed in scores of other county elections between 1689 and 1715 or later. The fact that a Stanley or a Lowther could command a seat in Lancashire or Cumberland does not invalidate the general picture. Most counties were uncontrollable, the prey to party divisions, until a combination of costs and Whig dominance brought about treaties among the leading families, by which the representation was divided between the parties. When such treaties proved impossible or collapsed, party was still an issue. See Eric G. Forrester, *Northamptonshire County Elections and Electioneering, 1695–1832*, Oxford, 1941, 7: 'What we find in Northamptonshire is not an aristocratic coalition intended to procure the election of nominees as Knights of the Shire, but, on the contrary, groups of landowners – both peers and commoners – ranged against each other on party lines'; also R. J. Robson, *The Oxfordshire Election, 1754*, Oxford, 1949, 47–51; C. Collyer, 'The Yorkshire Election of 1734', *Proceedings of the Leeds Philosophical and Literary Society*, 1952, vii (1), 53–82.

from 1689 to 1715. At this time poll-books, although becoming far more frequent as the techniques of electoral control were being actively exploited by politicians and their parties, were still far from being in general use. And we know too that the organization of freeholding tenantry by the gentry developed during the virulent contests that took place between 1689 and 1714. Many of the aristocracy and gentry of large estates were already doing their best to whip up their freeholders during the great Exclusion crisis from 1679 to 1681, but the process had not gone very deep. For example, Colonel Robert Walpole mounted his horse and rode alone to Norwich on 2 February 1679, as he did for all subsequent elections, at least until 1689. His son, however, by 1715, organized his freeholders like a regiment. He paid them 8s. for their horses, 7s. subsistence money for themselves; the old and infirm went by wagon that was also well stocked with refreshment, for it included a four-gallon barrel of brandy; the whole cavalcade, colours flying, was preceded by trumpeters. His father never spent more than two guineas on a county election; Robert Walpole's bill in 1715 was £110 13s. 7d.[29]

Although the control of county voting certainly becomes more systematic between 1689 and 1715, the number of freeholders who would, and did, vote as they pleased was very large. Also, there was a very considerable number of politically active minor gentry or prosperous yeomen, call them what you will, who needed to be consistently canvassed. Sometimes a man might be able to influence one or two votes apart from his own, and this class was numerous, but there were still many freeholders who decided their own vote, even as late as 1714.[30] If this were not so, the swings from Tory to Whig and back again, which are a feature, during this period, of country election

29. C(H) MSS., Account Book 15, for Colonel Walpole's expenses; Vouchers, Disbursements of Mr John Turner, Jr, 10 February, 1715, for Robert Walpole's.

30. Leicester Museum, Braye MSS., nos. 2895, 2899, 2900, 2902, 2903, 2904, 2905, 2907. It is obvious from these canvassing-lists that a floating vote existed, particularly in the large villages and small country towns such as, in Leicestershire, Hinckley, Mountsorrel, Husbands Bosworth, Lutterworth, etc.

contests as well as of the boroughs with large electorates, would be incomprehensible. In such elections party is of supreme importance, and it makes nonsense of Professor Walcott's thesis that politics of this age are nearer to those observed by Namier for the mid-eighteenth century than to the two-party system of Feiling or Trevelyan. His work has led to appalling confusion.

The upshot of this struggle over the electorate was to endow many boroughs with two franchises, both of which had been accepted at one time or another by the House of Commons, thereby creating a precedent and an opportunity for local political factions to fight each other.[31] Here indeed is the grass roots of party, for whichever group could dominate the Parliamentary elections could dominate the borough, and that meant profit and power. But the point needs reiteration; by the end of the Exclusion crisis more men had become involved in Parliamentary politics in the constituencies than ever before in the history of Parliament, and this is the basis both of party and of political instability. The situation was complicated and made more rancorous by the purges of the corporations undertaken during the Commonwealth and Restoration, to which I shall return later.

Naturally, the obstreperous temper of the House of Commons had led the Court to consider expedients other than restricted franchises and new Parliamentary boroughs: the first was slow and unreliable, the second signally failed.

Throughout the 1670s the Commons became immensely sensitive to the tactics used by the Court to circumscribe their activities or to reduce their capacity for independent criticism. Naturally, they feared secret influence and they called time and time again for a statement about expenditure from the Secret Service fund. Much of their detestation of Danby sprang from the belief, not without foundation, that he was building up an

31. A typical example is New Windsor, which was consistently contested during this period on the basis of two franchises. In Liverpool the two contesting parties were known as Old or New Charter men; likewise in Plymouth. See *The Norris Papers*, ed. Heywood, ix, 25 n.1; *The Journal of James Yonge*, ed. F. N. L. Poynter, 1963, 205-6.

effective Court party – by family alliance, by local loyalties, by common conviction about policy maybe, but also, the opposition rightly suspected, by a judicious use of money as well as place. And of the corruptibility of the Commons, contemporaries had less doubts than later historians.[32] There were too many gentry of very modest means whose sufferings during the Commonwealth, combined with their present economic difficulties, made them regard royal bounty as no more than their due. The attempt was made in 1675 to incapacitate placemen from sitting in Parliament, or at least force them to seek re-election, but without success.[33] In the first Exclusion Parliament, however, a Bill was introduced to make it illegal for any Member to accept an office of profit during Parliament; and this was followed a few days later by a furious attack on Sir Stephen Fox and the taking into custody of Peregrine Bertie as the Crown's agent for corrupting the Commons.[34] Dissolution prevented further actions, but the next Parliament was in no better temper than its predecessor and passed the following resolution without a voice being raised in protest:

That no member of this House shall accept of any office, or place of profit from the Crown without leave of this House: or any promise of any such office, or place of profit, as such time as he shall continue a member of this House . . . and that all offenders herein shall be expelled this House.[35]

Perhaps it was in the forlorn hope of undercutting Danby that the opposition tried to secure a resolution on 13 March 1677 to

32. *A Seasonable Argument to Persuade all Grand Juries to Petition for a New Parliament or A List of the Principal Labourers in the Great Design of Popery and Arbitrary Power,* an annotated list of placemen, pensioners, and creatures of the Court, reprinted in *English Historical Documents, 1660–1714,* ed. Browning, 237–49.

33. Grey, *Debates,* iii, 53–5, 29 April 1675. For Danby's party, see Browning, *T. R. Hist. S.,* 4th ser., xxx, 21–36.

34. Grey, *Debates,* vii, 213, 8 May 1679; 316, 23 May 1679.

35. Ibid., viii, 225. Vaughan thought this resolution would 'prevent ulcers in your own bowels'. The situation was, of course, more complex than the simplicities of Vaughan allowed. Many offices were granted for life: Sir Robert Howard, a bitter enemy of Danby, was Auditor of the Exchequer, but for life and could not be dismissed, in spite of his opposition to the Court: Baxter, *Development of the Treasury, 1660–1702,* 27.

revive the old statutes concerning payment of wages to Members, the last full-scale debate on this topic for nearly two hundred years.[36] It failed, of course, as it was bound to fail when the scramble to get into Parliament was steadily driving up the price that men were willing to pay for the privilege, but it is a further indication of the sensitivity of the opposition to threats to the independence of the Commons and of the need to prevent, by any means, the corrosion of its liberty that they felt, quite correctly, was taking place. Henry Powle, Sir Henry Capel, William Sacheverell, and the rest were as sensitive about the privileges of Parliament as any Hampden or Eliot. They were quick to see the danger of a Member being pricked as High Sheriff of his county, which was the fate of Sir Edward Jennings in November 1675. As Sir William Coventry said, 'If one be made, fifty may be made, and so fifty settled in the country, and he need not tell you how fifty votes would have carried things as they are not now carried . . . so it concerns the Parliament that you have not the gap open to root up all your privileges.' And this threat seemed so real that the country party won a victory: it was declared a breach of privilege for a Member to be made a sheriff.[37] Similarly, the opposition had denounced that other novel tactic of the Court, tried a little earlier than the pricking of Jennings as sheriff, which was this: the date of the recall of Parliament for the autumn session of 1675 had been communicated to Members favourable to the Court by the Secretaries of State. By such means the Court hoped doubtless to get a little breathing-space and to secure the passage of essential business, a trick tried with success in 1664 when Charles II obtained the repeal of the Triennial Act. The Commons declared, immediately they met, that they should be summoned by Proclamation only.[38] This was, of course, mere shadow-boxing, and the real confrontation between Court and country took place on more fundamental issues.

By 1678, Parliament had been in existence for nearly eighteen years; growing more intractable with age, it had been disci-

36. Grey, *Debates*, iv, 237–40.
37. Ibid., iv, 16–27, 16 November 1675.
38. Ibid., iii, 367–72, 27 October 1675.

plined, if not controlled, by a sharp use of the royal prerogative. Adjournments and prorogations quickly put an end to unseemly debates, wanton impeachments, or long wrangles about grievances whether of religion or standing armies or taxation or waste in the Navy. The Commons, of course, leapt at any chance to question the royal prerogative, and in 1677, after Charles II had left Parliament prorogued for over a year, the opposition tried to claim that the Commons were automatically dissolved.[39] To no avail; lacking systematic organization, with scarcely a vestige of a Whip, the country party could fall apart in dissension as easily as it could fuse in anger. And to many independently-minded lawyers such as Sir John Maynard, royal prerogative was a fact of law, not a mere whim of Charles II. So this time the opposition failed, and this power to prorogue remained the King's trump card in his conflict with Parliament, along with the power to dissolve. The country party came nearer to success in 1678 when both Lords and Commons debated a petition requesting the King to dissolve Parliament. It was lost by two votes and the King's fury left no one in doubt what was at stake. Yet dissolution had to come. The full weight of the Popish Plot, with the mounting hysteria of London and the country at large, proved too great even for a monarch of Charles II's dexterous pliability. The subsequent general elections were fought with bitterness, and almost everywhere the extended franchise came into action, and it must be emphasized once again that more voters were involved in the elections of 1679–81 than ever before in the history of Parliament. Moreover, the Exclusion Parliaments, in the brief time they had for action, did their utmost to confirm these elections made on wider franchises. Had they secured the exclusion of James II and obtained sufficient Parliamentary time, a wider franchise, combined with electoral reform, would have reached the Statute Book; for the country party realized well enough that there was no other way of securing their power in the political life of the nation.[40] But that was

39. Grey, *Debates*, iv, 61–77, 81–95.

40. Jones, *The First Whigs*, 213; Grey, *Debates*, iv, 3: Sir Richard Temple 'would not have one chosen that has not an estate of £500 p.a.' (12 November 1678).

not to be. The violence of the Plot, the hesitation of Halifax and many other members of the Lords, combined with Charles II's own superb sense of timing, defeated Shaftesbury and his supporters, who never possessed half the coherence of purpose that is often attributed to them. Most country members, terror-struck with Popish spectres, were totally preoccupied with Exclusion. They did not have, however, an army of grievances in Church and State such as their fathers had enjoyed in 1641. Exclusion was in a sense a crisis of detail, not the symbol of a clash between two opposing interpretations of the constitution, nor did it possess those mounting overtones of class conflict that had marked the struggle between Charles I and his Parliaments. Perhaps that is not quite exact. The far-seeing Shaftesbury, Powle, and others were sensitive enough to royal intentions to realize that, for the future, constitutional safeguards would be needed to protect the role of Parliament, and this could be done only by statute. They never had the time or the opportunity to develop their programme. Habeas corpus alone reached the Statute Book, and that by luck. The Exclusion Parliaments met for weeks, not months or years, and this crippled the opposition. Similarly, the discontented in the City and among the country gentry were certainly involved in the violent reaction to the Plot and in the vociferous demand for Exclusion, but the objects of their animosity were precise – James II and Catholics and France; it never generalized itself into an attack on monarchy and aristocracy as such.⁴¹ Had the

41. 'These ministers in the government are Machiavels – one of these two things: this must come to a stand, or we must come to blood. There are but two sorts of monarchy in the whole world: one absolute without limitation, as that of France, where subjects are at the disposal of the King for life and limb, and to invade other nation's property for the luxury of the court: and little men of low fortunes are the Ministers of State – and whoever does that I shall suspect him of absolute monarchy. Cardinal Richelieu would not suffer so great a man as the Duke of Montmorency, but cut off his head, and another churchman succeeded him who suppressed all the great men of France, and all to support absolute monarchy' (Sir Henry Capel, 7 January 1681): Grey, *Debates*, viii, 264. Xenophobic, intolerant, dogmatic, Sir Henry Capel is typical of much of the support given to Shaftesbury and Exclusion, and the sentiments could better be described as those of an English *frondeur* than those of a Roundhead. Capel

crisis continued, the division in society might have run deeper. As it was, by skilful exploitation of the prerogative power, Charles II weathered the crisis, but only by acknowledging that he and his ministers had lost all control over Parliament. He knew that he could not call another without first taking action at the most important and dangerous level of all – the control of elections themselves. Or rather his policy had to go further than that; he needed to bring about a change in the distribution of political power at the local level and to control it more closely; only then were Parliamentary elections likely to go his way. The traditional methods of influence and patronage were, he realized, quite insufficient. He needed to control, destroy, or diminish a dangerous segment of the new and growing electorates.

The method that he adopted – the remodelling of corporation charters – was not new. It had been used by Oliver Cromwell on one or two occasions to maintain a sympathetic minority in control when the populace had been antipathetic to his régime.[42] At the Restoration the need to dispossess Independents and Presbyterians and to prevent their return to power by a popular vote had led to its extension, and in 1661 the Commons insisted that the appointment of all Recorders and town clerks be approved by the King, who furthermore made it quite clear that he would favour the restriction of the Parliamentary franchise in chartered boroughs.[43] The Corporation Act of 1662 set up a special Royal Commission, empowered to remove

also hit hard at Halifax, 'who will go with or against Popery as the torrent drives him': ibid.; HMC, Beaufort MSS., 112. After the Revolution Capel proved himself an excellent oligarch when, as Deputy-Lieutenant of Ireland, he managed the Irish House of Commons with dexterity and skill. See his letters to Shrewsbury, HMC, Buccleugh MSS., ii, 62–519, *passim*.

42. B. L. K. Henderson, 'The Commonwealth Charters', *T. R. Hist. S.*, 1913, 3rd ser., vi, 129–62. The two boroughs were Reading and Colchester, but Henderson places far too large a construction on the evidence when he writes: 'we may infer that Cromwell, as early as 1656, had perceived what the later Stuarts realized and afterwards practised more extensively, namely that in the corporate towns there lay the possibility of a more effective control of Parliament.' There is no evidence that Cromwell ever intended to pursue a consistent policy of borough charter manipulation in order to secure a favourable Parliament.

43. *Cal. S. P. Dom.*, 1660–61, 582.

corporation officials and fill vacancies. The Duke of York led the Committee of the Lords concerned with the Bill, which deliberated in his apartments at Whitehall Palace. Both he and his brother met their first rebuff in this vigorous policy towards the Parliamentary boroughs, when the Commons refused to make the Board of Commissioners permanent and fixed a term to its appointment.[44]

So the Court was for a time restricted to this shadow-play with the Commons: adroit use of controlled elections; trial balloons such as Newark; the private letters to friends; the skilful use of pension, of loyalty, of patronage of every variety from jobs for relations to a gracious speech at Court. But all had failed. By 1680 the electorate was completely out of control, and Charles II had been reduced to his prerogative powers.

As soon as the hurricane was over the old policy was revived with a vengeance. Quick action was needed to overturn the country party before it could consolidate its power. The Whigs had been more successful in the constituencies than in the House of Commons. In some Parliamentary boroughs, even with tiny corporations, they had secured a majority. At Leominster, for example, a borough that was ruled by the twenty-five members of the corporation, fourteen were 'fanatics'.[45] Elsewhere their political influence had been extended by their own decisions in Parliament in respect of the franchise, but such victories could be regarded only as precarious, for a royalist-dominated Commons could just as easily reverse them. Also, it would be quite wrong to think of the country party swamping the constituencies during the elections of the Exclusion Parliament. They won, quite handsomely in some constituencies, but in others only by the skilful exploitation of every electoral trick, and in many towns they had only a bare margin. In every borough and in every country that they had won, there was, as Charles II and

44. J. H. Sacret, 'The Restoration Government and Municipal Corporations', *EHR* (1930), xlv, 232–59. For the Corporation Act, see *Statutes of the Realm,* 13 Car. II, c. i.

45. *Cal. S. P. Dom.,* 1684 (8 October); also Ogg, *England in the Reign of Charles II,* ii, 635. Ogg was one of the few recent historians who have given a proper weight to the remodelling of corporations.

his advisers realized, a party thirsting for revenge and hungry for the political power of which they had been deprived. Indeed, it was this situation, which was to continue for another forty years, that provides the basis of local party strife.

The aristocracy, too, was as evenly divided as the gentry: the violent hatred between the Townshends and Pastons in Norfolk, or Hastingses and Greys in Leicestershire, is well known,[46] but their quarrels were mere symptoms of a widespread division in all counties. So Charles II could be certain of considerable support at every level to render the corporations more amenable to the Court.

The Court's policy was quickly revealed. James II was an ardent advocate of borough reorganization, but even before he was re-established in London in May 1682, the government had shown its hand; or rather begun to put into resolute action a policy already decided. As early as December 1679, a committee of the Privy Council had been set up to investigate the lists of Justices of the Peace with a view to a further purge, and a circular letter had been dispatched requesting that the Corporation Act be put into force, and reports of action taken sent to the Privy Council. By the autumn of 1681, the surrender of corporation charters had begun in earnest, usually spurred by the threat of *quo warranto* proceedings, but not always; many corporations realized quickly enough that the tide had turned and got down on their knees, in full regalia, to surrender the old or accept the new.[47] Few resisted, and most that did failed; all that they achieved was an increased financial burden. These legal costs were extremely heavy – the borough of Beverley, only too eager to please, spent £438 13s. 4d. in getting its new charter, and had to borrow both in London and from their local patron to meet the cost.[48]

46. For Norfolk, see J. R. Jones, 'The First Whig Party in Norfolk', *Durham University Journal*, 1953, N.S., xv, 13–21; for Leics., Plumb, *VCH Leics.*, ii, 102–20.

47. Ogg, *England in the Reign of Charles II*, ii, 635–6.

48. *Beverley Borough Records, 1575–1821*, ed. J. Dennett, *Yorks. Arch. Soc., Rec. Series,* Leeds, 1932, lxxxiv, 174. In consequence, the Whartons, who were Tories, secured a stranglehold on the borough for the next thirty years.

For the rest of Charles II's reign the process continued. Small boroughs, of course, were easy game; they had little inclination to saddle themselves with the heavy legal costs that a struggle with the Court would involve. The majority of chartered Parliamentary boroughs with small electorates had been remodelled by the time Charles II died. The larger boroughs proved less easy. The battle royal with London, which effectively destroyed Shaftesbury's party in the City Corporation and drove many of its members into exile, is well known; other large towns struggled to preserve their privileges. Nine hundred petitioned in Norwich against surrender; at Bristol, Nottingham, Hull, and Newcastle there was resistance, yet, perhaps, less than might have been expected, and some large towns such as Plymouth capitulated at once.[49] The indications were that the balance of political forces had been closer during the Exclusion crisis than the success of the country party might lead one to believe. Also, of course, the country party possessed very little effective organization; the Whigs usually consisted of a small number of burghers, sustained by a section of local gentry, with only the loosest contacts in ideas and actions at the county, let alone the national level. And they could be, as in Norfolk, sharply divided among themselves even at the most critical times.[50] The supporters of the Court were, perhaps, no more numerous, and the balance in all corporations seems to have been held by moderates who were strongly influenced by events. Nevertheless, this ruthless attack by Charles II on the very base of Parliamentary liberty aroused a surprisingly small amount of immediate opposition.[51] True, voices were raised in the 1685 Parliament, but on one issue only, that royal charters had been granted to boroughs that had a prescriptive right to

49. Ogg, op. cit., ii, 635. For Plymouth, see *The Journal of James Yonge*, ed. Poynter, 188–90.

50. Jones, *Durham Univ. J.*, N.S., xv, 19.

51. The best detailed account of a Parliamentary borough during this period is the admirable but neglected article of Philip Styles, 'The Corporation of Bewdley under the Later Stuarts', *Birmingham Historical Journal*, 1947, i, 92–133.

return Members to the House of Commons. The debate was adjourned to a Saturday and so not continued.[52]

Charles II's policy had proved successful, for opposition to the Court during the 1685 election was very fitful and strong only in places. A candidate at Scarborough was arrested for attempting to poll the freemen. At Bridgwater it was thought that the new charter would be challenged; similar troubles arose at Sandwich and St Albans, but considering the number of boroughs that had been remodelled, the opportunities for a contest were not taken by the broken and dispirited Whigs.[53] Furthermore, at this time James II commanded widespread support, particularly among the aristocracy. His Lord-Lieutenants were reliable men, such as Norfolk, Newcastle, Plymouth, Brooke, Winchilsea, Dartmouth, or Rutland, who possessed great estates and considerable clientage in their counties. They were prepared to use all their influence to secure the return of Court candidates. They did their best to obtain the cooperation of the leading gentry to prevent contests in the counties, which the government realized presented the greatest danger. The Duke of Norfolk brought all his influence to bear on the Norfolk gentry to get them to decide on candidates favourable to the Court and to avoid a contest, and he succeeded impressively. Gentlemen as diverse in their political sympathies as Sir Christopher Calthorpe, who became a non-juror, and Colonel Robert Walpole, who was a strong Whig, agreed without discussion on two Knights of the Shire favourable to the Court. By such methods the political temperature was lowered, contests avoided, and the electorate evaded.[54] In

52. *JHC*, ix, 721, 27 May 1685. There is no record of the debate; Anchitel Grey did not sit in the 1685 Parliament.

53. The number of chartered boroughs that returned Members to Parliament was about forty, but this category contained most of the populous towns whose opposition to the Crown had been strongest; hence a reversal from Whig to Tory in these boroughs was of prime importance. Although valuable work has been done by Professor George on the remodelling of corporations, a definitive study covering the whole period is still needed.

54. B. Cozens-Hardy, *Norfolk Lieutenancy Journal, 1676–1701*, Norfolk Rec. Soc., 1956, xxx, 63–6.

the capable hands of Sunderland, backed by the passionate interest of the King himself, the royal management was both more systematic, more comprehensive, and more successful than at any other election of the seventeenth century.[55] And the result was a compliant House of Commons. As Barrillon forecast, it did not remain so, largely because management with the Commons proved as feeble as management of the elections had been effective.

With the single-minded obstinacy that was such a marked trait of James II's character, having failed with the 1685 Parliament, he could think only of an intensification of remodelling. The *quo warrantos* soon started up again and purges, dominated by a Board of Regulators, were quickly under way. This time the policy was thorough. Agents of the Board undertook a circuit of corporations. Their task this time was to report not only on chartered corporations, but on the political situation of all Parliamentary boroughs, with a view to strengthening the Court's influence. Dr Nehemiah Cox set out for Wiltshire and Dorsetshire with James Clarke; Benjamin Dennis and Richard Adams undertook East Anglia; Wade, Jones, and Andrews left for the western counties; although the names of other agents are not known, their reports exist, as do their instructions, which were comprehensive. Not only were they to survey the political complexion of Parliamentary boroughs and decide whether further regulation was necessary and feasible, or who should or should not sit for boroughs where intervention was possible, but also establish a permanent King's agent in such boroughs – men who could be relied upon to disseminate propaganda in inns and coffee-houses as well as report on anything taking place that might be to the Court's prejudice, particularly of course of any libels in print.[56] Action quickly followed. At least thirty-five boroughs were regulated between 10 March and 17 September 1688, ten by *quo warranto* proceedings, seven by the powers acquired by the Court in revoking ancient charters, and others by a mixture of regulation and threats of a future *quo*

55. Kenyon, *Robert Spencer, Earl of Sunderland, 1641–1702*, 113, 114–15.
56. Sir George Duckett, *Penal Laws and Test Act in 1687–8*, 1882–3, i, 194–7.

*warranto*. Buckingham, a borough with a tiny electorate of thirteen, had three mayors removed and a threat of *quo warranto,* with the possibility of legal costs soaring beyond the corporation purse, before it finally surrendered. At Barnstaple, Bridport, Chester, and Wells the entire corporation was removed by a single order, and it is no wonder that men talked of the 'Dissolution of the Corporations'. Such a response was indicative of the growing resentment felt at James II's policy; alienation of all sections of political influence either at the national or local level had taken place very rapidly between 1686 and 1687.[57] Men who had happily gone down on their knees to offer Charles II their charters grew stiff-necked and stubborn in 1688. The corporation of Grantham is a case in point. On 30 June 1684 they had offered up their charter to the King 'unanimously on a full voat'. The new charter gave the Crown the right to remove the major officers; so naturally a compliant corporation elected two Tories in 1685.[58] But by September 1687 Grantham was no longer docile; royal agents reported that Sir William Ellis, who had been rejected in 1685, now possessed the greatest influence in the borough. He would be returned for Parliament with anyone he cared to name.[59] Action was taken and a *quo warranto* served on the corporation in April 1688, but the corporation resolved to resist, and began to collect funds for the purpose. In June, the King used his powers under the charter and removed six aldermen, that is half of them. Opposition continued for a time, but it was partially overwhelmed, and a new charter was issued in September. The corporation ignored it and the mayor named in it never acted. Before the Crown could respond to this situation, it had been overtaken by events. Sir William Ellis became Grantham's Member of Parliament in 1689.[60]

57. R. H. George, 'The Charters Granted to English Parliamentary Corporations in 1688', *EHR*, 1940, lv, 47–56.

58. G. H. Martin, *The Royal Charters of Grantham*, Leicester, 1963, 21. The Tories were John Thorold of Grantham and Thomas Harrington of Boothby.

59. Duckett, op. cit., i, 146.

60. Martin, op. cit., 21–23. Sir William Ellis, 2nd Bt. of Wyham and Norton, Lincs. (1654–1727), M.P., Grantham, 1679–81, 1689–1713. He

Ellis's father and uncle had been Roundheads; he himself was married to a daughter of Richard Hampden, and he had been an ardent exclusionist. So much for all the King's efforts at Grantham to secure a complacent corporation! It should be stressed again that in 1684 Grantham had been complacent. Although there were boroughs such as Beverley that meekly accepted regulation, many resisted, and resisted strongly;[61] by the autumn of 1688, however, the majority of chartered boroughs were in what James II and his Board of Regulators regarded as safe hands. The men who now dominated the corporations were, however, precariously placed. Often Dissenters, sometimes Catholics, but usually intransigent royalists, they mostly lacked any broad political influence in their neighbourhoods; and frequently their climb to power had been marked by outbursts of violence.[62]

During this period James II and his advisers turned their attention to local political power in a wider sense than the Parliamentary boroughs, which they could influence by charter. They wanted to secure control over the county representation if they could do so; more than that, they wished to see local society dominated by men on whom they could rely absolutely. So the Lord-Lieutenantships were purged; peers such as the Earl of Rutland in Leicestershire, who had been sympathetic to the remodelling policy of the early 1680s, were thrust aside and replaced by their hereditary enemies – in this case the Earl of Huntingdon, who was completely sympathetic to James II. Elsewhere Court hacks – Preston, Dover, Jeffreys, Petre – acquired Lord-Lieutenancies. The pattern of a century was broken as savagely as it had been at the time of the Civil War. As with the Lord-Lieutenants, so with their deputies; out they went in purge after purge, the Justices of the Peace following the

voted consistently Whig: in 1690, 1703, 1704, 1710, and probably in 1713. There is no evidence of his ever defecting from the strict Whig Junto line. See also Godfrey Davies, 'The By-Election at Grantham, 1678', *Huntington Library Quarterly*, San Marino, Calif., 1943-4, iv, 179-82.

61. *Beverley Borough Records, 1575–1821*, ed. Dennett, *Yorks. Arch. Soc., Rec. Series*, lxxxiv, 178; George, *EHR*, lv, 51-2.

62. Styles, *Birmingham Hist. J.*, i, 113-14.

Deputy-Lieutenants. Not since the Norman Conquest had the Crown developed so sustained an attack on the established political power of the aristocracy and major gentry. But the attack, which after all had begun in the 1670s, had to be renewed again and again, for each onslaught alienated a new group of gentry until men as loyally royalist as Sir John Reresby, the ardent High Anglican, dedicated Tory, Governor of York, wrang their hands in despair. Reresby just could not understand a policy that turned out such men of substance as Sir Henry Goodricke, Christopher Tancred, Sir John Kaye, and Sir Michael Wentworth, men whose acres were so broad that they could command dozens of the minor gentry and hundreds of freeholders, and replaced them by men who possessed scarcely any land in England, let alone in Yorkshire, and by one man, at least, who by reputation could neither read nor write.[63] Such a reversal of power caused tempers to flare, and at times was accompanied by riot and violence.

By September 1688 this policy had so obviously failed that James II switched rapidly into reverse. The traditional men of power were restored, recent charters cancelled, new Commissions of the Peace promulgated. But it was too late; not only were events destroying James II and his narrow circle of advisers, but also the total alienation of the majority of the aristocracy, gentry, and commonalty lost him the slightest hope of mass support, so that when the Revolution came, he was rejected by the nation, by Tories as well as Whigs – indeed, by everyone. Even the Clarendons, Rochesters, and Ailesburys realized the forlorn nature of their cause. True, neither the aristocracy nor the gentry rose *en masse* against James II, and it has been calculated that only 10 per cent of the peerage gave William III active support during his march on London. This is not surprising;

63. *Memoirs of Sir John Reresby*, ed. Browning, 584. The fact that Sir John Kaye was a Whig and Sir Henry Goodricke, who shortly afterwards arrested Reresby, a follower of Danby, was of little significance to Reresby, compared with the fact that men so well landed as they were should be deprived of their traditional status in society. Therein lay the enormity that had to end in disaster. Reresby, however, realizing how James II was cutting his own throat, was more worried than the gentry who were displaced. They were well aware that times were about to change.

in the autumn of 1688 James II possessed an excellent professional Army, based on London; the militia had been deliberately neglected for more than two years; the Lord-Lieutenants
who controlled it were James II's most ardent supporters. It
must have struck even the meanest intelligence among the
aristocracy that James II could only be beaten by a professional
army; hence the need for William III rather than a civil war.[64]
Nevertheless, when the crisis came, it was the Dutch professional
army that men joined and James II's from which they deserted
in flocks; and the reluctance of such pillars of James II's Court as
the Duke of Beaufort or the Earl of Bath to stir themselves, the
ease with which Nottingham and Halifax changed sides at the
last opportune moment, underlines, if underlining be needed,
the total rift that had taken place between James II and the
natural political establishment of the country. The universality
that permeates the Revolution of 1688 arose not only because of
James II's specific attacks on the Anglican monopoly of the
Church, the Army, Navy, and universities, or from his determi-
nation to secure toleration, but also because of his outright onslaught on the very basis of political power, which if successful
would have made the Stuarts as absolute as their French or
Spanish cousins. It is this attack on the natural leaders of society
in their country neighbourhoods that must be regarded as the
most fundamental cause of the Revolution of 1688.

The drive towards absolutism on the part of Charles II and
James II involved more, of course, than an attack on Parliamentary franchise. As we shall see, a deliberate, conscious drive
had taken place to secure administrative reform and to plan the
armed forces on the French model. In consequence, one of the
critical features of the Revolution was the fear that new methods
of administration and the innovating administrators would not
survive the political crisis. The danger for the future political
stability of England in 1688 lay not only in the independence of
Parliament, but also in the likelihood that an effective executive
would be overwhelmed and the machinery of the State circum-
scribed at every turn. Whether this would happen or not depended on how far the country party, whose resurgence was a

64. Kenyon, *The Nobility in the Revolution of 1688*, Hull, 1963, *passim*.

political fact as soon as James II restored the charters, could establish its authority at the centre of political life. The Parliamentary situation seemed to favour them. William III was pledged to regular and freely-elected Parliaments. The situation in almost all Parliamentary boroughs was full of opportunities for the radicals. The possibility of prosecuting the lackeys of the Board of Regulators and that far larger body of Tory-inclined corporation men, who had surrendered their charters with such alacrity in the early 1680s, seemed to men like William Sacheverell almost a certainty; prosecution meant proscription and a world safe for Whigs. Such hopes, however, were to be quickly dashed. Parliament needed to be preserved; that was agreed, but little else.

The Revolution of 1688 marks one more failure of the Crown to secure control over the legislature. It was an emphatic act by the gentry to insist on the maintenance of their local power and their peculiar institution – Parliament; for that is what they meant by those clauses in the Bill of Rights that stressed the need for frequent Parliaments and free elections (by free elections they did not mean elections free of their influence, but of the King's). The supreme authority of Parliament was also stressed in the new Coronation Oath, and to make doubly sure that Parliaments met regularly William III's supplies were initially granted for a few months only.[65] And like Magna Carta of old,

65. The Commons were very divided about the propriety of granting William III the same supplies as James II, and W. A. Shaw made a vitriolic attack on the muddle created by the Commons. See W. A. Shaw, *Cal. Treas. Bks., 1689–92*, 1931, ix (1), lxxxiv–lxxxv: 'At the end of 1694, therefore, the ultimate position was that the Grand Revolution of 1688 had made a hopeless muddle of the country's finance as far as concerned the fixed peace revenue or King's revenue of the country. It had neither granted that revenue for life, nor adopted the alternative principle of yearly grants. It had not considered the peace revenue as a whole, one part it had granted for life, other parts it had granted for term of years, other parts it had not considered or granted at all save by mere inoperative resolutions. . . . To represent the ultimate outcome as the triumph of a Whig or constitutional or republican idea of starving the Crown in order to make it dependent on the Parliament is simply moonshine.' Shaw loved effect and hated the Whigs. He quotes Grey's *Debates,* throughout which runs one refrain from the back-benches: 'If you give this revenue

the Bill of Rights had its sanctions clauses – there was to be no standing Army and Protestant gentlemen were to be allowed arms; the right of rebellion is implicit. The gentry had asserted their rights. To whom those rights would belong was, however, a matter not of unity but of discord. Years of conflict had created two bitter factions among the gentry – Whigs and Tories, and these parties were not merely in conflict about ideological matters – the extent of religious toleration, the role of prerogative, and the like. They were fighting for power in the constituencies. The gerrymandering that had gone on in corporations and counties for more than a decade had, in the vast majority of boroughs, created two parties bidding for control, which meant power over charities, jobs, property, real estate, and freeholds of all kinds, as well as Parliamentary influence. All this was to give teeth to the party conflict, and to increase the instability of English political life, which is such a marked feature of politics from 1688 to 1715. There was a solid economic and social basis to the conflict between Whig and Tory, which represented not so much a conflict of ideology in a national sense, although that had importance, but personal and factional vendettas at the local level. Every manoeuvre to bring Parliament to heel had failed; in 1689 the Commons enjoyed a freedom and an independence that they had not possessed since 1641. As well as freedom, they had acquired a certain, continuing place in government; no year was to pass without their meeting, and this they knew would be so. And after the execution of Charles I and the flight of James II, few could dispute where sovereignty ultimately lay. The problem of the control of Parliament seemed to have been solved to the satisfaction of its backbenchers – that control was impossible. Parliament, it seemed,

---

for three years you will be secure of a Parliament' (Sir Thomas Clarges, 21 February 1689): Grey, *Debates*, ix, 123, a sentiment that was constantly reiterated in the Commons debates on the revenue. The muddle was due on the Commons' part to a desire to underpin the authority of Parliament, yet give the King a reasonable supply of money for the war, but also to a lack of management by the Crown. The fact that the Whigs wished to give a term of years to parts of the revenue in order to make certain both of Parliaments and of accountability of ministers is as clear as daylight and no moonshine.

was free to harry monarchs, topple ministries, cut supplies, refuse taxation, concern itself with peace and war, formulate those constitutional changes that it felt necessary for its protection, and generally ride rough-shod over the administration. For the next twenty-five years the pattern of politics resembled this description: governments teetered on the edge of chaos, and party strife was as violent as anything England had known since the Civil War. The Revolution, however, strengthened the two processes, the development of oligarchy and the growth of the executive, which were in time not only to reduce the power of the independent Member, but also to secure single-party government, and this was to achieve that subjugation of the legislature that the Stuarts had frequently attempted but never achieved.

# CHAPTER THREE

# THE GROWTH OF OLIGARCHY

IT proved easier to win a revolution than secure it. Within twelve months the country party registered a number of defeats, and by February 1690 the King had decided to see whether a fresh general election would bring him a more amenable Parliament, or, rather, one with a less intransigent core, for the Convention Parliament, in full session, was moderately rather than violently Whiggish. The Bill of Rights, which in the first flush of the Revolution promised to be a comprehensive constitutional document, had been quickly watered down to a string of condemnations of James II's actions, followed by a number of hopeful generalizations about the way in which executive power should be used in the future. The ultra-Whigs protested at such flabbiness; as William Sacheverell urged the Commons, 'Since God hath put this opportunity into our hands, all the world will laugh at us if we make half a settlement. . . . Secure the right of elections and the legislative power.'[1] What was worse, from a Whig point of view, was that little punishment was meted out to those who had been responsible for the destruction of their party after 1681. To their chagrin they failed to obtain their cherished Corporation Act by which those responsible for surrendering charters, or acting under the new ones issued by Charles II and James II, would have been incapacitated for seven years from playing any part in corporation affairs – an essential step if the world was to be made safe for the Whigs. The issues were perfectly clear to Sacheverell's supporters and their opponents. Serjeant Maynard, that aged relic from the Long Parliament, told the House in a voice so frail with age that Anchitel Grey could scarcely hear him, 'If there be no penalties, you had better like what King Charles and King James did. If these surrenders stand, they may make what

1. Grey, *Debates*, ix, 83.

Parliament they will at Court.' Or as Foley put it more violently, 'We have ill ministers, and they are concerned that the same thing may be done again. Men have done all they can to annihilate their corporations, and we must not annihilate but restore these men.' His sarcasm was wasted. The Tories were well enough aware that proscription would mean their ruin, and they also knew that their policy of moderation was William's policy. They surveyed their own necessities with a warm and generous feeling. 'If all these', Sir Henry Goodricke, Danby's henchman, told the House, 'whom avarice, force and easiness have induced to surrender their charters, if all these must be left out, whom will you have to act; whom will you have to choose Parliament men? None. Harmony must save us.' But the chance had been lost, and a bitter struggle in the chartered corporations was inevitable.[2]

The failure of the extreme Whig party was due to a variety of causes. The success of William III's invasion had followed so rapidly on James II's reversal of his charter policy in October that little or no time had been available in many constituencies to undo the years of preparation by his secretaries: over 45 candidates, for example, out of 102 recommended by Sunderland in the summer of 1688 were returned to the Convention Parliament in 1689.[3] Probably less than a third of the Commons were old exclusionists, and the balance of power was certainly held by men who had never previously sat in Parliament, and significantly

2. Grey, *Debates,* ix, 513–18. Not that the question of charters was buried by the defeat of Sacheverell; the country party harked back to the question as soon as the new Parliament met. On 14 May 1690, Sir John Lowther told the Commons: 'I think those were great Crimes in the last Reigns, of surrendering charters, and those men not called to account. We were told then to lay all things asleep: but if you will look into grievances, look into the last occasions of your ruin, not only into 1678 but 1684, and the rest.' And in the same debate Shadrack Vincent added for good measure: 'Since I see it is now the fashion to name Privy Councillors, I will name another who I desire may be turned out. He that delivered up the charters in Cornwall. I mean the Earl of Bath': Grey, *Debates,* x, 144 and 141 (*bis*), mis-numbered.

3. Add. MSS., 35,516, fos. 50–54; Plumb, 'Elections to the Convention Parliament', *Cambridge Historical Journal,* 1937, v, 241.

their names are not to be found in the two division lists – one Whig, one Tory – which throw light on the more intransigent groups in the Commons.[4] The Whig situation in the House of Lords was weaker still. Only with considerable reluctance had the peers been brought to accept the idea of a vacancy of the throne, and they were totally uninterested in making the world safe for the country gentry. They had burst back into the lush pastures of Court favour, and their attention was consumed by far more serious business than constitutional principles. Most of them had been happy enough with the late Charles and early James. The majority of the peers found it difficult to accept William III with whole-hearted grace; and the wrangles about regency, vacancy, and abdication had displayed clearly enough their yearnings for a fixed and immutable world. What had broken their spirit was their steady exclusion by James II from authority in their neighbourhoods and from the rich pickings of executive office. Now all was changed; and although their loyalty might be dubious, their appetite was not. The Spencer House Journals, the notebooks of the Marquis of Halifax, in which his conversations with William III are recorded, are concerned principally with questions of place – who should get what – and the aristocratic professionals and their henchmen created the major problems; be they suitable or unsuitable, niches and rewards had to be found. Although William III thought the Duke of Northumberland a great blockhead, he had to have a troop of horse and be sent to Holland; young Hampden might be weak in the head, but the offer of an embassy was important; Delamere was repugnant to the King, but he became Lord-Lieutenant of Cheshire; Sir Henry Capel, Lord Essex's brother, was thought to be incompetent, but he moved steadily up the ladder of promotion.[5] As to Danby, said William III, 'hee knew not what to make of him. All his kindred and dependence voted against him. He could not live with a man at that rate.' But live with Danby, William did. He could not escape him. In the next five years Danby moved first to a marquisate, then a duke-

4. Ibid., 240–41.
5. Foxcroft, *The Life and Letters of the First Marquis of Halifax*, ii, 200–52.

dom, and he stayed in office until 1699, enjoying both salary and perquisites, although at times without the power it conferred.[6] The aristocracy and gentlemen of influence were back where they belonged, at Court and in office. They were never to be dislodged again by any narrow clique of purely King's friends; instead, so deeply entrenched did they become, as decade succeeded decade, that neither social change not extension of the franchise made much difference. They were still there in the reign of Queen Victoria. Although it has long been realized that the Revolution of 1688 could be expressed in the equation 'property equals power', this is too coarse a statement to describe the reality. What the Revolution did was to confirm the authority of certain men of property, particularly those of high social standing, either aristocrats or linked with the aristocracy, whose tap-root was in land but whose side-roots reached out to commerce, industry, and finance. And their authority was established not so much because Parliament became a continuous part of government but because they settled like a cloud of locusts on the royal household and all the institutions of executive government. For these prizes, they fought each other – at least for thirty years or so after the Revolution – after which Walpole sliced up the cake for them and reduced their quarrels to bickerings about the crumbs.

In 1688 the natural oligarchs lacked the social and political cohesion that they were to acquire in the middle decades of the eighteenth century, though even then ambitions and jealousies were common enough, but in the late seventeenth century the divisions in their ranks went deeper. Often this sprang from local situations.

Apart from the procreative efforts of Charles II, much of the peerage was a late Stuart creation, and sometimes this had led to sharp struggles for leadership: in Norfolk, the Townshend family, always of importance but never of pre-eminence, had become in the reign of Charles II first barons, then viscounts, and they had challenged the Pastons, a much older family, for the leadership of the county, a challenge that had led to violently

6. Foxcroft, op. cit., 206; also Browning, *Thomas Osborne, Earl of Danby*, i, 504–48.

contested Parliamentary elections and deep divisions among the minor gentry and yeomanry. Likewise in Leicestershire, although the Manners had acquired their earldom of Rutland in Tudor times, yet a hundred years later the Hastingses still regarded them as interlopers. The politics of Lancashire and Cheshire were embittered by the hatred of the Earls of Derby for the Earls of Warrington.[7] And usually, although not uniformly, these animosities were strengthened by political division: the Pastons, Hastingses, and Derbys were Tories, their enemies Whigs; indeed, after 1678 party divisions were as sharp in the House of Lords as in the Commons, yet on the Whig side less bedevilled by factional subdivisions. But the Whigs enjoyed only a bare majority in the Lords, and that only after the first years of William III's reign; his promotions to the episcopal bench, the elevation of the eldest sons of several Whig peers, and the decision of such undertakers as Portland, Godolphin, Sunderland, and finally Marlborough to support the Whigs rather than the Tories, gave the Whigs their small preponderance.[8] The uncertainty of their majority led them to a far closer degree of organization, through race meetings and country-house parties, than might have been the case had they enjoyed a larger majority; and their hard core – the Junto – showed a greater dexterity and flexibility than their Tory rivals, who lacked their coherence. But the Tory cause, with the prospect of Queen Anne's succession, was never a hopeless cause until 1716. The aristocratic Tories were struggling for the right to dominate the Court, to control the executive, and to acquire supremacy in local affairs. These were such solid prizes that they naturally gave an edge to party strife. Also, they commanded widespread support throughout the nation; indeed, usually far more than the Whigs.

Both at Westminster and in the constituencies the fight for power was on, and the peerage was more active in general

7. Jones, *Durham Univ. J.*, N.S., xv, 13–21; also 'Restoration Election Petitions', ibid., 1961, N.S., xxii, 49–57; R. W. Ketton-Cremer, *Norfolk Portraits*, 1944, 22–57; Plumb, *VCH Leics.*, ii, 109 ff.; HMC, Kenyon MSS., 234–5.

8. A. S. Turberville, *The House of Lords in the Reign of William III*, Oxford, 1913, 7–15.

elections, if contemporaries are to be believed, than ever before. Be that as it may, one fact is certain: there were more general elections to be active in. Between 1689 and 1715 twelve general elections were fought, only one less than for the rest of the eighteenth century; indeed, more general elections took place in that short time than in any other period of Parliamentary history, before or since – a fact unmentioned by historians, yet of immense significance. Not only were general elections exceptionally frequent, but they were strongly contested. Scarcely a borough avoided a poll, and the majority were fought time and time again.[9] This was true of the counties, and of boroughs with large electorates, medium electorates, and, significantly, of tiny electorates. Only in the two decades immediately preceding the Reform Bill of 1832 were Parliamentary seats of all kinds so fiercely contested, but even then not so frequently.

In my opinion, this electoral struggle had a profound influence on the growth of political stability and on that drift to oligarchy which no amount of special pleading can eliminate from mid-eighteenth-century politics. It is necessary to consider the contests for Parliamentary seats more closely. Parliamentary seats may be categorized in three main groups: counties; boroughs with large electorates (above five hundred); and the narrow constituencies with less than five hundred voters. And it is instructive to compare what is happening between 1689 and 1715 with the situation at the general elections of 1754 and 1761 – to compare, that is, the unstable and the stable worlds.

Firstly, the counties. In 1754, five counties went to the poll; in 1761, four. (In many counties, representation followed a traditional pattern of compromise. The Whig aristocracy named one Member, the Tory country gentlemen the other.)[10] Between

9. Plumb, 'Elections to the House of Commons in the Reign of William III' (unpublished Ph.D. thesis, Camb. Univ. Lib.). The evidence of contested elections in this period is exceptionally scattered; certainly, the number of known contests must be far less than the number that took place. For Queen Anne's reign, see Speck, 'The Organization of the House of Commons, 1702–14' (unpublished Ph.D. thesis, Bodleian, Oxford), ii, 422–30.

10. Namier, *The Structure of Politics at the Accession of George III*, 65, 70–71.

1689 and 1715 the situation was entirely different. There was very little compromise. At the election in 1690 twelve counties, at least, were contested; in 1698, twenty-two, perhaps twenty-four, were fought; in 1702, twenty; in 1705, twenty-eight; in 1713, thirteen.[11] Some counties were repeatedly contested. During William III's reign, Essex was contested at five out of six general elections and twice at by-elections.[12] From these facts alone it is obvious that a bitter struggle for political power was taking place. As the eighteenth century drew on, the battles in the counties were fought either to victory or stalemate. The cost, too, particularly of large counties, became so prodigious that, even though the gentry were organized to underwrite much of the candidate's expenses, the total sum proved such a burden that every effort was made to secure a compromise and avoid the expenses of a contest. But after the Revolution there was little desire for compromise, and the violence of county contests, alive with virulent propaganda and intensive canvassing, are sufficient evidence of party strife.

On the other hand, in the constituencies with large electorates, that is boroughs such as Westminster, Southwark, Bristol, York, Coventry, and Norwich, there is very little difference in the number of contested elections in the two periods. With

11. 1690: Berks., Cheshire, Essex, Herts., Middlesex, Norfolk, Oxon., Somerset, Suffolk, Warwicks., Wilts., Cardiganshire.

1698: Beds., Cambs., Cheshire, Durham, Essex, Glos.(?), Hants., Herts., Lancs., Leics., Middlesex, Norfolk, Northants., Northumberland, Notts., Oxon., Rutland, Somerset, Staffs., Suffolk, Surrey, Warwicks.(?), Worcs., Yorks.

1702: Berks., Bucks., Cheshire, Cumberland, Essex, Glos., Leics., Middlesex, Norfolk, Northants., Notts., Shropshire, Somerset, Suffolk, Surrey, Wilts., Worcs., Westmorland, Brecon, Flintshire.

1705: Beds., Berks., Bucks., Cambs., Cheshire, Cornwall, Essex, Glos., Hants., Herts., Kent, Lancs., Lincs., Middlesex, Monmouthshire, Norfolk, Northants., Northumberland, Somerset, Suffolk, Surrey, Sussex, Warwicks., Westmorland, Wilts., Worcs., Yorks., Breconshire.

1713: Beds., Bucks., Glos., Hants., Hunts., Kent, Monmouthshire, Rutland, Shropshire, Surrey, Sussex, Wilts., Carnarvonshire.

12. All general elections, except that of 1700–1701; the by-elections were in January 1693 and February 1694. By Queen Anne's reign the battle was dying down; it was contested only in 1702, 1705, and 1710.

electorates running into many hundreds of voters, they were too difficult to manage by the usual methods of influence and patronage; yet, at the same time, the cost of a contest never became prohibitive. Further, certain boroughs, particularly Westminster, Southwark, and Bristol, quickly assumed a specialized character for politicians. The elections in these boroughs were regarded as indicating the trend of public opinion, and, in consequence, whenever there was the slightest rise in political temperature during the eighteenth century, they went to the polls. Like the counties, however, in William III's and Queen Anne's reigns, they were more strongly fought and emphatically on party lines.

But in the third category – the narrow constituencies – the difference between the two periods is more remarkable. There were about one hundred and fifty boroughs in this category, and by the reign of George III they enjoyed a very large measure of electoral peace.[13] There were, of course, occasional ruffles on the surface. In a fit of pique the Cornish borough of Grampound threw over the Edgcumbes after many decades of allegiance to them, and flurries of this nature occurred in the small boroughs of the South-West from time to time as decade followed decade in the eighteenth century. They were usually due to deaths of patrons or managers or sudden hunger for new men on the part of the handful of electors. At times they were invaded. At Bishop's Castle Lord Clive used his enormous fortune to buy out the Warings, who had been established there since the beginning of the century. It cost him over £30,000 and even for a nabob it was expensive. But in most of these boroughs the marriage of patron and voter had been strengthened by long years of mutual gratification, and divorce was rare. In 1761 only fifteen of these boroughs went to a poll.[14] Between 1689 and 1715 there was bitter rivalry, many broken engagements,

13. Namier, *The Structure of Politics at the Accession of George III*, 126. Namier gives the figure for 1761 as 148; in the earlier period the franchise was less well defined. 1761 was, of course, a very quiet election; nevertheless, I feel the contrast to be a valid one: ibid., 160.

14. Ibid., 294, 344–55; Sir Lewis Namier and John Brooke, *The House of Commons, 1754–90*, 1964, i, 228–9, 361–2.

and a great deal of promiscuity, and there were many boroughs that deserved the Duke of Richmond's stricture on New Shoreham – that it was 'a new whore that is anybody's for their money'.[15] In 1690, seventy boroughs, at least, were contested; in 1698, sixty; in the reign of Queen Anne, between fifty and sixty at each election.[16] And it was unusual for any borough to go for many years without a contest.

In the infinite variety of election documents relating to these narrow constituencies it is not common to find much mention of the political or religious differences that might have swayed either the candidate or the voter.[17] This does not mean that either candidates or voters were devoid of principles in religion or politics, or unaware of them in others.[18] Indeed, many a narrow constituency followed the periodic swings from Whig

15. E. and A. Porritt, *The Unreformed House of Commons*, Cambridge, 1903, 9.

16. Plumb, 'Elections to the House of Commons in the Reign of William III' (unpublished Ph.D. thesis, Camb. Univ. Lib.), 124 ff. These are very conservative estimates, for there is no comprehensive political correspondence similar to that of the Duke of Newcastle for the later period, and the evidence for many contests must be still buried in private archives or forever lost.

17. In the elections for county seats or large boroughs, political or religious attitudes are often mentioned, but the contrast with the smaller boroughs is marked. An interesting and illuminating example occurs in the election correspondence of Sir Robert Walpole and his father. Although there is considerable material relating to Castle Rising, a small borough in Norfolk, neither politics nor religion are mentioned, but in the correspondence relating to King's Lynn, Norwich, and Norfolk, political considerations are frequently discussed; see Plumb, *Walpole*, i, 57–9, 103.

18. Ibid., 104; C(H) MSS., J. Turner to Robert Walpole, 8 May 1702. (The fact that Walpole had supported his uncle, Horatio Walpole, a Tory, at Castle Rising worried Walpole's Whig friends at King's Lynn.) 'But how farr the Rising Election may influence I cannot be certaine. It is easy for those that wish us ill to say they are made property of and tools only to serve a turne, and everybody knows what is done at Rising [it being so near] as well as if it were here, and what objections [one side] may make of our turning with the wind, contrary to former practises.' In none of the letters or documents relating to elections at Castle Rising in the C(H) MSS. or the MSS. of Sir George Howard of Castle Rising is there any mention of the political beliefs of Horatio Walpole.

to Tory or back again that marked the general elections of this period, even though they seemed to be quite firmly under the control of a patron. In 1702, the corporations of Brackley and Buckingham, the former having thirty-three voters, the latter thirteen, deserted Lord Wharton and turned to the Tories; in 1710, a handful of electors in Marlborough turned from their Whig patron, the Duke of Somerset, and elected a Tory. Of course, these tiny electorates were divided by ancient conflicts based on party lines. In Buckingham there was always an anti-Whig minority; the dedicated Whigs usually dominated and could persuade the less dedicated to go their way, doubtless stressing the advantages of their excellent connexions, which, after all, had provided the town with an excellent gaol and town hall; but in times of acute party division the wobblers could leave them, join the Tory minority, and so swing the election. And obviously, the mood of the country at large could swing the wobblers' votes. But except in times of acute crisis,[19] the attitude of candidates in these small boroughs to representation quickly became entangled in their ideas of property and social status, and it was questions of interest, influence, and ownership, or of patronage and profit, that were usually uppermost in their minds when they talked and wrote about their constituencies. But when elected most of them were good Whigs or good Tories, picking up their perquisites, and fighting for their way of life, according to the fortune of their parties. And although it is difficult for us, they found it easy to conceive of general elections in political terms, even though it seldom entered their heads to do so in regard to their own activities in a particular borough.

19. Walcott, *English Politics in the Early Eighteenth Century*, 39–40. Walcott stresses that Buckingham and Brackley were 'usually' under the influence of Lord Wharton, which is true but conceals the truth. Walcott's thesis attempts to deny the influence of the two-party system and to replace it by the concept of factions; hence the adverb 'usually' conceals the fact that these boroughs could be influenced in their decisions by party convictions. For the divisions in Buckingham, which by 1702 were at least twenty years old, see Francis and Margaret Verney, *Memoirs of the Verney Family during the Seventeenth Century*, 2nd ed., 1907, ii, 380–97. For Marlborough, see Mary Ransome, 'Parliamentary History, 1689–1832', *VCH Wilts.*, 1957, v, 213.

The battle in the narrow constituencies was a battle for power between two parties, between two conceptions of the function of Parliamentary government, but it was often fought in personal terms.

Men had wished to control Parliamentary representation long before 1689. Both Shaftesbury and Danby had built their parties on a geographical basis, on the control of representation where their prestige and wealth – and the prestige of their friends – carried most weight.[20] But Danby and Shaftesbury were playing for the highest stakes – the control of England's political destiny. Men who had less to gain or lose were disinclined to invest great sums of money either in the candidature of their clients or themselves, owing to the uncertainty of the duration of Parliament – whether it would last ten years, ten months, or even ten days.[21] This erratic factor in the life of Parliament checked the growth of systematic patronage, whose prerequisite is regular, but not too frequent, elections. This was secured first by the Revolution of 1688. Since 1689, Parliament has met every year. By 1690, it was obvious that this would be so. From 1695 the government was obliged by statute to hold an election at least once in every three years.[22] There was a clear-eyed appreciation of this new situation and an understanding that in future the way to political power, office, or sinecure would, in most cases, lead through Parliament. As Peregrine Bertie wrote to his brother, the Earl of Lindsey, concerning the candidature of his nephew Philip at the Stamford by-election in 1694:

It is a great thing if he carryes, may be of great advantage to him, and make the Court look upon him with better eyes. . . . [For] Courtiers must venture their fortune and they can have no better lottery than our House to push their fortunes in.[23]

Rather than giving advice, he was echoing a family sentiment, for between 1689 and 1715 twelve Berties pushed their way into

20. Browning, *T. R. Hist, S.,* 4th ser., xxx, 30–31.
21. F. and M. Verney, op. cit., ii, 381.
22. 6 & 7 Will. & Mar., c.2.
23. HMC, Ancaster MSS., 249–50.

Parliament[24] and each one got a winning ticket in the lottery, though the luckiest was Peregrine himself, who in 1694 was enjoying places and sinecure worth £2,000 p.a.[25] Lesser families cherished the same hopes as the great ones. In April 1705, Tom Leigh wrote to his brother, Peter, the Tory proprietor of the borough of Newton in Lancashire:

.. I'm sure it will be of the last ill consequence to me if I desist and not renew my request to you for your assistance at Newton once more. ... If the new Parliament prove but a good one, as there is all the reason in the world to believe it will, then it is most certain the tide must turn, and if so, whoever is out of the House is out of the way to be provided for.[26]

It was the knowledge that concrete returns might reasonably be expected that made men prepared to invest larger and yet larger sums in elections. But this, of course, was not the only reason for the outburst of contests that followed the Revolution. Both the attitude of the Crown and the violence of party feeling

24. Hon. Albemarle Bertie: Lincs., 1705–8; Cockermouth, 1708–10.
   Hon. Charles of Uffington, Sr: Stamford, 1685–1711.
   Charles of Uffington, Jr: Woodstock, 1705–8; Stamford, 1711–22.
   Hon. Henry of Chesterton: Westbury, 1678–9; Woodstock, 1681; Oxford, 1685–95; Westbury, 1701–2; Westbury, 1702–15.
   Hon. Henry: Beaumaris, 1705–27.
   Hon. James: Woodstock, 1695–1705; Middlesex, 1710–34.
   Montagu, Lord Norris: Oxfordshire, 1689–99.
   Hon. Peregrine, Sr: Stamford, 1665–78, 1685–7; Westbury, 1689–90.
   Hon. Peregrine: Boston, 1685–7, 1690–98, 1701–5; Truro, 1705–8; Boston, 1708–11.
   Peregrine, Lord Willoughby: Lincs., 1708–15.
   Hon. Philip: Stamford, 1694–8.
   Hon. Robert: Westbury, 1695–1702, 1702–8.
25. Bodleian, Rawlinson MSS., D.846, fos. 1–3.
26. Lady Newton, *Lyme Letters, 1660–1760*, 1925, 225. Thomas Leigh of Lyme (1765–1717), M.P., Newton (Lancs.), February 1701–13, second son of Richard Leigh of Lyme, Cheshire. His brother, Peter, a Papist, was patron of the borough. Immense pressure was used by Leigh and his friends to secure him an office, but he failed. Ironically, Tom Leigh appears to have been a casualty of the Tory Land Qualification Act, 1711, designed to keep our Whig carpetbaggers: ibid., 220–40.

played their part. In 1689 and in 1690, the Crown and its servants could not use openly and effectively the great influence that it possessed, and for two reasons. William III's manifesto had stressed the need for free elections – free, that is, from the methods of James II. The memory of thorough purges, of nominations being forced on boroughs, was far too recent for William III and his ministers to attempt even to exploit the Crown's patronage. In addition, of course, there was the further difficulty of William III's early ministries being composed of Whigs and Tories; indeed, the Treasury, which embraced so much patronage, was often divided between Whigs and Tories, which further added to the confusion in the exploitation of Crown influence. In consequence, for most of William III's reign Crown patronage was used tentatively, as an example will show.

In 1690, the Earl of Shrewsbury, who was Secretary of State, sent this letter to the corporation of Dover:

I understand the Earl of Torrington has written to Dover on behalf of Sir Charles Hedges, Judge of the Admiralty, that he may be chosen to serve in Parliament. Tho' I do not pretend to have any interest in the place, or so much as to intermeddle in elections, yet from the knowledge I have of the gentleman's worth, I cannot but wish he may succeed.[27]

Hedges was not elected. The corporation preferred James Chadwick, a Kentishman of modest means, and Thomas Papillon, a wealthy London merchant, who early in his career had bought up a large estate at Acrise, just outside the town.[28] An ardent Whig, he had represented the borough during the Exclusion Parliaments. And yet, as Sir Lewis Namier pointed out:

27. *Cal. S. P. Dom.*, 1689–90, 414.

28. James Chadwick: M.P., New Romney, 1689–90, Dover, 1690–97. His wife was the eldest daughter of Archbishop Tillotson. Chadwick was a discreet Whig who became, through the good offices of Somers and Godolphin, a Commissioner of the Customs in 1694.

Thomas Papillon (1623–1702): M.P., Dover, 1673–81, 1689–95; London, 1695–1700. A leading London merchant and Commissioner for Victualling the Navy who had fled to Utrecht in 1684 to avoid paying a punitive fine of £10,000 imposed for his part in defending London's charter. See *DNB*; A. F. W. Papillon, *Memoirs of Thomas Papillon of London, Merchant, 1623–1702*, Reading, 1887.

There was a castle at Dover, there were forts, ships, trade and packet boats, which, in terms of patronage, reads: The Lord Warden of the Cinque Ports, the Ordnance, the Admiralty, the Treasury (through the Custom House), and the Post Office.[29]

But Shrewsbury and Torrington were too cautious to use what by 1761 had become the commonplace political pressure put by the administration on its local officials. It might be argued that Shrewsbury was being foxy, preferring two thoroughgoing Whigs to a civil servant of mildly Tory disposition. I doubt it. Shrewsbury was not only lazy but very diffident. And Torrington was neither. By 1700 the memory of James II was receding and the government was becoming less reticent in the use of its power. Using methods that would have seemed familiar, if crude, to Newcastle, the government attempted to win control of both seats at Dover. It was too late. They failed to dislodge the Papillons, who had established an interest that was to last for three generations.[30]

The Hedges case was not an isolated case. In December 1700 William Ellis, an Under-Secretary of State, wished to enter Parliament. His keenness and his unwillingness to leave anything to chance can be judged by the fact that he became a candidate for four boroughs – Harwich, where the government influence might be regarded as very strong; Steyning, which was enjoying the fruits of a struggle between Sir John Fagg and the Duke of Richmond; Malmesbury, which was one of the battlegrounds of Wharton and Abingdon; and one other seat.[31] At Harwich he

29. Namier, *The Structure of Politics at the Accession of George III*, 121. Sir Charles Hedges renewed his attempt to secure a seat at Dover in 1700. He employed his under-secretary, William Ellis, and a local agent, William Mackay, and used all the influence he could muster. He was successful, but only to fail again in the election of 1701: Add. MSS., 28,886, fo. 200; 28,887, fos. 374, 388.

30. Namier, op. cit., 121–2.

31. Add. MSS., 28,927, fo. 127. The Duke of Somerset, who refused to support him at Steyning, had discovered to his cost that his interest in that borough was very slight: ibid., 28,886, fo. 168. For Malmesbury, see the Marquess of Lansdowne, 'Wiltshire Politicians (*c.* 1700)', *Wiltshire Archaeological and Natural History Magazine,* Devizes, 1932, xlvi, 75–7.

cut no figure at all; at Steyning and Malmesbury the chief combatants paid no attention to him. At the fourth borough, whose name cannot be traced, the patron told Ellis that unless the government requested him to do otherwise, he intended to elect his son-in-law. Obviously, Ellis could not secure any help whatsoever from the government, for he failed to reach Parliament.[32]

It might, of course, be argued that Ellis and Hedges were exceptional cases, but there is stronger evidence than this, and of a more marked type. The outburst of Lord Cutts, Governor of the Isle of Wight, concerning the activities of his deputy, Major Morgan, at Yarmouth is particularly revealing of the Court's weakness. Writing about him to the Secretary of State in 1693, he remarked:

The Corporation would be entirely the Governor's if Major Morgan didn't oppose it, a thing unheard of in any former reign as it is indecent and contradictory to reason for an officer in the King's pay to put his own private affairs or inclinations in the balance with his master's service.

In 1761, Major Morgan would only have done so at the risk of his advancement in the Army. However, Major Morgan came to no harm. But even after Cutts, five years later, had come to terms with Morgan, he failed at the election to rouse the government's interest sufficiently to get them to nominate Members.[33]

32. Add. MSS., 28,886, fos. 123, 158, 178, 180, 185, 187, 204; Bodleian, Carte MSS., 223, fos. 296–8, 302.

33. HMC, Frankland–Russell–Astley MSS., 77, 95. Cutts was also sharply reprimanded by the Secretary at War, William Blathwayt, for quartering two companies of soldiers at Yarmouth during election time. William III expressly forbade it, as such an action was bound to set the House of Commons aflame: ibid., 85. The situation was no better in 1695, when Henry Guy wrote to Portland, on 30 July: 'I am informed and I am afraid it is too true that, although the predecessor of Lord Cutts did make all there for Parlt. that now it is so farre otherwise that hee will not be able to bring in himself': Nottingham Univ. Lib., Portland MSS. Guy was proved wrong, however, in one point; Cutts was returned for Newport (I.o.W.) after a contest. Cutts, however, elected to serve as Knight of the Shire for Cambs.: *Official Return of M.P.s* (1878), i, 575. In this election, however, Morgan dominated the elections at Yarmouth (I.o.W.) and Newtown (I.o.W.).

In the early years of William III's reign the ministry generally refrained from exerting the influence on elections that it possessed. Certainly, William III made deliberate progresses through the countryside in the hope of influencing country gentlemen and substantial burgesses towards candidates whom he favoured, but the detailed and deliberate exploitation of Crown and Treasury patronage was, to say the least, haphazard and irregular. It is true that as the years passed, it became less discreet and made its wishes plainer, but its initial neglect had fostered, rather than deterred, contested elections. Also, it should be remembered that most of William III's ministries were coalitions, which in itself made it more difficult to systematize government patronage in the interests of a single party. The situation changed in the reign of Queen Anne, when government interest was used much more effectively.[34]

The very nature of the narrow constituencies also provoked contests. Contests were often a process of definition. They gave a focus to personal rivalry and helped to settle it. They made men define for themselves exactly what value they placed on a seat in Parliament and, being human, candidates were often in two minds. And a divided mind usually meant a divided poll. Again, only time and experience could focus power and consolidate it in the hands of those groups of men who came to dominate these electorates. Naturally, at first, they fought among themselves, playing would-be patron against would-be patron – Whig against Tory. But this led to the definition of a stable hierarchy of power, to a known and recognized channel for the flow of guineas and favours.[35] Such a definition might last,

34. See Speck, 'The Organization of the House of Commons, 1702–14' (unpublished Ph.D. thesis, Bodleian, Oxford), ii, 313.

35. Many boroughs achieved a definition of power and influence during this period; for example, Old Sarum is not contested after 1715, Wilton contests cease after 1710, and although Calne is savagely fought between 1688 and 1715, the contests die out immediately afterwards: Ransome, *VCH Wilts.*, v, 208–30. A revival of contests in these small controlled boroughs develops after 1780 and gradually strengthens in the early nineteenth century as the political divisions in the country become sharper. Indeed, contested elections are the best indication of the strength of party passion in the country.

as at Castle Rising or Heytesbury, until the Reform Bill, but this was undoubtedly rare. Death of patrons, the division of estates, family quarrels among the managers resident in the boroughs, could upset ancient agreements. Also, the social prestige of Parliamentary influence was so great that an invasion of a borough might take place even though the odds were mostly against victory. But settlements usually lasted for several decades, and boroughs quickly settled down again after a contest. By such methods the growing electorate of the seventeenth century was checked, diminished, or rendered impotent.[36]

No matter how homogeneous the structure of society had been in 1689, a struggle for the control of Parliamentary representation would have taken place; the nature of the new situation and the frequency of general elections would have demanded it. As it was, society was far from homogeneous. The aristocracy and the squirearchy had many broad common interests that drew them together when they were threatened from without. But once they had obtained security and their privileged position in society had been established, the resentments, envies, and jealousies of the rich and not-so-rich could flourish with renewed rancour. With the growth and consolidation of great estates that came at the end of the seventeenth century, incomes of £10,000 to £20,000 a year were no longer rare. These allowed a style of life that was the envy and despair of the small squire. To make it harder to bear, some of these incomes were newly acquired. After a successful career in law, Sir Nathan Wright laid out nearly £50,000 on estates in Leicestershire and Warwickshire within three years. Among others, he bought up that of Sir William Villiers, whose family had been established in Leicestershire for centuries and many of whose members had sat in Parliament.[37] The representation of Leicester came as

36. The history of the Parliamentary boroughs of Cornwall and Devon given in vol. i of Namier and Brooke, *The House of Commons, 1754–90*, illustrates the pattern of a settled oligarchy.

37. Leicester Museum MSS., Account Book of Sir Nathan Wright. The memorial of Sir William Villiers at Brookesby reads as follows:

SACRED

To the Memory of S<sup>r</sup> WILLIAM VILLIERS Bar<sup>t</sup>. Descended from
A Race of Worthy

easily to Wright's son as the estates to his father. There were scores of men like Wright who had made fortunes in government service, in law, or in commerce, who were buying up estates partly as an investment but also to secure that position in society that came with the ownership of land. Parliamentary representation, or the control of it, was but a part of the same process. But it was natural that these men should be subjected to the hatred of the dispossessed – of those families who regarded themselves as the traditional leaders of the county.

Broadly speaking, therefore, the prerequisites for the violent contests in the small boroughs were these. Firstly, the Revolution made the government very cautious in the use of its undoubted power in elections. Secondly, the Revolution had established Parliament as the permanent and central feature of the body politic. It had become the obvious, and almost the only, way to political power. Thirdly, changes in land ownership were profoundly affecting the structure of local politics. New men of property wanted the social prestige that went with Parliamentary representation. Also, as the estates of the peerage grew both in extent and riches, their attitude towards the tiny boroughs nestling at their palace gates hardened to a benevolent despotism. These were conditions unfavourable to the squirearchy, who were inhibited from adopting a radical attitude to the

---

Ancestors Upwards of Five hundred Years Happily injoying Great
Revenue in this
County in a right Noble and Hospitable Use thereof; By whose much
Lamented Death is
determin'd the Male Line of the Eldest house of that Hon^ble. Name in
Great Brittain
to none of whom He was Inferior in all Accomplishments Requisite to
Adorn his Quality
He departed this life in the sixty seventh Year of his Age on the
twenty seventh day of Feb^ry
1711.12
Nathan Wright, the son of a lowly Leicestershire clergyman, had married early into the Leicestershire gentry (an Ashby of Quenby); he became Lord Keeper from 1700 to 1705. After starting as a Whig, he became a sound Tory, and it needs to be emphasized that the slide into oligarchy did not automatically favour the Whigs; Tories frequently won handsome rewards.

constitution by their political and religious traditions. But they put up a stern fight. They were not defeated by a lack of courage or by an unwillingness to spend what wealth they had. Nor did they lose in all cases. Human beings can be loyal as well as mercenary; for example, the Rashleighs of Fowey – a family of modest wealth – continued to represent this borough in the eighteenth century as it had in the sixteenth. Also, where numbers were strength, where they could pool their resources, where the conditions of franchise were favourable, namely in the counties, they often won and won handsomely.[38] In addition, during the reigns of William III and Anne they enjoyed the powerful support of a number of dedicated Tory peers – occasionally but not always, for in the battle for supremacy in a borough, Tory could destroy Tory and Whig, Whig. And there were times when the tide of political sentiment swept in their favour, when even a Wharton failed to maintain his hold on so small a borough as Buckingham.[39]

The great difficulty facing a man of moderate means, attempting either to secure or maintain an interest in a small borough, was the constant increase in the cost of fighting an election. In 1689, Samuel Pepys spent £8 5s. 6d. at Harwich; in 1727, Viscount Perceval spent £900.[40] In 1689, the borough was contested; in 1727, it was not. At both dates the number of voters was thirty-two. Weobley in Herefordshire was the scene of a very fierce contest between Colonel Birch and his son, who possessed large estates near the town, and the formidable combination of Edward Harley, Thomas Foley, and Viscount Weymouth. In 1690, Harley's election bill was about £70; in 1717, Weobley cost one candidate £719.[41] This difference in cost

38. Indeed, the Tories may be said to dominate the county seats. Speck calculates that in Queen Anne's reign the Tories controlled thirty-two English and sixteen Welsh county seats: op. cit., ii, 306. The situation in William III's reign was more confused, and the Tories were less deeply entrenched, for the 'Whig country' interest was much stronger.

39. Similarly the Duke of Somerset at Marlborough.

40. Bodleian, Rawlinson MSS., A.174, fo. 221; HMC, Egmont's Diary, i, 56.

41. Add. MSS., 34,518, fo. 57. This was Harley's expenditure on behalf of Thomas Foley. He himself sat for New Radnor.

is a critical one. £100 or less was a sum well within the compass of a large number of small landowners, local merchants, or even attorneys, but £500, £600, or even £700, which might have to be spent every three years or so, was quite beyond their means. Such expenditure would have imperilled their estates. It meant that in many boroughs electioneering was a hobby that only rich men could afford, and the rise in cost is perhaps the most important factor in the development of oligarchy. Of course, direct election expenses were not so heavy in the reigns of William III and Queen Anne as they subsequently became. The Septennial Act put up the price of Parliamentary property, for it became a sounder investment, but the costs of this period should be judged by both what had gone before and by the plight of the gentry, saddled as they were with high taxes, low rents, and poor harvests.

Nor did the cost of an election stop with the election itself. There was usually a second contest to be fought in Parliament. It was always open for the defeated candidate to petition Parliament against the return of his opponent either on the grounds that he had been returned on the wrong franchise or that he had used illegal methods to secure his election. About 75 per cent of contested elections went to the House of Commons for a final decision. The petitioners and defendants had to transport their witnesses to London and provide for them at their own expense and, naturally, to reimburse them too for their trouble. It was often a major operation. In 1690, Robert Harley had to obtain coaches from Oxford in order to bring his witnesses from New Radnor in Wales. There were a score of them, and this involved him in complicated and very expensive staging arrangements.[42] Apart from the journey he had to support them in London for a fortnight, and naturally reimburse them for their absence from home. One can understand why, when it was all over, Robert's brother wrote to his father:

42. HMC, Portland MSS., iii, 450, Robert Harley to Sir Edward Harley, 26 October 1690: 'None at Worcester could furnish me with a coach to bring up my witnesses, nor at Moreton. I have hired Mr. Moore's coach from Oxford: he has six able horses. I desire somebody may go with the witnesses to Worcester to settle them as to their coming up.'

The goodness of God in the disposal of my brother's election at the Committee deserves our most grateful acknowledgement.[43]

This additional cost helped to drive poorer men from the contest. In January 1689, Sir Richard Cust, a county Whig of small estate living in Stamford, attempted to get his son, Pury, returned for that borough. He was opposed by the Berties, led by the Earl of Lindsey, Tories all, and strong supporters of James II. They locked up thirty of Cust's voters on election day in order to make certain of the result. It was both a good ground for a petition and a propitious time for Whigs, but Cust could not afford it.[44] He said it was an expense he could not bear. Five years later, at a by-election, Sir Pury considered contesting the seat again. Peregrine Bertie told him bluntly that it would cost him £500 or £600 if he did, and in his letter to the Earl of Lindsey, he wrote with evident self-satisfaction: 'I believe Sir Pury Cust will not be willing to enter into battle with so great a family.'[45] He was right; the Custs refrained. They saved their remaining strength for the next general election. They were defeated. They petitioned and they were defeated again. For the rest of Sir Pury's lifetime his fortune was seriously impaired and he lived in straitened circumstances.[46] A generation later, but only after another disastrous attempt to regain their place at Stamford in 1734,[47] their fortune was finally restored by marriage to a great heiress, Anne Brownlowe, which brought friendship with the Duke of Rutland, a seat a' Grantham, and high office in the reign of George III. The story of the Custs is unusual only in its happy ending.

43. Ibid., 451.

44. Lady Elizabeth Cust, *Records of the Cust Family*, 1898–1927, i, 359. Sir Richard Cust's total rental was £706 12s. 6d. p.a., of which he spent £336 10s. n the maintenance of his household. £300 was allowed to his spendthrift son, Sir Pury: ibid., 250–51.

45. HMC, Ancaster MSS., 250.

46. Lady Cust, *Records of the Cust Family*, i, 375–8. The voting was:

|  |  |
|---|---|
| Hon. Charles Bertie | 202 |
| Hon. Philip Bertie | 174 |
| Sir Pury Cust | 124 |

47. Plumb, *Walpole* (1961), ii, 316–18.

The Poles, facing ruin at Honiton in Devonshire, owing to the cost, dropped out of the contests, and the following clause in the will of Sir William Pole, 4th Bt, drawn up on 6 May 1733, is significant:

My request to my son John and other persons to whom I have limited my manors etc. is that they will never stand as a Candidate or if chosen will never be prevailed upon to serve in Parliament for the Borough of Honiton.[48]

This was a curiously ironic twist of fate, for it was entirely due to the Pole family that Honiton had acquired Parliamentary representation in 1640.

The increase in the cost of elections was due to a variety of reasons. There was an increase in bribery. But bribery seems to have been more like a disease that struck down certain boroughs than a general condition of electioneering. True, a Bill was introduced to disenfranchise Stockbridge because its voters were so openly venal.[49] Wootton Bassett courted a similar fate. There the agent of Colonel Webb 'carried a bag of money through the town upon his shoulders with a pair of bagpipes playing before him'.[50] At Weobley in 1701 votes fetched over £20 apiece, which was regarded as a dear underhand bargain.[51] Although

---

48. *Report and Transactions of the Devonshire Association*, Exeter, 1934, lxvi, 254. The number of voters at Honiton in Queen Anne's reign was about three hundred. Later in the century this borough also ruined the Yonges. Sir George Yonge, who was forced to sell his Honiton estates, declared that elections had devoured a fortune of £240,000: ibid., 256. The Vincents heavily mortgaged their estates (afterwards foreclosed) through the expense of maintaining a seat at Fowey (1708–27): W. P. Courtney, *Parliamentary History of Cornwall*, 1889, 106.

49. *HCJ*, x, 295–6; xi, 37.

50. Ibid., x, 522–3.

51. HMC, Portland MSS., iv, 11. £20 was a high price, £10 more usual, and £5 not infrequent. The price of votes fluctuated but, from the evidence of Marlborough and Great Bedwin, steadily rose in Queen Anne's reign. Important men in a borough who could deliver other votes besides their own commanded high prices. It was rumoured that the Duke of Somerset paid £100 for John Smith of Marlborough and undertook to educate his son. Lord Bruce certainly paid Flurry Bowshire of the same town forty guineas for his vote: HMC, Ailesbury MSS., 208.

there is plenty of evidence of bribery, good sound evidence of candidates stating the price they have had to pay, it was not a widespread practice. By and large, voters attempted to veil their cupidity. The greatest expense of nursing any constituency was due to entertainment, fees, and donations.

Entertainment by the candidates of their chief supporters was centuries old. But before 1689 it was in general modest – wine for the corporation, with tobacco, beef, and beer for the chief inhabitants. With the scramble to get into Parliament candidates were naturally encouraged to be lavish, and in consequence they very rapidly educated the appetite and palates of their supporters. On St Peter's Day, 1698, Alexander Popham provided his supporters among the thirty-two voters at Bath with this meal:

2 venison pasties, 2 haunches boiled, 2 chines of mutton, 4 gees, 4 piggs, 12 Turkey chickens, plain chickens and rabbitts sans number and abundance of clarett and sherry.

A ball followed for the ladies, and

in the evening there were glass windows broke on purpose that the glaziers that were not worthy to eat with them might have some benefit by the matter.[52]

This was an unexceptional, modest entertainment; in 1693 Guicciardini Wentworth was ready to spend between £200 and £500 on entertaining less than one hundred voters at Clitheroe on behalf of the Hon. Philip Bertie.[53] In December 1701 Thomas Coke ran through £133 in a few days at Derby.[54] And as decade followed decade the cost of entertainment soared. By 1784 food and drink at Chester for three thousand electors cost the Grosvenors £8,500 (£14,000 had been demanded); in addition, cockades cost £1,300. Who else but the Grosvenors could afford it, so who else but a Grosvenor could represent Chester?[55]

52. Reference lost.
53. HMC, Kenyon MSS., 273–5. Wentworth was secretary to the Chancellor of the Duchy of Lancaster, Lord Willoughby D'Eresby, whose brother, the Hon. Philip Bertie, was standing as a candidate. He failed.
54. HMC, Cowper MSS., ii, 445. In 1695 it was said to have cost Mr Vernon £700 to lose Derby town: HMC, Portland MSS., iii, 573.
55. Gervas Huxley, *Lady Elizabeth and the Grosvenors*, 1965, 85–6.

Entertainment, however, was only the atmosphere in which friendship and loyalty between candidate and voter could thrive. The proofs were more solid, more durable.

Firstly, there were the fees. With the establishment of regular elections and repeated contests, the corporation officials began to develop a proper sense of the value of the services that they rendered. At Buckingham, Sir Richard Temple had been accustomed to give 10s. to the clerks who wrote out the polls and to the serjeant, and 2s. 6d. to the cryer, ringers, and gaoler.[56] By 1700, the following rates were commonplace: £10 to the clerk for entering votes; two guineas was customary for mace-bearers; five guineas to bailiffs and constables. The host of minor officials were paid in proportion. And, of course, the candidates paid for any booths, tables, or books that might be required.[57] By 1715, £50 to £100, according to the size of the borough, could be reckoned as reasonable outgoings to officials.

But more important than fees were donations, and they were much more expensive and not necessarily confined to election times. (More often than not they were a highly speculative investment.) At Rochester, Sir Cloudesley Shovell and Sir Joseph Williamson built a town hall; fearing that a town hall would be insufficient, Williamson also endowed a grammar school for boys.[58] At Wigan, Mr Warren offered to provide the corporation with a water supply, as did Lawrence Carter at Leicester.[59] Gifts of plate, mortgages, and almshouses were other mementoes of the bond that tied a candidate and his corporation

56. Godfrey Davies, 'The Political Career of Sir Richard Temple (1634–1697) and Buckingham Politics', *Huntington Library Quarterly*, San Marino, Calif., 1940–41, iv, 77 n. 120. The total cost in 1688 at Buckingham was a mere £12 12s. 8d., per candidate. At Castle Rising in 1689 ringers got 10s., fiddlers 10s., drummers 5s., and 'Holbertmen' 5s. between them; the trumpeter received 2s. 6d. As there were so few voters and no contest, a clerk was not needed: Sir George Howard MSS.

57. E. and A. Porritt, *The Unreformed House of Commons*, i, 181–201. Shaftesbury had wished to saddle these expenses on the county and pay for them by means of a rate. An attempt had been made in 1679 to fix the sheriff's fee at 2s. 6d., but it failed: ibid., 183.

58. HMC, Bath MSS., ii, 176.

59. HMC, Kenyon MSS., 278.

together.[60] And of course, these forced benevolences were not limited to election times only. The drain of guineas was perpetual, and the more a corporation received, the greater became the sense of its own value until by the middle of the eighteenth century corporations became as brazen as Tewkesbury or Oxford. In 1766, Oxford suggested that its candidates discharge its debt of £5,670 as a condition of re-election.[61] In 1753, Tewkesbury demanded that the candidates should contribute £1,500 each towards the repair of roads, an offer accepted by two rich London merchants, and so their old Member, Lord Gage, who had represented the corporation for twenty-two years, was ignominiously turned out.[62] As each decade of the eighteenth century passed, it became more difficult for anyone but a man or family of very solid wealth to face such massive expenditure.

But there were other demands, which wealth alone could not provide: in a world devoid of competitive examinations or interviewing boards, the prospect of employment in offices, great or small, depended above everything else on knowing, or being approved by, the person who could bestow the office. Loyalty had long been expected from clients, but now many clients' hands were strengthened because they could trade their vote. Patrons and borough-mongers might demand a place in the royal household in return for supporting a ministry, but they also expected the right to bestow a certain amount of patronage on their corporation, for its voters expected their pickings. As soon as Sir Thomas Pelham, the father of the Duke of Newcastle was made Commissioner of the Treasury in 1698, begging letters began to pour into his office. They range from a round robin signed by the Lord-Lieutenant of Cornwall and fourteen M.P.s, pressing the claims of one of their party agents for a land-waiter's place, to a letter from Sir Rowland Gwynne, who was more concerned with recouping his own losses after a bitter and expensive struggle with the Harley–Foley group at New Radnor. He solicited places for two men who 'have been

60. E. and A. Porritt, op. cit., i, 158–63, gives numerous examples, and the list could be massively extended.
61. Namier and Brooke, *The House of Commons, 1754–90*, i, 357–8.
62. Ibid., 292.

active in the late revolution and are withal married to two of my sisters'.[63] Parsons, too, throughout the country were waking up to the fact that they could best forward their professional career by using their increasing leisure for electioneering politics. After working for him at Maldon, the Rector of Woodham Waters wrote to Montagu, Chancellor of the Exchequer: 'I proposed the honour and favourable representation to the King but this is all the design I have in my application to you.'[64] Obviously, men who had plenty of opportunity to make respresentations to the King were regarded as admirable and desirable candidates, and especially so in the small seaports where each voter might expect a place either in the Customs or Excise or Post Office. And as soon as the government began to recover from the excessive caution created by the Revolution, it did not find much difficulty in securing the loyalty of boroughs such as Harwich, Orford, and East and West Looe, boroughs that in the reign of William had been in the hands of county families.

In giving and providing an M.P.'s work was never done, no matter how absolute the control of a borough might appear to be. At Aldeburgh in Suffolk, Sir Henry Johnson, a rich East India merchant (who married his daughter to the Earl of Strafford) frightened away a local Tory, Sir Edward Turner, Kt, after two sharp and expensive contests in 1689 and 1690.[65] The nomination of both seats remained in his hands until he died, but his correspondence shows that he himself felt no such certainty and that the maintenance of his interest was a constant and expensive preoccupation. His brother William lived at Aldeburgh and kept an open house for him, and the entertain-

63. Add MSS., 33,084, fos. 92, 93.

64. Ibid., 15,903, fo. 114.

65. The right of election was in dispute, as to whether or not nonresident freemen could vote. Sir Edward Turner's agent, Thomas Godfrey, tried to get a sight of the charters to settle the issue, but they were kept under lock and key at Framlingham, some fifteen miles from Aldeburgh, by the town clerk. In 1690, there were about 150 freemen voters; by 1754 they had dwindled to 50, another example of the decline of the electorate in the eighteenth century: Earl Winterton MSS., letters of Thomas Godfrey to Sir Edward Turner. For Sir Henry Johnson's correspondence, see Add. MSS., 22,248.

ment provided seems to have been both lavish and uninterrupted. Sir Henry was expected to use his influence to extricate Aldeburgh men pressed for service at sea and to buy shares in all craft built by local shipwrights. Clerkships in the East India Company were known to be in his gift, and Aldeburgh seems to have been teeming with ambitious young men with a passion for the East; they were all relations of voters. The local gentry, who began by calling him 'A whoremaster and no gentleman', got used to him and then began to exploit him. They borrowed his yacht when they wanted the benefit of sea air and encouraged him in his judicious habit of sending them rarities from the East. It was, of course, a game that could know no end, and after 1689 the Parliamentary voters and those who controlled them realized that the vote was the basic coin for traffic in influence.

Naturally, they became keen on restricting its circulation and limiting the number of voters to as few as possible. It is not surprising that after 1689, borough after borough diminishes the number of freeman voters or forgets to admit any at all. Hastings, for example, admitted only two each year, and both were expected to provide a sumptuous banquet for the corporation – so naturally they were drawn not from Hastings but from London or the county, and after 1715 they were usually rich clients of the Duke of Newcastle. Severe restrictions in the making of freemen appear at Ludlow in 1698, at East Retford in 1701, at Plympton Erle in 1702, and so on.[66] In these boroughs the number of freemen was reduced to a handful – a great convenience for all concerned. Other corporations deliberately restricted the number of voters by raising the freeman's admission fine.[67] By such methods the electorate was gradually whittled away.

66. E. and A. Porritt, *The Unreformed House of Commons*, i, 72–3.

67. The reverse method also was used at times – the creation of large numbers of freemen for a specific election. Often these were non-resident so that the candidates would need to pay their expenses in travelling to the election. Usually, of course, these became occasions for considerable treating and disguised bribes – the hire of horses and coaches at excessive rates. Or the non-resident freemen were reliable friends of the patron who could be expected to pay their own expenses; for example, Sir Charles

Many boroughs had two franchises that at some time or other had been accepted by Parliament as the true franchise for electing Members. Between 1689 and 1729, when the question was closed by the Last Determinations Act, a large proportion of the narrow constituencies were contested on this question of franchise.[68] Two things are clear. One is that it was the Tories, and the old-fashioned Whigs who were associated with them in the New Tory party, who were being elected on the wide franchise, defending it, and fighting for it. There are exceptions, but they are rare.[69] The second is the corollary of this, that Whig Parliaments decided time and time again in favour of a narrow franchise. Further, there can be very little doubt that many of the boroughs that come into the category of narrow constituencies were created by the decision of the Commons between 1689 and 1729. It was only to be expected. Twenty-four voters were easier to control than three hundred, three hundred easier than three thousand. And those voters who survived the restricting process were always the influential members of the corporation, usually the mayor, aldermen, and common councilmen, and of course they gained too: there was less dilution of profit.

What is less well realized is that many corporations were convulsed between 1680 and 1720 by a constitutional crisis: two franchises, two differing concepts of the necessary structure of a corporation, had provided a natural focus for factional strife at the local, and party strife at the national, level. The violence of party feeling, of Whig hatred for Tory and vice versa, arose

---

Blois made fifty-nine of his friends freemen of Dunwich: HMC, Various Collections, Dunwich MSS., vii, 106–7; E. and A. Porritt, op. cit., i, 60–68.

68. For some years after 1688, a few boroughs possessed not only two franchises but two charters, e.g. Dunwich, which was contested in 1689, 1690, 1691 (by-election), 1695, and 1698, after which the charter difficulties are settled and no further contests take place: HMC, Various Collections, Dunwich MSS., vii, 104–6. Other dual corporations were Orford, Aldeburgh, Thetford, Plympton Erle, Ludlow, and possibly Tewkesbury.

69. Styles, *Birmingham Hist. J.*, i, 92–133.

from the battle of power in the constituencies. So many misconceptions of party are current because the constituencies have
been ignored; it is simpler and easier to play with genealogical
tables. Nevertheless, these battles, protracted as they were,
usually lead to victory or defeat, to settlements and treaties, and
so to an end of crisis and party strife. And as borough after
borough settled into decades of electoral peace, the electorates
vanish; political rights are of little value if they cannot be
exercised. Usually such rights remained profitable; contest or
no contest, treating and pleasing went on, but political principles
ceased to play any part in the electoral life of most small boroughs.

The rising cost of elections, the intricate system of spoils and
influence, the narrowing franchise, forced the borough-
monger or patron to a greater dependence on the government,
be it Whig or Tory. Many were impoverished by the excessive
cost and needed outdoor relief for themselves or their families;
and in the end many of them wanted cash to keep themselves
afloat, and they had to trade the right of nomination of their
boroughs to the Treasury. This last stage was accomplished in
1727 when Newcastle bought his right of nomination at Wen-
dover from – ironically enough – the great-great-grandson of
John Hampden. It is possible that this had happened before.
Nothing comparable to the Newcastle papers exists for the
earlier period, otherwise we might find that the burden of
building and supporting an electioneering interest without
direct financial aid had become too great before 1727. But in
the absence of other evidence, 1727 must be regarded as marking
the further stage in traffic for seats.

Fundamentally, the effect of this spoils system was to make
government support essential. So long as there was a possibility
of a Tory government, many oligarchs wavered in their political
sympathies, and Harley used great skill by holding out the bait
of office to the more important of them. In order to secure John,
Duke of Newcastle, and his twelve seats, he made him Lord
Privy Seal. Such an empire could probably demand ministerial
office in any government, and in order to maintain that empire,
office was also essential for it. But Newcastle remained Whig at
bottom, attended the Cabinet but little, and corresponded with

Hanover.[70] The same is true of Somerset, who lingered on for a time with Harley. There were many lesser men who, in order to protect their expensive preserves, were willing, like Newcastle, to moderate their principles, if not reject them entirely. So long as events were going Harley's way, they went with him, but as soon as the tide turned they deserted: opposition was a luxury that as time went on fewer and fewer were able to afford. It was only by such allegiances that Harley could achieve or maintain power, yet the strengthening of oligarchy was fatal to the Tory attitude to government. The same is true of elections. The prospect of success, of a Tory Parliament, encouraged many Tories to contest elections, but it also encouraged them to lavish expenditure, to bribery, to kidnapping, to violence and riot, to all those methods that their own propagandists were denouncing as corrupt because these Tories knew that nothing was more certain to destroy the traditional place in politics played by the man of modest property. They knew that the struggle was critical, but the party as a whole would not face the implications of it. And, in consequence, they exaggerated or distorted what was happening and based their political programme on secondary issues. However, they were haunted by another spectre as well as the growth of oligarchy – the growth of the executive, the placemen and pensioners whom they regarded as the bought lackeys of the Crown.

70. Plumb, 'The Organization of the Cabinet in the Reign of Queen Anne', *T. R. Hist. S.*, 1957, 5th ser., vii, 144.

# CHAPTER FOUR

# THE ROLE OF THE EXECUTIVE

METHODS of government frequently get out of phase with the changing needs of society. The Tudors, by a remarkable mixture of princely authority, Prerogative Courts, Parliamentary participation, and the delegation of local power to the gentry, created a flexible and effective system of government that enabled them to maintain power during a religious and social revolution of considerable complexity. By early Stuart times these social and religious revolutions had become increasingly difficult to control by the methods of the Tudors. Subject to constant attack, partially destroyed between 1641 and 1642, and submerged by the Commonwealth, the Tudor system nevertheless re-emerged at the Restoration, crippled but alive. Even though the Prerogative Courts had been abolished, the supremacy of the Crown in executive matters had been reaffirmed; the judicature, too, remained under royal control. The monarchy might have been bullied and battered, yet it emerged victorious in 1660, its powers undefined. By 1661, the Church and its bishops were re-established in their old authority. Yet there was a difference. Both Parliament and the gentry had increased in authority, if not in a sense of responsibility. The defeat of the Major-Generals and the re-establishment of the old electoral system of Parliament are as significant as the abolition of the Prerogative Courts or the restoration of Church and monarchy. The gentry were as opposed to newfangled methods of centralized government as of old. The result, for the second half of the century, if not chaos, was constant crisis. The problems of executive power, however, haunted Charles II more constantly than they did James I. At the same time the necessity for effective government continued to grow. The Navy of Charles II and his tiny Army created logistic problems that were massive in comparison with those of his grandfather; unlike James I his days were increasingly flooded by the correspondence of an ever-extending diplomatic service; business in all Departments of State continued to multiply, and with its multiplication came the need for a larger and larger budget. But the expansion of the work of government in the reign of Charles II was, however, trivial compared with the flood released by the Revolution, which involved Britain in almost continuous war for twenty-four years. By Queen Anne's reign the Navy consisted of over 200 ships and about 50,000 seamen. Fleets sailed the Baltic, the Mediterranean, and the Caribbean; others protected the Channel and blocked Brest and Dunkirk. In addition, the Navy had to organize complex convoy arrangements for British merchantmen. An army of over 40,000 soldiers was under the command of Marlborough in Flanders, and significant bodies of British troops were also engaged in Spain; the network of alliances was more complicated than any in which Britain had previously been involved. All these services – naval, military, and diplomatic – required a massive communications network. And, of course, they required more than communications; all services clamoured for money, and the government was faced with raising unheard-of sums by taxation. A large and expanding fund of credit became one of the first necessities of government. Also, during these wars Britain began to take on some of the financial burdens of its allies and to permit the raising of foreign loans for military purposes in London.[1] So large and complex a development in armament and finance meant not only an increase in civil servants but also changes in methods of government, and the period between 1689 and 1715 witnesses a rapid growth in administration, of which the full emergence, on the one hand, of an effective Cabinet system and, on the other, of an independent Treasury, are perhaps the most important. What made, however, for administrative flexibility did not always lead directly to political stability.

Much of the success of the French monarchy in the seventeenth century had been due to the construction of an effective central administration. Of course, by modern standards, it was

1. Sir George Clark, *War and Society in the Seventeenth Century*, Cambridge, 1958, 67.

both corrupt and inefficient: the sale of offices, the prevalence of bribery, the loss of revenue by tax-farming and tax exemption, the locust crowds of aristocrats and their hangers-on in all Departments of the State, bred a sense of luminous decay; yet this is illusory. Bribery, corruption, low tax yields, these had been a commonplace of governments for centuries; what was new was the systematization of bureaucratic methods, the greater reliance on factual data in the formulation of policy, and the far greater employment of professional administrators. The monarchy of Louis XIV, from the King downwards, was, by seventeenth-century standards, exceptionally professional. And the stability of France derived from its government.[2]

In contrast to France, the growth in England of the efficiency and power of the executive bears little direct correlation to the achievement of political stability with which it was to be intimately related. As might be expected, the central organs of government develop first; stability follows. And of course, the size of the executive, and the numbers of its employees, are not the only factors that helped to encourage political stability; methods of recruitment, the origins and connexions of personnel, and even the interrelation of duties all have their part. So does the absence of reform, and it is vital to remember that although the executive grew with great rapidity between 1689 and 1725, there was little or no reform: offices were created in abundance; next to none, except at Court, were abolished. Equally important to growth in extent and activity of the executive are two other factors: firstly, unanimity of attitude among office-holders, for without a large measure of unanimity, as we shall see, no executive can act as a stabilizing agent; secondly, harmony between offices, or the successful emergence of a dominant office. Both happened in England. The Treasury became the dominant office for domestic affairs, the Secretary-ship for foreign; between them they possessed the control of all major business, and when the holders of these offices were close allies, the strength of the ministry became formidable. There

2. See Menna Prestwich, 'The Making of Absolute Monarchy, 1559–1683', in *France: Government and Society,* ed. J. Wallace Hadrill and J. McManners, 1957, 105–33.

remains, however, the question of the kind of government that the executive supplies, its efficiency, its harmonization with the economic, political, and social attitudes of those whom it governs, and finally the confidence it can inspire, or the control that it can exert, on the legislative body to whom it may be finally responsible.

For centuries the fulcrum of executive power had rested on the monarch and his court; indeed, during the Middle Ages, and perhaps even later, stability of government had depended, to a very large extent, on the effectiveness of the monarch himself. The personality of the monarch, his grasp of administration and of policy as well as his judgement in choosing ministers, had also been a political factor of the greatest importance in Tudor and Stuart times. It is necessary to stress that Burleigh and Walsingham no more chose themselves than Buckingham or the Duchess of Portsmouth, although their choice obviously derived from a different spring. It used to be argued that the foreign birth and upbringing first of William III, then George I, and the femininity of Queen Anne, led to a devolution of royal power into ministerial hands, and that the result was Cabinet government, the emergence of a Prime Minister, and a shift of power away from the Court to Parliament, and that this fading of the influence of Court and monarch helped to bring about a much more stable political world. This, however, is far too schematic. In considering the influence of the executive on the growth of political stability, this so-called constitutional development requires to be dealt with. Both James II and William III were dedicated, hard-working monarchs with a natural interest in, and flair for, administration – kings of whom even Louis XIV might have approved. Whenever he had an opportunity, William III attended not only Cabinet meetings, but also meetings of the Treasury Board, the Admiralty, even the Commissioners of Customs and Excise; if anything, he was even more thorough in his application to business than James II. Indeed, his whole upbringing in Holland had not only made him hard-working but also an addict of committee government.[3] Yet neither James II nor William III could secure a stable or

3. Stephen B. Baxter, *William III*, 1966, 272-3.

efficient executive; both kings were constrained by frequent ministerial changes, and most of the committees of government of William's reign, from the Treasury to the Board of Trade, proved to be hotbeds of faction. They were rampart with party strife and personal antagonism. Such division had a deleterious effect on policy as well as on administrative competence. Indeed, William's reign is marked by very rapid ministerial changes.[4] William III failed to achieve not only stable Parliamentary government, but also a stable executive. At times, as in 1690 or 1694, this brought about such a paralysis of government that the war was nearly lost. Yet as time went on, there was a steady improvement both in the range and nature of administration, and *even* at the ministerial level there developed constitutional devices that made for great competence in business, of which the growth of Cabinet government is the most important.

William's frequent absences abroad, and the inability of Mary II to attend to the detailed daily routine of government business, swollen as it was by war and the increased diplomatic activity that war generated, gradually led to a more constant and sophisticated use of the Cabinet Council, in spite of William III's initial distrust of such a body. This was largely due to Sunderland who, like Walpole, strongly disapproved of large Cabinets, which created opportunities for factions to develop. In 1693, William III, on his advice, designated a smaller war committee to bear the brunt of administration. There is no need here to delve into the complex history of the Cabinet. I have done that elsewhere.[5]

4. For example, thirteen Commissions of the Treasury were issued between 1689 and 1702, and eleven Commissions of the Admiralty – these within fifteen months, between January 1691 and March 1692. During the same period there were ten Secretaries of State.

5. For the Cabinet, see Jennifer Carter, 'Cabinet Records for the Reign of William III', *EHR*, 1963, lxxviii, 95–114; Plumb, *T. R. Hist. S.*, 5th ser., vii, 137–57. 'A cabinet council of 12 or 13 men, of which no one takes himself to be particularly concerned in the general conduct of affairs where there is neither secrecy, despatch nor credit, is a monstrous thing.' (Sunderland to Portland, 27 June 1693): Kenyon, *Robert Spencer, Earl of Sunderland, 1641–1702*, 263 n.1. A year later, on 13 July 1694, Sunderland expressed himself even more forcibly to Portland about the Cabinet: '... it was not proper immediately to forme a Newe C[abinet] Counsell upon the breaking the old. You know my Proposition was alwayes the 5

What the Cabinet succeeded in doing in the reigns of William III and Anne was to create a machine that kept the daily business of the war moving, in spite of the factional struggles, conflicts of opinion, and personal animosities, which were checked but never eradicated. It did impose, however, some administrative order in the political chaos at the centre. Every perceptive statesman, like Sunderland, saw the desirability of a smaller body united by political attitude and personal loyalty; no statesman could achieve it. The early Cabinets of George I were as riven by personal jealousies and political differences as those of William III and Anne, for by 1717 the conflict between Sunderland and Stanhope on the one hand and Walpole and Townshend on the other cleft the Cabinet in two. Indeed, political stability was not brought about by the emergence of Cabinet government. It could as easily provide a platform for dissension as iron out differences, and Walpole quickly realized the danger of regular meetings of large Cabinets. And so Walpole reduced the Cabinet to virtual insignificance. He met privately with the Chancellor, the Privy Seal, the President of the Court, and two Secretaries, and settled business. Papers that they had agreed were not signed by the King in open Cabinet, as had been the usual practice in Queen Anne's reign, but privately in his closet.[6] At

---

officers who now Meet and the *1st* Commissioner of the Treasury and no one man more but your selfe, for if any body else is admitted a great Many More must and then the whole thing will be ridiculous. Other persons should never be called but as the business requires it, and I will Positively say the Government can not be carryed on any other way': Nottingham Univ. Lib., Portland MSS. Sunderland, not Walpole, is the true architect of Cabinet government in England.

6. Plumb, *Walpole,* ii, 197; Peter King, *Life of Locke,* 1830, ii, 'Notes on Domestic and Foreign Affairs', 50, 52, 84, 86. King, the Lord Chancellor, writes in 1729: 'The Duke of Newcastle told us that the King being to go tomorrow, and having appointed the Queen Regent, he observed that we [i.e. the Lord Chamberlain, the Lord President, the Lord Privy Seal, the remaining Secretary, and Sir Robert Walpole] would meet, as there would be occasion, and that we should not tell anyone extra of the message or of this, or of any other meeting that we should have, because there were some other that might expect, to whom it was not fit that every-thing should be known': ibid., 86. William III's attitude had been almost identical to this when he tried to restrict State business to his chief officers

times, of course, the Cabinet had to meet – for the formal draft of the King's Speech, for the pardoning of criminals, for the approval of preliminaries and treaties, and on those occasions when Walpole thought that a ventilation of business with a large group was requisite. Unity among the six chief ministers of the Crown was easier to achieve than with a large Cabinet, and if not achieved Walpole forced a resignation, as he did with Townshend in 1730. And by these methods, which it must be emphasized were a departure from the Cabinet government as practised in previous reigns, Walpole created a centre of gravity at the heart of the administration. Failure to achieve this by either William III or Queen Anne and their reliance on a large Cabinet Council had been a major factor in the political instability of their reigns. Every Cabinet from 1689 to 1714 rapidly disintegrated into faction; their composition rarely remained stable for more than a year. The complex needs of the war, the absence of William III, and the sex and incapacity of Queen Anne kept them in being; it required a monarch of George I's perspicacity and firmness to reduce their significance and so take a major step forward towards political stability. The period 1720–39, a period of maximum political stability, is marked by a decay of Cabinet government.

The withdrawal of the monarch from business, which conventional constitutional histories have stressed as a major factor in constitutional development in the early eighteenth century, and which, by the delegation of power into the hands of ministers,

---

in 1694, a procedure to which Normanby, a member of the Cabinet, violently objected. 'It is true, that I did promise my Lord Normanby, that when there was a cabinet council, he should assist at it: but surely this does not engage either the Queen or myself, to summon him to all the meetings, which we may order, on particular occasions, to be attended solely by the great officers of the Crown, namely, the Lord Keeper, the Lord President, the Lord Privy Seal, and the two Secretaries of State. . . . I do not see that any objection can be made to this arrangement, whenever the Queen summons the aforesaid officers of the crown, to consult on some secret and important affair' (William III to Shrewsbury, 22 May 1694): W. Coxe, *Private and Original Correspondence of Charles Talbot, Duke of Shrewsbury*, 1821, 38–9. This, of course, marks the triumph of Sunderland's view of the Cabinet.

helped to create a more effective and stable administrative system, is no less a myth. Certainly, Queen Anne did not attend to the details of administration as did William III; her age, her lack of intellectual capacity, precluded that, but she was constantly involved in the process of government. It is a surprising fact that she attended more Cabinet meetings than any other monarch in our history; indeed, no meeting was a Cabinet without her and she averaged over one a week for her entire reign – usually these were on Sunday and lasted for several hours. In addition there were privy councils, certain meetings with her ministers in the closet which were not mere formalities, and she showed a lively and at times obstinate interest even in the details of Army commissions; she saw ambassadors, both formally and informally, and undertook personal correspondence with her royal relations.[7] And under the pressure of her servants she intervened decisively, some might say disastrously, in politics. But she and her husband were not difficult to manage; yet the waywardness of her emotions, her addiction to intrigue, and the fact that she did choose and dismiss ministers, added to rather than subtracted from the political instability of her governments – after all, the crisis of 1710 was partly her doing.

With the accession of George I, the situation did not change; indeed, it became more involved. George I brought with him a small body of highly trained German political advisers whose opinion he held in high respect; they were not idle, and concerned themselves with the details of appointment as well as policy. Both Bothmar and Bernstorff were deeply involved in matters of domestic as well as foreign policy.[8] Although

7. See the various Cabinet memoranda of the Secretaries of State. Harley's: BM, Portland MSS., Loan, List 4, 29/9; Charles, Earl of Sunderland's: Blenheim MSS., C1–16; Dartmouth's: William Salt Library, Dartmouth MSS. A further large batch of Dartmouth memoranda (Dartmouth MSS., 742/vi/2–4) has come to light since I published my article on Queen Anne's Cabinet. They run from 19 June 1711 to 14 June 1713. They do not in any way modify the views put forward in that article (cited above, p. 97, n. 1). Queen Anne attended sixty-two Cabinet meetings between 18 June 1710 and 17 June 1711. For her interest in Army commissions, see Plumb, *Walpole*, i, 153–5.

8. F. Bonnet, the Prussian Resident in London, reported on 24 De-

excluded from the Cabinet, by October 1715, if not before, Bernstorff was secretly receiving regular reports of its discussions from Lord Chancellor Cowper through his wife.[9] On matters of diplomacy in Western Europe, ambassadors reported more fully to the Germans than they did to the English Secretaries of State.[10] Although many English ministers regarded this entry of Hanoverians into English business as inevitable, others, such as Walpole and Townshend, were infuriated, and both Bernstorff, Bothmar, and the King's mistresses, as well as minor figures such as Jean Robethon, the King's private secretary, and Mohammed and Mustapha, his highly intelligent Turkish factotums, were the centres of intrigue, creating new stresses in the politics of the Court that in the end led to political crises. In addition to the Germans, there was also the Prince and Princess of Wales, the centre of a rival Court, within three years spectacularly at loggerheads with the King, and in close contact with the opposition. Here was no withdrawal by the monarchy from politics, no sudden growth of political stability at the centre through the King's inability to speak the language of his country or understand its customs. In 1717, ministerial politics involved the Crown as deeply as in 1710.[11] The character of the King and his alleged withdrawal

---

cember 1714 that 'La première connaissance de toutes les affaires vient aux ministres d'État de Bernstorff et de Bothmar': Wolfgang Michael, *The Beginnings of the Hanoverian Dynasty*, 1936, 374.

9. Herts. PRO, Panshanger MSS., Lady Cowper's Diary, October 1715; the passage revealing this fact was omitted from the published Diary. Lady Cowper writes: 'It was an employment I was not fond of but as it was at the request of B. Bernstorff and that I thought he was right in getting all the information he could I consented to it as did my Lord Cowper.' For this and the influence of the Germans in general, see J. M. Beattie, 'The English Court in the Reign of George I' (unpublished Ph.D. thesis, Camb. Univ. Lib.), 347–54.

10. Ibid., 351; HMC, Polwarth MSS., i–ii, *passim*.

11. Language was no barrier. George I wrote and spoke French fluently as his first language. Bernstorff told Lady Cowper that the King understood neither Latin nor English. The English ministers either spoke French fluently, like Carteret, Townshend, Newcastle, etc., or haltingly, as did Walpole. Nevertheless, Walpole wrote French quite fluently; a long letter from him in his own hand to the Duc d'Orléans,

from business may be dismissed as irrelevant as a factor in constitutional and political development after 1714. Political stability did not begin at the top; Court, Cabinet, and Closet were reached last, and were always to remain vulnerable. Stability began at the grass roots, in the constituencies, in the Departments of State, in the failure of the Commons to check the stabilizing processes that were to undermine its capacity for anarchy. And perhaps the most important of all is the expansion of the executive, which grew, not independently of the legislature, but partly within it.

Between 1680 and 1720, the executive underwent a number of profound changes, and it is necessary to consider them in some detail. The most striking, perhaps, is the changed relationship between the Court and the Departments of State. In contrast with the seventeenth century, by the early eighteenth the Court was dwarfed in size of personnel employed by the Admiralty, the War Office, and the Treasury (including the Exchequer, Customs, and Excise). The Court had, in fact, diminished absolutely as well as relatively. In the reign of Charles I, excluding the households of the royal children and the Queen, Charles I's servants above and below stairs, in the stables and wardrobe, and including the Gentlemen Pensioners, as well as the Yeomen of the Guard, had numbered about 1,480. By the reign of George I the number had dropped below 1,000.[12] The Yeomen of the Guard had diminished from 200 to 119; the number of servants below stairs, under the control of the Lord Steward, had dwindled steadily from 305 to 160. William III and Anne had abolished

---

dated 15 August 1723, is to be found in the Archives du Ministère des Affaires Étrangères, Quai d'Orsay, Corr. Pol. Angleterre, cccxlv., fo. 288. I am indebted to my pupil Mr Paul Fritz for this reference, which is further evidence destructive of the old myth that George I and Walpole could only converse in dog-Latin. Jean Robethon, the King's private secretary, was bilingual: Herts. PRO, Panshanger MSS., Bernstorff to Lady Cowper. For the large number of audiences that George I gave daily to his ministers, see Algemeene Rijksarchief, The Hague, Hensius Corr., 1867, L'Hermitage to Hensius, 18 December 1714.

12. G. E. Aylmer, *The King's Servants, 1625–42*, 1961, 27; Beattie, 'The English Court in the Reign of George I' (unpublished Ph. D. thesis, Camb. Univ. Lib.), 7.

a number of offices – Esquires of the Body as well as various sporting offices. Some offices, although in theory they still existed, were not filled; others had ceased to have much importance. The Gentlemen of the Privy Chamber had not only lost their salaries but also their right to free diet. However, the office still possessed attractions both for patron and the patronized; no Gentleman of the Privy Chamber, being a menial servant of the King, could act as sheriff, juryman, or militiaman, and more important still he could not be arrested for debt. And so we find the lists filled with M.P.s, ex-M.P.s, or immediate relations of M.P.s; indeed, it is rare to find in the early eighteenth century a name that does not belong to the political establishment in these lists. Perhaps the most decisive change, however, took place in the Hall. In Charles I's reign there had been forty-six posts; by 1714 they had been reduced to five and George I abolished four of these. Other departments had gone out of Court as the Board of Works had done; its work was almost entirely under the control of the Treasury. Similarly, the functions of the Treasurer of the Chamber had been curtailed, except for his payment of the King's Messengers, a body that had grown through the increase of diplomacy.[13] In spite of this contraction the Court remained large but its significance changed. Socially, and for the highest reaches of politics, it was still the most important of all institutions; its patronage was of *great* importance for Parliamentary politics and it provided a haven of privilege and profit for a number of landed families of political influence.[14] Men of business often obtained experience in service at Court, and many others acquired additional salaries, by holding minor office, to those that they drew from their departments.

13. Ibid., 5–8, 37.

14. William Le Fleming of Rydal Hall, Westmorland, eager to be presented to George I, wrote as follows to James Stanhope: 'I cannot but wish that for his present Majesty's good, you would not refuse introducing any gentleman to him that have either served him well, or but been zealous for his service, or that are likely to be brought to be affectionate or well inclined to him. For a word, or a smile or but a nod from a King, or but from a great man often influences much': PRO, *S. P. Dom.,* 35, viii, fo. 82, quoted in Beattie, op. cit., 22 n. 42. Even to be near the fountain of patronage was patronage!

And yet it had ceased to be the major provider of office, great and small; its range of patronage could no longer compare with the Treasury, possibly not with the Navy, or even in time of war with the Army and its ancillary activities. So perhaps it is not surprising that the number of M.P.s holding Court office in this period was never very great. In 1701, there were seventeen M.P.s holding household posts; in 1742, after the fall of Walpole, the same number. In George I's reign they rose, after Sunderland's fall and when Walpole had a grip on affairs, to twenty-four.[15] In addition, of course, to the M.P.s, the household provided office, increased status, and solvency to a significant segment of the House of Lords. Indeed, perhaps its greatest importance lies in this fact. About a quarter of the effective membership of the Lords in George I's reign had, often in addition to other posts and offices, positions at Court. In many ways these twenty-five to thirty peers, fortified by a disciplined bench of bishops and usually underpinned by sixteen representative peers of Scotland, formed, after 1722, the kernel of ministerial stability in the Lords. This should be strongly stressed, because the House of Lords as a factor in politics is so constantly ignored.

Throughout William III's reign, and to a lesser extent under Anne, coherence and unity were no more to be found at Court than in the Commons; but the open bitterness between Sunderland, Leeds, and Wharton would have been unthinkable after 1722. Of course, personal animosities arose – Carteret hated both Townshend and Walpole – and he had his sympathizers; again, after 1727, there was a small watchful group, the old friends of George II as Prince of Wales, who waited for Walpole to make a mistake. Even the bishops and representative Scottish peers had their moments of doubt, and the bishops even made an occasional fluttering gesture of independence,[16] but the difference between the Court in 1700 and in 1727 is dramatic and indisputable. By 1727 there was a Court party, firmly under the control of the minister, and for the ordinary course of politics utterly reliable; and this included the richest, the most powerful and widely connected aristocrats. By 1727 the anti-Court

15. Beattie, op. cit., 410–18.    16. Plumb, *Walpole*, ii, 299–300.

aristocracy was trivial in numbers and negligible in influence, and constantly dwindling. Neither Charles II, James II, William III, nor Anne had achieved this.

Furthermore, the household was by the 1720s more extensively, if loosely, linked with Parliament than ever before in its history; the twenty-four M.P.s who held Court posts in 1726 are not a sufficient indication of this involvement. Of the ninety-one men who, at one time or another, were Gentlemen of the Privy Chamber to George I, over a half were fathers or sons of M.P.s or related to them, or had been at one time or another Members of Parliament themselves. And this is largely true of all posts of moderate social distinction at Court.[17] From the time of the Revolution, Parliament itself, because it met yearly, had become a much more desirable place to sit in for the socially distinguished families, for those families, indeed, that had in the past naturally gravitated towards the Court. This at first did not lead to great political homogeneity among the courtiers, but the potentiality was there. Offices, great and small, were open to purchase, both in William III's and in Anne's reigns; again, neither William III nor Anne were committed to any set of ministers for long, so patronage in the household eddied with the tide, sucking in and casting out Whig and Tory in all their complicated varieties. In George I's reign, however, direct purchase of important Court appointments had virtually ceased, even if bribery had not.[18] Competition for patronage remained intense, and the Duke of Chandos spent well over £14,000 in bribes in less than four years; these were given to George I's German ministers and one of his mistresses.[19] The lack of purchase, however, made dismissal easier for politi-

17. Even menial offices could play a useful part. Robert Walpole's daughters were being educated in 1714 at Madame Nezeareau's school in Chelsea; in the same year, immediately after the accession of George I, her husband, Charles, became a Sewer of the Chamber.

18. There was but one attempt, by the Duke of Chandos to buy the Duke of Montagu's office – the Great Wardrobe.

19. C. and M. Baker, *The Life and Circumstances of James Brydges, First Duke of Chandos*, 112, n. i. He obtained a peerage for his father, the deanship of Carlisle for his brother, and the reversion of a Court post for his son.

cal reasons, and therefore political control tighter. After 1689, and even more after 1714, the ebb and flow of political power between Parliament and Court becomes stronger; more of the political establishment of the nation are to be found at Court, and courtiers themselves became steadily more entangled in the routine of Parliamentary government. Also, the social role of the Court for Parliamentary families acts as a cement, binding the two institutions together.[20]

The Court, however, could not satisfy the aspirations, social or pecuniary, of a political nation that was constantly growing in size and authority. Ultimately political stability is created by a sense of possession – that power is being satisfactorily transmuted into authority. A vital factor in the growth of political stability at this time lies, therefore, in the fact that the institutions of executive government expanded at a rate that was capable of absorbing or obliging, and thereby satisfying, an effective segment of the political nation.

Two facts need to be stressed. The number of men employed by the government grew faster between 1689 and 1715 than in any previous period of English history, and perhaps at a rate not to be equalled again until the nineteenth century. The volume of government business grew equally fast, and in so doing touched directly the lives of more people than ever before.

The greatest expansion of the executive occurred in the Treasury. Not only did the Treasury expand, it also secured control over all sub-departments that were concerned with the Revenue – Customs and Excise – and other departments connected with taxation. Furthermore, the Treasury enhanced its

20. This is well illustrated by the actions of George I, after his quarrel in 1717 with the Prince of Wales. For the next three years George I became, contrary to his earlier practice, extremely active socially, dining frequently in public, providing public tables at Hampton Court and St James's, going frequently in large parties to the Opera – all of this being to counteract the pull of his son's rival Court. And, of course, he let it be known that all who attended his son's Court would not be viewed with favour. The social life of George II and Queen Caroline from their earliest days in London had been politically tinged. Snobbery being as prevalent as it is, social life at Court provided a source of cheap patronage. See Beattie, op. cit., 344–406.

power by securing a greater degree of independence than any other Department of State.[21]

Charles II's reign had witnessed important reforms in the internal organization of the Treasury. Sir George Downing had been responsible for a thorough reorganization of the Treasury records and for the introduction of Dutch ideas on taxation and financial policy. A succession of exceptionally able civil servants, both major, such as Henry Guy or William Lowndes, or minor, such as William Snow or Robert Squibb, brought a necessary air of professionalism to its work, a tendency that was encouraged by a number of very able statesmen – Danby, Rochester, Godolphin, and Harley – whose political careers were closely associated with the Treasury. 'Between 1660 and 1702 the Treasury office grew from something approaching the personal retinue of a magnate into a professional body of civil servants.'[22] By comparison, the power of the Exchequer waned, and it was the Treasury that secured freedom from control not only by the Secretaries but also by the Cabinet. At the same time dependent bodies – Customs, Excise, Mint, and Tax Office – were brought under its own direction, a development that was rendered more effective by the abolition of tax-farming in the reign of William III. Furthermore, the growth of the Treasury office, because it was freer from sinecures and offices held for life, enabled men of talent to rise rapidly in the service of the government. One should not, however, paint too rosy a picture of this administrative revolution. In the Exchequer, at least, sinecures abounded. Sir Robert Howard, as bad an administrator as he was poet, could not be removed from his post as Auditor of the Exchequer, which he had bought and so held for life. His security permitted the luxury of political opposition to the King. The Exchequer also provided a notable

21. Unlike all other government business, Treasury business scarcely, if ever, came before the Cabinet. In more than one thousand Cabinet memoranda that I have studied I have only come across two or three doubtful examples. Treasury business was settled directly with the monarch by the Lord Treasurer or First Lord. For the Treasury, see Baxter, *The Development of the Treasury, 1660–1702*, and E. Hughes, *Studies in Administration and Finance, 1558–1825*, Manchester, 1934.

22. Baxter, op. cit., 257.

army of offices that were discharged by deputy, and so provided outdoor relief for the lucky families that held them. Few, however, were as fortunate as the family of Walker, who held the office of Usher of the Exchequer. It had been granted this office in perpetuity by Henry II, and members of the family were still drawing their stipends in William III's reign. Corruption, too, was rampant enough. It took the Crown the best part of a hundred years to recover the £12,000 of which it was defrauded by Sir William D'Oyley. Both Henry Guy and William Lowndes, Secretaries of the Treasury, left, considering their origins, surprisingly large estates, and Guy's arraignment for bribery probably had a stronger basis than political animosity. Peculation at a lower level was endemic and the cumbersome regulations for the supervision of financial transactions never worked efficiently. It would be quite fallacious to depict the Treasury in the reigns of William III and Anne as an efficient, well-ordered, and thoroughly competent service.

Nor was its policy always enlightened. In general, William III obtained his money cheaper than Charles II; his knowledge of banks and banking, combined with his urgent need for money for his troops, gave him a personal interest in the Treasury's activities that may be measured by his frequent attendances, when resident in England, at the Commission. The foundation of the Bank of England, which had William's support, gave greater flexibility and security to the country's monetary system than it had ever possessed before, and as the years passed, permitted a greater exploitation of the nation's credit, which vastly stimulated the national economy. And no doubt too, the appropriation of taxes, irritating as it was to William III, also helped to create a sense of financial probity. Yet against this must be placed the follies of the Recoinage, which created unnecessary financial stringency and much human suffering, and a taxation system that at times took on more the appearance of bingo than a carefully calculated national policy. That perhaps is unjust. The land tax, as first announced, was a serious attempt to introduce what was virtually an income tax, and even in its final form, as a tax based largely on fixed property, it provided an important source of revenue that, in spite of the complaints of the country gentry, bred rather than destroyed confidence and made borrowing easier and cheaper. The cost of the war was so great and the need for raising revenue so constant that the search for new taxes did, however, take on some aspects of a lottery. All suggestions were welcomed by the Treasury, from amateurs as well as expert economists such as D'Avenant. Any adventurer with an idea that seemed viable was encouraged to promote it. Normally he produced pamphlets extolling the virtue of his tax – the ease of collection, the justice of its incidence – and as Parliament assembled he circulated the Members, then lobbied them. If the Treasury, approving of the idea, succeeded in getting it through the Commons, the promoter could then expect a rich reward. He always secured a place in the collection. By such means Thomas Neale made and lost a fortune out of the salt tax.[23] Taxes rained on commodities – trawlers, hackney cabs, servants, plate, paper, glass – yet the increase in William III's reign was small by comparison with that in Queen Anne's; between 1702 and 1714 more customs were levied on new commodities than had been imposed since 1660.[24] Most of these new taxes increased the work of the Customs and Excise, but others, such as the land tax and salt duties, required new and elaborate organizations; a few, such as licences for hawkers or hackney cabs only required commissioners, an office, and one or two clerks. Yet the overall result was a huge extension in the number of people employed by the government in the collection of taxes. By 1718, 561 customs officers were employed in the Port of London alone, but in addition to these about 1,000 were employed on a part-time basis, and it was from this pool that regular officials were usually recruited. In the outports, in addition to seventy-two who had their offices by patent, and who

23. *DNB*; Hughes, *Studies in Administration and Finance, 1558–1825*, 176–7. John Kynvin was responsible for suggesting duties on paper, which was based on his experience of Spanish methods: Baxter, *The Development of the Treasury, 1660–1702*, 58. The Treasury Books contain a multitude of suggestions for taxation, and so do the private papers of Godolphin, Harley, and others. Sir Robert Walpole continued to receive similar propositions throughout his ministry.

24. E. E. Hoon, *The Organization of the English Customs System, 1696–1786*, New York, 1958, 26.

were usually sinecurists discharging their duties, if they had any, by deputy, customs officers were plentiful enough. Plymouth had fifty-four, plus a hundred part-timers who enjoyed the delightful title of 'extraordinary men'; Dover forty-three regular officers; Dartmouth twenty-five; Liverpool fifty-five; and Great Yarmouth forty-three, in addition to three patent officers and fifty-six extraordinary men, an establishment of an astonishing size for so small a port; though perhaps the twelve regular officers required at Fowey was equally remarkable.[25] Multifarious as the customs duties had become, the number of officials had grown more rapidly, and for reasons that were as often political as financial. As with the customs, so with excise, salt, hides, and the like: revenue officers sprouted like mushrooms between 1689 and 1714. 389 were employed on salt duties (a few of these were also customs collectors, but there were extraordinary men in salt as well as in the customs); about 500 were employed in collecting taxes on hides. For every county there were distributors of 'stampt vellum' who received a poundage of 18d., and were free to employ under-distributors. And, of course, the land tax involved a very considerable number of gentry. The land-tax commissioners became men of great power in their counties. The method of assessment was that used by Charles I for ship money and followed by Cromwell, Charles II, and James II for poll taxes. Each county was assessed; the commissioners then assessed individuals in order to meet the government's demand on the county. Within a few years of its establishment it became clear that the land tax was unlikely to be abolished so long as the burden of a large Army and Navy had to be borne, and the commissioners and receivers for the land taxes became exceptionally powerful in local politics.

The vast increase in the number of men involved in the administration and organization of taxes led, naturally enough, to very considerable corruption. At the centre there was plenty of dishonesty, peculation, and incompetence, but, even so, an earnest attempt was made to keep a disciplined control of excise, customs, and land-tax officials in the localities. It proved, how-

25. These figures are drawn from John Chamberlayne, *Magnae Britanniae Notitia*, 1718. See also Hoon, op. cit. *passim*.

ever, to be the work of Sisyphus, as a few cases will illustrate: Briggs and Blofield, both close friends of the Walpole–Townshend faction in Norfolk, were £17,000 in arrears in 1695; Robert Peters, the receiver for Hertfordshire, went bankrupt in 1713 owing the government £26,000;[26] the swindles of three M.P.s – Burton, Duncombe and Knight – in 1698, by falsely endorsing Exchequer bills raised upon the land tax, outraged the tolerant commissioners. The salt collection was less corrupt than the land tax, but far from free of it, and the depredations of Robert Bell of Newcastle in Queen Anne's reign were notorious.[27] The customs and excise officers were in a sense bribed by the government to be honest. After all, they received half the value of any seizures they made; nevertheless, owing to the lowness of their salaries and their dependence on fees, corruption, connivance at smuggling, and illicit trade were endemic among them.[28] The extent of corruption, however, is not a matter of vital concern in this context. What is important to stress is that after 1689 and throughout the reigns of William III and Anne the number of people employed by the government in the collection of taxes, and deriving profit from it either legally or illegally, increased with exceptional rapidity. The profit cannot be denied. Although the yield of taxes steadily fell before 1714, the number of men employed in their collection constantly rose. Far more men, therefore, were being drawn into a direct and profitable relationship with government than ever before. Fields ripe for patronage were constantly opened or extended. Two final points, therefore, should be made before turning to other administrative developments. Incompetent, corrupt, ramshackle, antiquated, and ill disciplined as the English system of finance and taxation was, it nevertheless worked adequately enough to meet the huge demands of William III's and Queen Anne's wars; and neither monarch was ever in the dire financial straits that had confronted all the English rulers of

26. W. R. Ward, *The English Land Tax in the Eighteenth Century*, Oxford, 1953, 49–50.

27. Hughes, *Studies in Administration and Finance, 1558–1825*, 189.

28. Hoon, *The Organization of the English Customs System, 1696–1786*, 211–18.

the seventeenth century, including Cromwell. There were plenty
of short crises, but interest was met, debts paid, and revenue
found, and as the years passed, the financial solvency and
stability of England was secured; this must be regarded as a
factor of prime importance in the growth of political stability.
Indeed, it has long been recognized as such. Equally important,
but less remarked, is the growth of personnel profitably engaged in government employment. These people, as we shall see,
were drawn from the politically conscious part of the nation, and
the political nation was extremely conscious of them.

The huge sums raised by increased taxes and large loans on
the public credit were mainly spent on the Army and Navy.
By 1714, the British Navy was the largest in Europe, and it
employed more workers than any other industry in the country.
Its expansion between 1689 and 1697 was dramatic. Ships
increased from 173 to 323, and tonnage from 101,892 to over
160,000; by 1714, although the number of ships had fallen,
their size had increased, for the tonnage was up to 167,219
and their fire-power had also increased.[29] Such an expansion
not only stimulated all the ancillary industries, but also greatly
increased both the number of serving officers and the number of
men employed in administration; after all, the clerical business
of the Admiralty and the Navy Board doubled between 1689 and
1697.[30] Indeed, increase in business forced the Admiralty to buy
the core of its present site and to build large new offices; to the
indignation, if not the surprise, of the House of Commons, the
seller of the land appeared as the Secretary of the Navy at
Portsmouth. In addition, a new dockyard was opened at
Plymouth, strengthening the potential government interest
there; increased work in shipbuilding and refitting created new
and lucrative opportunities for the dominant economic and
political groups in major ports along the coast, from Bristol to
Hull. Nor was this all. Groups of London merchants dominated

---

29. John Ehrman, *The Navy in the War of William III, 1689–97*, Cam-
bridge, 1953, xx; the following paragraphs are greatly indebted to Mr
Ehrman's excellent study. See also J. H. Owen, *War on Sea under Queen
Anne*, Cambridge, 1938.

30. Ehrman, op. cit., 554.

victualling, and the Baltic merchants grew fatter on their swelling yearly contracts for tar, timber, and hemp. Opportunities for economic and political power to fuse abounded everywhere. Of course, these were not taken at once. At the Admiralty itself there was a core of highly professional civil servants – led by James Southerne, William Bridgeman and Josiah Burchett – who ought, at least, to share the glory accorded to Pepys as founders of the administrative methods at the Admiralty, which lasted for centuries. And the Navy itself still offered opportunities for a successful career, unaided by patronage or favour; both Sir Cloudesley Shovell (perhaps the most delectable combination of names in naval history) and Sir David Mitchell had risen from cabin boy to admiral by their skill and courage alone. Yet the days of such mobility were numbered; able men were to continue to rise in the Navy throughout the eighteenth century but exceedingly rarely without the support of a political patron or the advantage of family connexion. Already the value of promotion in a political context was well appreciated, as appreciated as the political potential in naval activity in the boroughs and seaports, but, at least during William III's and Anne's reigns, there were two parties at Court, and a spoils system developed that turned the higher posts of the Navy into a curious game of snakes and ladders. But the point that needs to be stressed here is that this vast extension of naval activity provided new pastures, rich in political potential, capable of providing increasing affluence and power for the political nation – pastures that quite obviously could be better cultivated under moderately disciplined procedures of oligarchy than in the semi-anarchic conditions of party and factional strife.

The same was, of course, true of the Army. In a sense its expansion was more dramatic than the Navy's; also, its need in men, money, and armaments were very much the preoccupations of William III himself, who always took a somewhat jaundiced view of the huge expenditure that the Navy required. Immediately after the Revolution, 10,000 troops were raised and in spite of the temporary reductions imposed by Parliament in 1697, the British Army had risen to at least 70,000 by 1711, and the number of its regiments had almost quadrupled since the days of James II, when the foundations of Marlborough's army were laid.[31] With the growth of the Army there had developed a much more complex, sophisticated, and numerous administration. The outstanding figures, as with the Treasury or Navy, were professional civil servants, exceedingly efficient by the standards of their day, none more so than William Blathwayt; like Pepys they were avaricious, open to bribery, and willing to moderate their pursuit of efficiency if it conflicted with private gain. The system of purchase, gradually abolished elsewhere, remained in the Army, and colonels and captains reimbursed themselves with a total disregard of military efficiency; food, clothing, armament, were as deficient in quality as the muster-rolls were in men. The Army was as luminous with corruption as any Department of State, and yet it worked more efficiently than it had since the days of Cromwell. And it was still open to talent. The hatred of the House of Commons for standing armies displayed both in 1689 and 1697 bred a sense of insecurity of investment that may have caused some fathers to hesitate before buying a commission for their sons. Moreover, plenty of officers were killed, providing at least temporary advancement in the field for able junior officers without influence. But by the end of Queen Anne's reign times were changing. Although the yearly passage of the Army Bill was still to provide an exercise for oratory for long-winded back-benchers, the fact of a permanent Army, tiny by European but large by British standards, had been accepted, and in consequence the investment by the upper classes in Army commissions became heavier, and promotion without influence or riches increasingly rare. The turning-point came in 1711, when the Tory government, in order to restrict his patronage and increase their own, forbade the Commander-in-Chief, Marlborough, to grant promotions in the field and insisted that all sales and purchases of Army commissions must, in future, be sanctioned by the Crown. Thereafter promotion by seniority or by political favour, and usually the latter, became the sole routes for advancement in the Army.[32]

31. C. Dalton, *English Army Lists*, 1892–1904, 6 vols; J. W. Fortescue, *A History of the British Army*, 2nd ed., 1910, i, 556–8.

32. I. F. Burton, 'The Committee of Council at the War Office: An

As with the Court, Treasury, and Navy, closer links were forged between the Army and Parliament. In the Parliaments of Charles II or James II, a general was a comparatively rare bird; in William III's, Anne's, and George I's Parliaments there were enough to make a small lobby. In 1701, thirty-nine Army officers sat in the Commons, as many as there were merchants;[33] and that, of course, only represents the core of the Army's involvement in Parliament: in addition to administrative officers such as Blathwayt and contractors such as Sir Stephen Evance, there was an ever-growing number of Members of the Commons whose sons or brothers or wife's relations were pursuing their fortune, and sometimes their fame, in the ranks of the Army.

No pastures were so rich, so lush, so promising of sweet increase, as the two armed forces or the taxation system, but elsewhere the waste was being taken in and laid down to grass sufficient to support a small band of well-born families. As with so many affairs of state, England slowly adapted French methods in diplomacy and established representatives in most courts in Europe; until the Revolution diplomacy had largely been a matter of grand, extraordinary embassies by an ambassador for a particular purpose – treaties, marriages, compliments to new sovereigns, and the like – or the use of accredited agents, sometimes but not always British. After the Revolution, although somewhat delayed by the reluctance of Catholic powers to acknowledge William III, England began to establish regular diplomatic representation, with a proper embassy staff, at all the major, and most of the minor, courts of Europe. William III appointed eighty diplomatic representatives, Anne one hundred and thirty six. Although there was a decline with the

---

Experiment in Cabinet Government', *Historical Journal*, Cambridge, 1961, iv, 78–84, and I. F. Burton and A. N. Newman, 'Promotion in the Eighteenth-Century Army', *EHR*, 1963, lxxviii, 655–68. As the authors write, 'Birth without fortune . . . describes the typical social background of an army officer under Anne'. This could be applied as a maxim to most fields of patronage in Augustan England.

33. Walcott, *English Politics in the Early Eighteenth Century*, 165. This figure is probably an underestimate, as it is based on Dalton's *English Army Lists*, which are very deficient.

return of peace in 1713, and a number of regular posts were reduced to mere agencies again, the process was reversed in the reign of George II and numbers rose again.[34] Not only were there more opportunities created for diplomats, but the service itself became much more professional. 'A regular hierarchy of ranks was organized and stabilized: salaries and allowances and methods of paying them were regularized . . . promotion from grade to grade became possible, if not always rapid and regular enough to satisfy aspirants.'[35] Even so, the diplomatic service never aroused intense cupidity; the rewards were not great; years in St Petersburg or Constantinople brought a sense of chill to the most robust temperaments, and few could view with equanimity a career spent at minor German courts. The pasture provided by the diplomatic service never grew lush. Yet it had its uses: it was compatible with membership of Parliament; it created, or so many diplomats hoped, a sense of obligation, an increased claim for a job at home; and it also provided for ministers a method of translating the important but difficult without the ignominy of total disgrace. And, of course, as well as the diplomats, there were the secretaries, the chaplains, the clerks – a small, new area of minor patronage for which there was never room enough.[36]

More important, perhaps, than the growth of the diplomatic service was the expansion of employment in the colonies. This, of course, had grown steadily throughout the seventeenth century as one West Indian island after another was brought within the control of the English government. New colonies had been founded along the east coast of North America and passed from proprietary to royal status; but after the Revolution,

34. D. B. Horn, *The British Diplomatic Service,* Oxford, 1961, 44.
35. Ibid., 13.
36. A typical example of the use of the diplomatic service is the fate of Thomas Burnet, son of Gilbert, Bishop of Salisbury, who naturally had claims on the Whig establishment. He spent the best part of four years besieging mistresses and ministers for a job. His hopes were for a minor Court post (he was already a Gentleman Waiter), and he was highly delighted when, at last, he obtained a consulship at Lisbon. See *The Letters of Thomas Burnett to George Duckett, 1712–22,* ed. David Nicol Smith, Oxford, 1914.

again with the methods of Louis XIV very much in mind, the Treasury and the Auditor-Generals rather than the Board of Trade gradually secured greater administrative and political authority in the colonies.[37] Indeed, the growing interest of the Treasury in colonial affairs was only partially financial, for there was little expectation that dues to the Crown would yield any revenue; they were in fact so small that they were only appropriated once, in 1699. What was at stake was authority and patronage – authority, which strategy required, and patronage, which was becoming an ever-increasing necessity. Any job that could be controlled by the government was rapidly becoming a matter for concern. The steady extension of royal authority led to an equally steady increase in numbers of revenue officers, customs officials, and postal clerks; the judiciary also increased and, owing to the war with France and Spain, so did the Army and Navy in the colonies. Neither did the Treaty of Utrecht provide much retrenchment. Fears of France and an aggressive attitude towards Spain kept the strategic necessities of the colonies alive throughout the long period of peace. As a field of political patronage, the colonies were made to yield their dividends. William Blathwayt secured quite lucrative offices for six of his relations.[38] Naturally, only high offices such as governorships attracted the politically powerful, but in any discussion of patronage it is unwise to limit its influence on politics to the number of peers or Members of Parliament directly involved. Often they were but the agents of extended families, hungry for jobs.

The growth of opportunity for political patronage was not limited to the institutions and professions briefly described in this chapter. During this period, both legal and ecclesiastical appointments, always subject it is true to political necessities, became more entangled with Parliamentary politics than they had been before.[39] This is particularly true of the Church; the

37. For the spread of Treasury influence and the steady extension of royal authority in the American colonies, see Jacobsen, *William Blathwayt*, 160–85.

38. Ibid., 348.

39. A typical example is the case of the three vacant bishoprics in 1708,

situation with regard to preferment has been fully exposed by
the late Professor Sykes and requires no reiteration. In 1701,
thirty-four lawyers out of the sixty-two in Parliament held a
legal office of some importance, and many of the others acquired
them in subsequent years.[40] The relationship between Parliament and the legal profession grew closer still, and remained
close, even when the number of practising lawyers in Parliament
declined in the later eighteenth century.[41]

There are two major fields of patronage that I have not discussed – Ireland and Scotland. Both greatly influenced Parliamentary politics in different ways. There was little growth of
place in Ireland, but, of course, a thorough purge after the
defeat of James II, and a greater consciousness of the need to
maintain control of political authority and the Irish establishment remained a vital concern for all ministries, and was dominated as much by Englishmen as by the Anglo-Irish. Scotland,
after the Union, suffered some intrusion of Englishmen into
Scottish places of profit, particularly in the Customs and Excise,
which were remodelled on the English pattern, but later, and
frequently enough, jobs had to be found for the Scots in London
– the Todds, for example, dominated the Post Office for much of
the eighteenth century.[42] Both these developments affected the
overall pattern of political stability, but they are not of great
importance in the context of the present chapter.

Two factors, therefore, emerge. The years immediately
following the Revolution witnessed a considerable extension
of government activity and efficiency, although this must not be

---

when the Junto attempted to force Godolphin to appoint three loyal
Whigs, a step that was frustrated by Queen Anne, and they got only one,
Trimmell, at Norwich. A situation such as this could not have arisen in
Charles II's or James II's reign.

40. Walcott, *English Politics in the Early Eighteenth Century*, 168–71.

41. Namier, *The Structure of Politics at the Accession of George III*, 42–5.
Namier estimates their number in 1761 as about forty.

42. Riley, *The English Ministers and Scotland, 1707–27*, 36–74. This book
illuminates admirably the nature and growth of patronage. Godolphin
preferred to use able administrators, but time and time again political
necessities forced him to choose a man on grounds of patronage rather
than experience.

exaggerated; the increase was in terms of what had gone before. This, with victories in the field, gradually bred confidence in the political nation – in the ability of the government to govern and to win its wars.

The growth of the executive had also created more places, and in the ensuing scramble for patronage, political considerations more often than not dominated the decisions as to who should get which place. But between 1689 and 1715, there was no single-party government; there were two parties, *pace* Mr Walcott, and many factions, and the scramble for place did not immediately lead to political stability – indeed, quite the reverse, for during this period there grew up the beginnings of a spoils system. It was never fully comprehensive, but it helped to keep party and factional animosity alive. After 1689, all Catholics were naturally purged from office, and with them went non-jurors; after 1696, those who would not sign the Association were scheduled to follow, but if the customs service is anything to go by, the process was slow and inefficient. Whigs had a rough time in 1702, and again in 1711 and in 1714. Bolingbroke swore he would have every Whig out of office within six months.[43] Of course, these purges were a hit-and-miss affair, and a discreet Tory or Whig, whether in a high office or a smaller one, could survive for years. Godolphin was rarely out of office between 1689 and 1710, and William Blathwayt was only out of office for a few months after the Revolution until the Whigs finally purged him in 1707. Others survived frequent ministerial changes because they held their offices for life. Nevertheless, swings in party fortunes could play ducks and drakes with place-holders. Members of Parliament became conscious of the risk of office. For example, a dozen or so Tory place-holders who voted for Bromley as Speaker in 1705 were summarily ejected from office.[44]

Even with the extension of place, the majority of M.P.s, however, had little or no share of patronage. This growth of the executive was viewed with disquiet by the back-benchers, who were contracting debts and mortgaging their lands to meet

43. Plumb, *Walpole*, i, 194.
44. W. A. Speck, 'The Choice of a Speaker in 1705', *Bulletin of the Institute of Historical Research*, 1964, xxxvii, 20–46.

the ever-increasing costs of elections. As scene after scene of corruption was revealed to them – exposure of frauds; swindles in the Treasury, Customs, and colonial accounts; deficiencies in naval supply – mouldy biscuits, bad beer; fraudulent Army contractors and false musters for dead men's pay – all of these things turned disquiet to anger and fed the flame of party animosity. There is thus a twofold result of this rapid growth of the executive: on the one hand, an intensification of factional strife at the centre, a more ferocious battle for power among the professional politicians, if not among the professional civil servants; and on the other hand, an increased bitterness between Court and country. For the independent squires or the back-benchers, the liberty of Parliament seemed to be threatened by this growing cancer in its midst, a mood that was quickly sensed and half believed by Robert Harley. It was exploited by him in order to influence party politics to the advantage of himself and his friends. For the whole of William III's reign and for most of Queen Anne's, the growth of the executive increased the instability of English politics, and the independent interests fought every inch of the way to prevent the domination of Parliament by the executive. The growth of place, like the growth of oligarchy, initially fed the rage of party.

# CHAPTER FIVE

# THE RAGE OF PARTY

'THIS I say; it is time for every man who is desirous to preserve the British Constitution, and to preserve it secure, to contribute all he can to prevent the ill-effects of that new Influence and Power which have gained strength in every reign since the Revolution; of those means of corruption that may be employed one time or another on the part of the Crown and that proneness to corruption on the part of the People, that hath been long growing and still grows.'[1] So wrote Bolingbroke in 1734 in his *A Dissertation upon Parties,* whose thesis was that increased taxation, brought about by the wars of William III and Queen Anne, had created fresh sources of patronage, and so defeated the major aim of the Revolution, which had been to secure the independence of Parliament. His hope was a renewed, reinvigorated country party – by 1734 a hope as utterly futile, as ridiculously unrealistic, as the rest of Bolingbroke's political philosophy. Yet it had not always been so. Bolingbroke's analysis was correct enough and his own early experience had demonstrated the power and effectiveness of the country party in action. The back-benchers, led usually by Tory or crypto-Tory groups, were quite as clear-sighted as Bolingbroke about the developments that were taking place between 1689 and 1714, and made resolute attempts to stop them. The rising cost of elections, the growth of government patronage, combined with inefficiency and corruption, so inflamed the passions of the average Member of Parliament that party strife became, between 1689 and 1720, as violent as at any time in our history. In this

1. Henry St John, Viscount Bolingbroke, *A Dissertation upon Parties,* 7th ed., 1749, 304-5. Also, 'There never was a juncture, within the memory of any who are now living, when the rage of parties ran higher than at this time': *Memoirs of the Life and Ministerial Conduct of Henry St John, 1st Viscount Bolingbroke,* 1752, 280.

rancorous upsurge of political feeling old lines of party division were blurred, if never eradicated, but a cleavage between Whig and Tory remained one of the basic facts of political history. The confusion, the complexity of politics in this period does not derive, as Walcott would have us believe,[2] from the absence of a two-party system, but from the failure of either party to secure effective domination over the other, a situation that was further complicated by the needs of two great wars. Coalitions were forced on both parties by circumstances; principles at times were moderated by events; and, of course, there were desertions and conversions, loss of nerve and beady-eyed compromise – all of which factors help to create a sense of confusion at the centre. At least for historians; contemporaries were less distracted and they rarely had difficulty, at least after the middle 1690s, in distinguishing Whig from Tory. When lists of Members of the 1713 and 1715 Parliaments were drawn up, probably for the enlightenment of George I's Hanoverian ministers, the compiler had no hesitation in dividing the majority of the House of Commons quite simply into Whigs and Tories.[3] And to politicians of these

2. Walcott, *English Politics in the Early Eighteenth Century*, 160.

3. Lincoln Record Office, Worsley MSS., 'Liste Exact du Dernier Parlement et de Celuyci avec de Remarques'. This very important list, written in the most beautiful calligraphy, was almost certainly intended for George I. It lists every Member as Whig or Tory, but does distinguish those Whigs who at times voted Tory and the somewhat larger group of Tories ('Whimsicals') who voted Whig. The Whigs who occasionally voted Tory are men such as William Lowndes, who as Permanent Secretary of the Treasury voted with the ministry whatever complexion it might have, a fact that the compiler notes. Whoever he was, his attitude to party is very sophisticated. He realized that it was the most important factor in politics, but also that interest, place, and ambition at the centre rendered its effect very complex in many individual politicians. His general remarks are so wise that they are given below in Appendix I (pp. 189–91) *in extenso*. This document will be published in its entirety by Mr Romney Sedgwick in his forthcoming volumes of the *History of Parliament*. Furthermore, recent analysis of division lists of Queen Anne's reign reveal a much more consistent voting pattern according to party principles than Walcott would allow, and this is particularly marked among the Whigs. See J. G. Sperling, 'The Division of 25 May 1711 on an Amendment to the South Sea Bill', *Historical Journal*, Cambridge, 1961, iv, 191–202; G. S. Holmes, 'The Commons Division on "No

two reigns, Whigs and Tories were as discernible as day or night.

There were broad party principles to which most politicians acknowledged allegiance, one way or the other. Of course, political commentators tried to give a more exact description, as, indeed, political commentators do today: Church Tories, country Tories, Court Tories – these help to explain the bias of a particular Tory. Again, the use, for the purpose of analysis, of Court and country interests is exceptionally valuable, for here is a real dichotomy, as we shall see, but it does not break the reality of either Whiggism or Toryism.[4] And the same is true of factions: whatever coalitions are made, factions remain Whig or Tory. As Feiling showed over forty years ago in his *History of the Tory Party* – which still remains the best political analysis of the period, the most profound, the most scholarly, and the most realistic – the separation and definition of party becomes clearer each year after the Revolution, and the only period of gross confusion was between 1690 and 1695, when the New Tory party, which was to base itself as solidly on the country interest as Shaftesbury himself, was being forged.[5]

Party, however, is easier to understand if political differences at the higher levels – such as peace and war, the amount of toleration allowed to Dissenters, the treatment of Ireland or the Union with Scotland, and the question of succession – are left on one side for the moment and the areas of bitter animosity in the structure of power explored in more detail.[6]

---

Peace without Spain", 7 December 1711', *Bulletin of the Institute of Historical Research*, 1960, xxxiii, 223–34; Speck, ibid., xxxvii, 20–46.

4. There is, perhaps, one exception here. In 1706, in a debate on a clause in the Regency Bill that repealed the clause of the Act of Settlement that would have excluded all place-holders from the House of Commons after Queen Anne's death and replaced it by a list of specified office-holders, a number of country Whigs voted with the Tories against this measure, although it was supported by the Junto. This, however, is the only considerable defection of Whigs that we know of during Queen Anne's reign. For an account of this debate and the country Whigs' attitude, see Camb. Univ. Lib., Add. MSS., 7093, fos. 72 ff.

5. K. Feiling, *A History of the Tory Party*, Oxford, 1924, 311 ff.

6. This is not to suggest that these great public issues were not of immense importance in dividing Whig from Tory; of course they were,

Traditionally, the conflict of power in seventeenth-century England had revolved about the role of the gentry, who had come to regard the House of Commons as their own peculiar institution which, if kept independent, could secure them a world to their liking. With this attitude to Parliament, they had maintained a loathing of standing armies – Cromwell's as well as Charles II's or James II's – a loathing based on the fear, not groundless, that they might have to fight again for Parliament. It was natural, therefore, that men who had opposed James II's tampering with the boroughs, or been supporters of Shaftesbury at the time of Exclusion, should view with equal concern the rising cost of elections, the growth of powerful oligarchical patronage in the boroughs, and the spreading influence of the aristocracy in county politics. The danger to the freedom of Parliament was, in their eyes, further increased by the proliferation of placemen and the growing opportunities for corruption in a tax system that seemed designed for their ruin. As Sir Charles Sedley thundered in the Commons in November 1691, 'The country is poor, the nation is racked, the courtiers hug themselves in furs, and the humble country gentleman is half-starved.'[7] His sentiments in that debate were echoed by both Whig and Tory, for in 1691 party politics were in flux. The old exclusionists – Garraway, Sacheverell, Lee – had been deeply disappointed by the Bill of Rights and by their failure to secure draconian measures against the Tories who had supported James II. They and their supporters felt that the Revolution was half complete. And they had their friends and allies at Court, for the leading Whigs, Shrewsbury included, did not take very warmly either to William III and Mary's obvious regard for Nottingham or their dependence on Carmarthen. Between 1690 and 1694 the Whigs were at a disadvantage at Court, and the prospect was far from remote that the King might establish

and a man's attitude to these matters was the quickest way of telling one from the other. It is, however, my contention that party strife goes deeper than a few great public issues and that it was symptomatic of deep divisions in the political nation and indeed reflected two bitterly opposing attitudes not only to the nature of political power but also to its social function and purpose.

7. Grey, *Debates*, x, 142.

his government on a purely Tory basis. Hence the Whigs were alert to the dangers of long Parliaments in which the effects of patronage might damage their future. They were also concerned by the growing number of placemen. Hence we find Whigs such as Shrewsbury in the forefront of the battle to secure a Triennial Bill, and the strongest opposition to it coming from the Tory Nottingham and the King himself. The Whigs, too, may have felt that frequent elections would strengthen rather than weaken their position in the Commons. About the Place Bills, pushed forward in this Parliament, the Whigs, or the bulk of them, were more circumspect; but what Whiggish support they achieved came from the old intransigents, the exclusionists, the immovable anti-Court, country Whigs and the new radicals associated with Harley. These years 1692–4 witness the beginning of a realignment of party forces in the Commons: the fusion between the Whig and Tory 'country' interests, which came about at a time when the members of the old country party – Sacheverell, Garraway, and Lee – died, so giving an opportunity for Robert Harley to emerge as the new leader of the opposition to the Court. But the changes in the *persona* of party go deeper than that. These are the years of the Whig party's volte-face. There emerged not only a New Tory party but a newly orientated Whig party, based on the House of Lords. 1690–94 had proved two things: first, that no Tory leader could secure effective leadership either in the Commons or at Court, and secondly that coalition government had been disastrous in the prosecution of the war. There was a fundamental contradiction in the Tory position, which Sunderland, back at Court, had been quick to realize. As he wrote to Portland in 1694:

I have so often repeated my opinion concerning Whigs and Tories that it is vain to do it any more, but I must however say, that the great mistake that has been made for five years together has been to think that they were equal in relation to this government, since the whole of one may be made for it, and not a quarter of the other ever can. Whenever the government has leaned to the Whigs, it has been strong; when the other has prevailed it has been despised.[8]

8. Kenyon, *Robert Spencer, Earl of Sunderland, 1641–1702*, 251.

Behind this acute analysis of Sunderland's lies a change in every way as dramatic as the rise of a new Tory party, and one ultimately of far greater consequence. The efforts of Shrewsbury on behalf of the Triennial Bill is the last stand made by any Whig leader to secure major constitutional change on behalf of the independence of the legislature. It is the end of Whig aristocratic support of those radical constitutional principles that stretch back to 1641.[9] Of course, many Whig aristocrats had been unhappy with their radical allies before 1688, and there had been an inner contradiction in Whiggism since the early 1670s. The right wing, represented by such peers as Viscount Townshend or the Duke of Rutland, had wanted power, not constitutional change, but events had forced them into a radical alliance with the anti-Court gentry. After 1694, all truck with the moderate radicalism goes. The Whigs solve their inner contradiction, as the Tories acquire theirs. After 1694, the Whig aristocracy is concerned not to limit but strengthen monarchy and authority. They oppose the reduction of a standing Army; they vote against the Act of Settlement; they actively negotiate the Act of Union with Scotland – a method of strengthening the Crown and increasing royal authority in the Lords and Commons, it should be remembered, that had been seriously considered by Charles II; they force through the Septennial Act; and they reduce the democratic franchise of the City of London. A strange Whiggery this! 1694 is one of the great watersheds in the development of party, far more significant than 1760 or 1794. From this time the Whigs, in constitutional principles, become deeply conservative but not, and this must be stressed, in political practice and management. There, they remained innovators. Whether consciously or unconsciously, the most powerful groups in the Whig party became preoccupied with the processes rather than the principles of government. They wanted to capture the government machine and run it. Of course, they had a policy, both long-term and short-term; but they felt that, given

9. One Whig peer, at least, remained loyal both to the Whig and his family's past – Anthony Ashley, 3rd Earl of Shaftesbury – but in Queen Anne's reign his views and attitudes seem curiously old-fashioned, as old-fashioned almost as Sir Roger de Coverley's.

the King's full patronage, they could make the government work both in the national interest and in their own. Personal strains and animosities continued within the Junto; intrigue among Whig leaders did not stop in 1694, nor close contact with the country Whigs abruptly cease. When it suited him Wharton could rouse his squires to action with the skill of a Harley. But this situation did not last long. With each passing year country and Tory became increasingly closely identified, and Whig and country further separated.

In the too ready acceptance of Professor Walcott's analysis of party, the emergence of a coherent, effective, and reasonably united Whig leadership has been overlooked. The Whig Junto saw its way to effective power through a more thorough exploitation both of the electoral system and of royal patronage. They realized quickly enough that they were a minority, and this imposed on them a unity that they might not otherwise have achieved, a unity that was deliberately strengthened by active social intercourse – race meetings and house parties in the summer and frequent junketings during the Parliamentary session at the Kit-Kat, founded in 1698. Their main strength lay in their territorial magnificence, enabling them to influence elections out of proportion to their numbers. Although, throughout the reigns of William III and Anne, committed Junto Whigs always remained a minority in the House of Commons, they were from 1694 onwards the largest coherent unit in the House of Lords, where, by 1713, their strength was such that Queen Anne could only obtain ratification of the Treaty of Utrecht by the unusual exercise of her prerogative in the creation of twelve new peers on 1 January 1712.[10] Yet, and this must be stressed, they were always a minority. And in this lay their party strength. They might quarrel, but they did not break into factions. In William III's

10. True, this opposition to the Crown was only achieved after a deal with the Tory Nottingham, and the government's position was further complicated by restiveness among the Scottish representative peers, but it was the coherence and unity of the Whigs that forced the Queen's hand. As Poulett wrote to Oxford, 'The Queen's enemies at present generally understand one another much better than her friends and servants': G. M. Trevelyan, *Peace and the Protestant Succession*, 1934, 193. See also Riley, *The English Ministries and Scotland, 1707–27*, 233.

reign they parted with much of their old country Whig support, with Jack How and his friends, but their leadership was never riven with the animosities that marked the Tory leadership – the bitter feuds between Nottingham and Leeds, the hatred of Bolingbroke and Oxford. It requires considerable ingenuity on Professor Walcott's part and a considerable opacity to the facts to factionalize the Whigs. His separations will scarcely bear analysis.[11] There were men of great power in the Whig party – the Dukes of Newcastle and Somerset are cases in point – who by the very extent of their possessions and eminence of social position acted in a more circumspect and courtly fashion, but, as I have shown elsewhere, reluctant as they were to follow Junto decisions, they could not bring themselves to support for more than a few months a Tory ministry.[12] Again, on those occasions, as in 1694 and 1708, when supporters of the Junto managed to obtain a foothold in a coalition ministry, they began to work, deploying all their skill, to obtain places for the rest of the Junto. At no time are the leaders of the Tory groups found working for each other with the same dedication.

This greater sense of unity was forced upon the Whigs by their minority position; so, in a sense, was their attitude to elections and patronage. From 1694 onwards the Junto began to take a much more practical attitude to place-holders. Henry Guy, the Secretary of the Treasury, was broken by Wharton; expelled from the Commons for peculation, his management of the Commons was taken over by the Junto and place-holders taught to learn the duties of their place, a system that was intensified in the next Parliament. A similarly dexterous use of the Assassination Plot was made by Somers in an attempt to secure a firmer political base for Junto Whiggery among the gentry. The loyal Oath of Association was imposed and a promise obtained from a reluctant William III for a thorough purge of the Commissions of the Peace. Again, in the election of 1695, Wharton conducted a more complex and vigorous campaign in his territories of Wiltshire, Buckinghamshire, Cumberland,

11. See my review of his *English Politics in the Early Eighteenth Century*, *EHR*, 1957, lxxii, 126–9.

12. Plumb, *T. R. Hist. S.*, 5th ser., vii, 137–57.

Westmorland, and Yorkshire than they had witnessed since the days of Exclusion, if not entirely with success.[13] The most notorious election bribery of William III's reign was perpetrated by the Whigs of the New East India Company, who attempted to suborn a number of boroughs in Wiltshire in 1700 and were expelled from the House for their pains. The Whigs, too, were often quicker than their rivals to print and circulate defamatory lists, and had so positive a success with their Black List of 1700 that most of the M.P.s on it lost their seats, a fact that Professor Walcott observes, but whose significance for the party conflict between Whig and Tory he fails to realize.[14]

Again, the great financial measures – the Recoinage and the foundation of the Bank of England – associated the Whigs in the public mind with the financial interests of the City. The Recoinage created immense hardship and naturally hardship bred suspicion that the difficulties of the country were to the advantage of the City financiers. As for the Bank, it was stamped with Whiggism from its inception. Naturally, the Whigs prosecuted the war vigorously; and it was prosecuted with high taxes. In Queen Anne's reign they were associated in the public mind with a reluctance to bring it to an end and to the country gentlemen the slogan 'No Peace without Spain' seemed merely a device for prolonging a war in order for the Whigs to enrich themselves and beggar the gentry. These factors – aggressive electioneering, a more ruthless exploitation of place, high taxes, vigorous war, close association with the moneyed interests of the City – helped to create in these years the Tory vision of a Whig, and to create those focal points of attack that were to become the stand-by of the country party. The fears, anxieties, and anger of the independent country gentlemen were intensified by a series of exposures of corruption. Not only was a well-known figure such as Henry Guy found guilty of financial dishonesty, but there seemed to be a never-ending stream of government peculations. Financial scandals

13. The Tories increased by two in Bucks. For Wharton, see Ransome, *VCH Wilts*, v, 208 ff., and the Marquis of Lansdowne, *Wilts. Arch. and Nat. Hist. Mag.*, xlvi, 60–81.

14. Walcott, *English Politics in the Early Eighteenth Century*, 90.

festooned the body politic like shingles. In May 1697, the Treasury office of Guy Palmes, the son of the Whig M.P. for Malton, was discovered to be £27,000 short. In spite of strong circumstantial evidence of forgery relating to the government receiver for Newcastle, and the obvious clerical incompetence, if not worse, of Palmes's clerk, Peters, and a later theft of £6,700 *in specie* from Palmes's office, Palmes kept his place. True, he was finally dismissed in 1702 – not, however, for incompetence, nor for tolerating corruption, but because he was a Whig. He was a sacrifice not to public morality but to party feeling, a mere pawn in the spoils system. The land-tax scandals equalled anything in the Treasury.[15] In 1695, Alderman Briggs of Norwich and Henry Blofield, the son of a Norwich hosier turned country gentleman, and a pillar of the Whig party, were £7,000 in arrears; in North Wales, Morgan Whitley owed the government £43,000 by 1699. Of course, not all peculators were Whigs; after all, Charles Duncombe passed as a Tory, and one of the most notorious land-tax scandals was associated with William Burslem, the leading Tory of Staffordshire.[16] But, and this must be stressed, the major scandals, whether in the Treasury, the tax offices, or the Army and Navy, were all too frequently associated with the Whigs – at least in the public mind – or with the regular servants of the Crown. The contracting scandals were particularly notorious – the beer, biscuit, and clothing provided for the Navy was a source of constant complaint; indeed in 1689, the fleet had to leave its station owing to the appalling conditions of its supplies and the House of Commons arrested the entire Victualling Board. Although there was some improvement, corruption continued.

The rising cost of elections, the proliferation of placemen, and the constant exposure of graft and corruption inflamed the attitude of the squirearchy, whatever its original principles may have been towards government and Parliament. The fact was that the minor gentry were being squeezed out of Parliament, and although they bore the brunt of the taxes, they were being

15. Baxter, *The Development of the Treasury, 1660–1702*, 157–65.
16. Ward, *The English Land Tax in the Eighteenth Century*, 49–52.

fleeced by courtiers, contractors, stock-jobbers.[17] To this must be added their natural suspicions of sophisticated metropolitan life, and their growing distrust of Continental wars. William III might be an improvement on James II, but he was Dutch and, therefore, suspect. Moreover, in the House of Commons, there was a considerable body of Members, basically loyal and patriotic, eager that the war should be won, but increasingly worried by the nature of government. More often than not, they were men of moderate estate, prominent in their localities, yet of no great influence and little hope of personal power or profit to themselves, uncommitted as they were to the Whig machine or to a Tory faction either, though their own principles might lean them towards the left or right. It was these Members to whom Harley began to direct his attention and to evolve a programme of opposition that exploited their resentments about corruption and taxation, and for which his supporters – Charles D'Avenant, Sir Bartholomew Shower, and others – began to draft a reinvigorating propaganda.[18] And so these years 1694–8, which saw the growing identification of Whig with placemen, projectors, and financiers, with an aristocratic group with strong commercial connexions who were willing to operate the machinery of government as they found it, also witnessed the marriage of Tory politicians to a political programme that was critical not only of the acts of government but also of the whole constitutional position, and pledged itself to the ancient seventeenth-century view that good government could never be secured until the separation of executive and legislature had been achieved. This programme possessed two major aspects: the purification of Parliament and the prevention of financial abuse.

The purification of Parliament required, so the extremists thought, three things: very frequent Parliaments, preferably

17. See Hughes, *Studies in Administration and Finance, 1558–1825*, 189, for the stimulus to militant Toryism given by the practices of corrupt local tax officials.

18. For Sir Bartholomew Shower's 'Reasons for a New Bill of Rights' and his election speech at Exeter in 1698, for which he was returned, see *Cal. S. P. Dom.*, 1698, 377–9. There he stressed his devotion to the Church, his dislike of Occasional Conformity, and his hatred of taxation.

annual; the total exclusion of all placemen, pensioners, contractors – indeed, anyone who was in any way obliged to the Court
or ministry in a pecuniary sense; and finally, that membership of
Parliament should be confined to men of substance, preferably
men of landed substance and not 'mere moneyed men'. There
was little or no sense of the injustice of the representational
system. John Locke had castigated the sheep-haunted districts
of Old Sarum that returned two Members to Parliament,[19]
but there was no agitation in the Commons to abolish Dunwich,
rapidly being consumed by the North Sea, or Gatton, where six
voters were moved in by wagon at the time of the election. The
only borough in William III's reign that came near to being
disenfranchised was Stockbridge, not because it was unrepresen-
tative, but because its open and notorious addiction to bribery
was too much even for a late seventeenth-century stomach.
Hindon nearly suffered a like fate in 1702 for the same reasons.[20]
Once the Triennial Bill became law, the demand for shorter
Parliaments was heard less frequently in debate and the country
party felt that they had achieved a real victory, as, indeed, in
some ways they had. Further successes came in 1696 with two
Acts, one against corrupt elections and another which dealt with
the procedure of Parliamentary elections. The preamble to the
first states quite categorically that its purpose is to put an end
to 'undue Elections of Members to Parliament by excessive and
exorbitant expenses contrary to the Laws and in violation of the
freedom due to the Election of Representatives for the Commons'. Any present, reward, or entertainment was made illegal
and the penalty was expulsion.[21] Evasion, however, did not

19. John Locke, *Two Treatises of Government*, ed. P. Laslett, Cambridge,
1960, 390.

20. *HCJ*, x, 36–7, for Stockbridge; for Hindon, Burnet, *History of My
Own Time*, v, 46–7. However, there was a suggestion, made by the Tory
country gentlemen, to disenfranchise all boroughs with electorates
of under fifty and give their representation to the freeholders of the hundred in which they were situated. This attempt was made in 1702, but it
came to nothing. The view of Sir John Trevor prevailed who said,
during the debate on Stockbridge, 'The House stands upon the ancient
constitutions, and I hope you will not remove old landmarks': Grey,
*Debates*, ix, 424.

21. *Statutes of the Realm*, 7–8 Will. III, c.4 and c.25.

prove difficult, for an election was considered only to have started once the writ had been received, and entertainment before its receipt was accepted as legal. That provided opportunity enough for most candidates. Within a few years, however, this Act was a dead letter and constantly ignored. The second Act, in addition to stopping the splitting of burgage votes, tried to prevent the irregularities of the sheriffs who, in collusion with their party, often suppressed the receipt of the writ, gave short or no notice of the election, or, if the voting was going badly for their party, switched it to a more favourable part of the county or one difficult of access.[22] All old tricks, practised by Whig and Tory alike, but, as the country interest realized, tricks that favoured the ruling clique, whichever complexion it might have, were in the end destructive of their own position. Apart from a standing order passed in 1701 which declared it illegal for any peer of the realm to take part in the elections to the Commons – and few standing orders can have been violated so promptly and so thoroughly with such complete immunity – no further effort was successfully made to erect stronger safeguards against the malpractices of electioneering, although attempts by back-benchers were frequent enough.

These two Acts were but part of a general scheme, engendered and piloted by Jack How, the blistering-tongued orator of the squirearchy, who insisted that the Whigs had deserted him rather than he Whiggery. His major support came not from his old allegiance but from the Tories or crypto-Tories like Harley. In addition to the measures passed, How hoped to secure a land qualification Bill and the exclusion of all place-holders.

How and his cohorts wanted a land qualification Bill in order to exclude merchants, financiers, and the like and also the younger sons of peers, who in many counties were beginning to

22. Typical examples are Somerset and Cardigan in 1690, where the polls, according to the defeated candidates, were suddenly switched to inconvenient places. The Sheriff of Wiltshire was more ingenious; he switched the poll to Salisbury where the smallpox was raging and so scared off the unwelcome voters: HCJ, x, 365, 368, 371, 428. The malpractices of sheriffs were very much on the minds of the supporters of the Bill of Rights: Bodleian, Rawlinson MSS., D.1079, fo. 18.

regard a seat as a part of their birthright. In 1696, the first Bill was pushed through by How, Harley, and their friends, only to fail in the Lords, when the King's disapproval of the measure carried weight. A subsequent Bill passed the Commons, but the ministry, almost entirely Whig, proved more effective in the Lords, and again it was thrown out.[23] The crusade, however, remained a very dear one to the country interest. Although it faded into the background during the long struggle about place-men, it was revived by Henry St John with the support of the October Club as soon as the Tories had secured an emphatic victory in the election of 1710, and the Land Qualification Bill was passed. Its passage was eased through the House of Lords by the exclusion of the eldest sons of peers from the operation of the statute.[24] Even so, Swift regarded it as 'the greatest security ever contrived for preserving the constitution'. It failed totally to achieve its aims. As a shibboleth it remained on the Statute Book for more than a century, and indeed was reinforced in the reign of George III. By 1717, however, a standing order of the Commons placed the onus, and therefore the costs of proof, on the petitioner, and even before that date, lawyers had devised conveyances by which putative Members could be fictitiously qualified over the period of their elections. In spite of Swift's high hopes, it proved to be useless.

The major attack by the country opposition, which by the late 1690s had become very largely the Tory opposition, on the growing influence of the executive, was directed towards place-men. The sinister role of placemen had worried the country party since the Long Parliament of Charles II; in the Exclusion Parliament of 1680, the Commons had passed, *nem. con.,* a resolution that any Member of the Commons accepting any office, place, or pension without the consent of the House should suffer im-mediate expulsion, a resolution that remained a dead letter.[25]

23. E. and A. Porritt, *The Unreformed House of Commons,* 168–9. £500 p.a. in land had long been the panacea of the squirearchy. Sir Richard Temple had pressed for it in 1675. See Grey, *Debates,* iv, 3.

24. *Statutes of the Realm,* 9 Anne, c.5. University Members were also excluded from its operation.

25. Grey, *Debates,* vii, 225.

But the old members of Shaftesbury's party – Lee, Sacheverell, Garraway – were still alive and very vocal in the 1690 Parliament, and it is not surprising that the back-benchers should have pressed for a Place Bill very soon after the Revolution, or that it should have been introduced in 1692 by a country Whig, Sir Edward Hussey, M.P. for Lincoln. It was as categoric as the old exclusionist attitude. All placemen were to be excluded. The Lords threw it out on 3 January 1693 by a narrow majority – two votes.[26] Ardently supported by Harley and Foley, who realized the great popularity of the measure, a similar Bill passed the Commons in 1694, and, amended to permit re-election, passed the Lords. Once again William III used his veto. Indeed, during these years, the mixed constitution was only saved by a forthright use of the royal prerogative. Otherwise, Parliament would have drawn closer to a Polish Diet than it did. Had the Land Qualification and Place Bills passed, the result would have been more backwoodsmen in the Commons, and greater reluctance towards taxation for the war, which in any case nearly ground to a halt in these years. England was near enough to political chaos; these measures would have given that chaos legal sanctity. Two further attempts in 1695 and 1700 at total exclusion were defeated, but in the 1701 Parliament, in which the Tory and country interest was overwhelmingly dominant, the famous clause that 'No person who holds an office of profit under the Crown, should be capable of serving in Parliament' was added to the Act of Settlement. Not to be brought into force until the death of Queen Anne, it was intended, of course, as Miss Betty Kemp has demonstrated in her excellent analysis of these Place Bills, to weaken the Hanoverians – which indeed was the major purpose of the Act of Settlement. Before it was brought into operation, however, it was repealed. In a sense the Tories had been hoist with their own petard and knew it. Harley, with experience of office, was acutely aware of the need of place; publicly he had been increasingly attracted by the more moderate policy of selective exclusion of placemen, and

26. Betty Kemp, *King and Commons, 1660–1832*, 1957, 54–6; James E. Thorold Rogers, *A Complete Collection of the Protests of the Lords*, Oxford, 1875, i, 106–7; Burnet, *History of My Own Time*, iv, 189–90.

the removal of those officers most likely to be under the thumb of the Treasury, and capable of influencing elections, finally triumphed.

The first success for this policy had been achieved in 1694 when the Stamp Commissioners were excluded from the Commons. The activities of revenue officers were heartily disliked, and it was easy to whip up antipathy to them. And the argument that the very nature of their office made them tools of any ministry seemed much more convincing in an age that had just turned from indirect farming to direct collection of taxation. In the Tory-dominated Parliaments from 1698 to 1702, further successes were achieved by the Tories on behalf of this deeply-felt attitude of the country interest. After an attempt to revert to farming had been thwarted, the Commissioners of Excise were excluded in 1699, and the Commissioners of Customs followed in 1701, but the greatest purge of placemen was in 1705. After hard bargaining, the Tories, led by Harley, agreed to rescind the all-embracing clause of the Act of Settlement in return for a long schedule of named offices – Commissioners of Wine Licenses, of Sick and Wounded, and of Transport; Commissioners of the Navy employed in the outports, governors and deputy governors of plantations, and a wide range of offices connected with the Navy; indeed, the list is an admirable indication both of the departments in which patronage had grown and of the fears and hostility of the squirearchy towards this growth. The only hope of getting such a measure through Parliament was to permit the office-holder to stand for re-election; any other device would have met with defeat in the Lords or been squashed by royal veto. This did not thoroughly emasculate the Act in the eyes of its promoters. They believed, or half-believed, that constituents could and would reject obvious placemen or men whose places might prejudice their independence.[27] And certainly, as Miss Kemp has shown, this Act was not entirely

27. Of course, the deeply committed country interest strongly disliked what they regarded not as compromise but selling the pass to the executive, and on this issue a number of country Whigs, led by Sir Peter King, joined with the opposition. An account of the debate will be found in Camb. Univ. Lib., Add. MSS., 7093.

without effect: it drove many office-holders to the comparative security of closed corporations, and others, unwilling to face the cost of a second election, desisted.[28] Yet it never incommoded any government and never seriously reduced the number of place-holders in Parliament. The drafting of the Act was loose, and new offices were usually decreed by the Commons to be outside its jurisdiction. By 1711, the Tory back-benchers were so dissatisfied with its operation that they pressed strongly for a further Act of total exclusion, but the ministry held them off and soothed their tempers with the Land Qualification Bill. Harley, after all, was doing his utmost at that time to extend patronage and bring it under the direction of the Treasury.

By the end of the reign of Anne this attitude to the constitution, of Parliament meeting regularly and being regularly dissolved, and consisting of well-to-do landowners, independent of ministerial control or the influence of place, had become orthodox Tory doctrine in spite of its long Whig ancestry, reaching back to the Civil War. And it was the espousal of these attitudes that gave the Tory leadership of Harley and then Henry St John such numerical strength. Just as Whiggery had in the middle 1690s begun to polarize about Parliamentary management and government finance, to wear an aristocratic, metropolitan, and courtly air, so Toryism had become increasingly identified in the eyes of the political nation as the party of the squirearchy: antipathetic to any system of Court management, highly suspicious of the executive, and strongly critical of government finance. Indeed, their attitude to finance helped the new image of the Tory party as much as its advocacy of Place and Pensions Bills or Land Qualification Acts.

Because two of its major incursions into high finance – the Land Bank and the South Sea Company – failed, the country party's attitude to finance has been regarded as inept, factious, and at variance with the economic needs of England at war. The problem was more complex. The need for money was realized on the back-benches as well as on the front, and Tory pamphleteers – particularly D'Avenant – were quite as active as the Whigs in canvassing methods of taxation to solve the

28. Kemp, *King and Commons, 1660–1832*, 59–64.

financial needs of the country. Harley's ability lay not in any economic insight or skill in monetary matters, but in the quick realization of the political capital that could be made out of opposition to the Government's financial policy. Harley, and those Tories and Members of the country party who supported him in the late 1690s, developed two major lines of attack: the injustice of the incidence of taxes, and the corruption and waste in their collection and expenditure. And as with the Tories' criticism of the growth of electoral oligarchy and the spread of patronage, the truth of their analysis can scarcely be denied.

There had been a serious attempt by the ministry in 1694 to devise a reasonably equitable system of direct taxation, by a system of poundage arising out of all property, whether of land, mortgages, houses, moveable goods, or offices, the armed forces alone excluded. Within two years the administrative difficulties had defeated the principle of the Act, which had become, at least for its major yield, a land tax. Furthermore, assessment had followed the traditional lines of subsidies: quotas were fixed for counties, and the county assessors fixed the quotas for hundreds.[29] This, of course, led both to injustice and to political corruption. Hundreds in which the political establishment was at cross-purposes with the establishment of the county often found themselves viciously assessed. Wherever the Whig or Tory parties controlled the assessors, then the land tax was, more often than not, biased in its incidence according to the political complexion of the taxpayer. As Sir Roger de Coverley observed, party spirit and the land tax made bad bedfellows.[30] When quotas were imposed the comment had been made 'that it will make great animosities within the county, one side endeavouring to ease themselves and load another'. This prophecy was rapidly fulfilled to the letter. In 1699 the rival factions of Yorkshire commissioners carried a dispute right to the House of Commons. In Brecon the authority of the commissioners' meeting was challenged on the flimsiest of

29. D. Ogg, *England in the Reigns of James II and William III*, Oxford, 1955, 402–5.

30. *The Spectator*, ed. Donald F. Bond, Oxford, 1965, i, 509.

pretexts. Staffordshire, Gloucestershire, and Cornwall were scenes of bitter conflicts.[31] In this battle, Tory successes appear to have been fewer than those of the Whigs. It was the Tories who carried out the greatest purge of Queen Anne's reign, in 1710, and in 1711 the Tories bayed for the blood of the land-tax commissioners. As well as being a measure of party strife, there can be no doubt that this conflict about the land tax helped to intensify party divisions in counties and boroughs. Also, it provided Tory propaganda with invaluable material, for they were naturally more aware of their opponents' enormities than their own.

The burdens of the war, the Tories argued, were borne by the small freeholder; he was being driven into mortgage and debt, and made to pay taxes out of all proportion to his wealth for wars that were being prolonged either in the interests of the Dutch (in William III's reign) or for Marlborough and the Whigs in Queen Anne's. It was a theme capable of more variations than Diabelli's and it did not require a Beethoven to invent them. They became the stock-in-trade of every hack Tory pamphleteer. Other taxes were drawn in: if increases in the customs did not open the sluice-gates of abuse, threats of excise did. Every political economist, from D'Avenant on the right to Locke on the left, believed excises to be the most just of taxes, partly because they extracted a mite even from the desperately poor. Yet the Tories and the country interest opposed them with such ferocity that the expansion of excise in William III's reign was limited to a few new articles, principally salt and hides, and a small increase was, in view of the necessities of the State, made in rates. The opposition to excises argued that they taxed necessities – beer, salt, leather, coal, and candles – and therefore weighed more heavily on the poor than the rich; that the powers given to excise officers to discover frauds led to the invasion of an Englishman's birthright, namely the privacy of his home; that they would provide such a regular source of income that

31. Ward, *The English Land Tax in the Eighteenth Century*, 35. See also *Memoirs of the Family of Guise,* ed. Godfrey Davies, Camden Society, 1917, 3rd ser., xxviii, 147, for the struggle between Guise and How for the control of Gloucestershire land-tax assessment.

the role of Parliament would be diminished and the power of the Court increased; that the plethora of officers required for the new excise duties would give new and maybe decisive patronage to the ministry in Parliamentary boroughs; and finally, excises were foreign, Dutch or French, or both, and therefore hateful, and when French, of course, symbols of tyranny and Popery. All these bugbears, which were used to frighten the nation in 1733, were stalking at large in 1700.[32] The effectiveness of such opposition propaganda, however, may be seen in the difficulties that the government had in 1694, when they only just secured an excise on salt and failed, for the time being, to get one on soap and hides.

Constant attacks, in Parliament and in pamphlets, identified the Tory party with bitter opposition to taxation and helped them to build up their impressive public support. The effect of this opposition, when taken in conjunction with its immense financial necessities, was to force the government to use other methods of raising money – lotteries, tontines, and the like – or resort to loans. Indeed, throughout Queen Anne's reign, when the Tory party was in the ascendant, except for a brief period between 1706 and 1710, no new excises were imposed; indeed, the only new tax was the stamp duty, imposed more for political than for financial reasons. Money was raised by increases in the rates of old taxes, borrowing, or by the exploitation of the gambling instinct. In order to borrow successfully, that is continuously and cheaply, the credit-worthiness of the government needed to be demonstrated. It was. The Recoinage, the foundation of the Bank, and above all the establishment of the Sinking Fund, gave a strength to England's financial system unmatched by any other European country except Holland – a fact rapidly appreciated by the Dutch who invested heavily in both the Bank and the Funds.[33] And for that, the bitter opposition of the Tory party to taxation was as contributory as the inventiveness of Montagu or the administrative efficiency of Godolphin. Most of the new financial institutions were of Whig

32. Plumb, *Walpole*, ii, 233–71.
33. C. H. Wilson, *Anglo-Dutch Finance in the Eighteenth Century*, Cambridge, 1941, 88–95.

origin – the Tories' contribution, particularly the Land Bank, failed miserably. True, the land tax and a few excises were imposed by mixed ministries, although the most important new excise – that on salt – was devised by Thomas Neale, a Whig entrepreneur and place-holder. These matters undoubtedly helped to identify Whig and finance in the public mind, an identification that was exploited by Tory propagandists and by Tory leaders bent on posing as the protectors of the freeborn Englishman from arbitrary taxation and tyrannical revenue officers.[34]

Between 1690 and 1710 the Tory party acquired a recognizable *persona*, based largely on the independently-minded squire's idea of himself. The Tory, apart from public issues, stood for free and frequent elections, sharp punishment for bribery and electoral corruption, low taxation, financial rectitude, accountability to Parliament, the exclusion of all place-holders, and sound land-qualification for Members. They also had a reluctance to large-scale Continental war and an aversion to Dissent; if the Hanoverians succeeded, then they were to be prisoners of Parliament, or rather of the Commons. That was the intention of the Act of Settlement. And there is no doubt that between 1690 and 1715 this political attitude commanded a majority both in the Commons and outside. Certain aspects of this policy were continually hamstrung by events: between 1690 and 1695 there was a real necessity to support William III in his wars

34. *The Works of the Rev. Jonathan Swift*, ed. John Nichols, 1801, iii, 6. *The Examiner* for 2 November 1710 is a splendid rhetorical denunciation of taxes and loans at the expense of the landed interest: 'Let any man observe the equipages in this town, he shall find the greater number of those who make a figure, to be a species of men quite different from any that were even known before the Revolution. . . . So that if the war continue some years longer, a landed man will be little better than a farmer of a rack-rent to the army, and to the public funds.' In my copy, which belonged to Macaulay and was given to me by G. M. Trevelyan, this *Examiner* is subjected to blistering marginal criticism, finally summarized in the single word 'Folly!' Swift, of course, was merely expressing better what had been long said. For further examples of this aspect of Toryism, see Michael Foot, *The Pen and the Sword*, 1957, and for the connexion between the Dutch and finance, which also aroused Tory horror, David Coombs, *The Conduct of the Dutch*, The Hague, 1958.

because of the danger of James II, whom nobody wanted back. The same is true in the early years of Queen Anne's reign, until the great victories of Marlborough in Flanders released the Tories from the strait-jacket of patriotism and permitted them to adopt their popular demands for peace.

In opposition to this, the Whigs had become much more closely identified with both aristocracy and government. They were committed to full-scale war and preoccupied by methods of financing it. Their smaller numbers gave them greater cohesion and their electoral disadvantages gave them a far keener interest in the exploitation of patronage and the manipulation of boroughs. Their only hope of success lay in alliance with the power of the Court and the Treasury. Both sides recognized the vast pecuniary advantages that would accrue to either party that succeeded for any length of time in dominating the political machinery either at the centre or in the localities, and that fact helped to exacerbate party strife as intensely as any differences about religious policy or the function of the legislature. Political power meant real things for both parties: jobs, influence, profit, the control of spoils. To deny this two-party division and to fail to see what they were really fighting for is to confuse the reality of early eighteenth-century politics. Of course, politicians and propagandists hoped to win power by the influence that their commitment to an attitude of life would bring them. The parties presented different images, *but they pursued a common goal* – not only the control and direction of policy but also the management of the political machinery of the country, which meant men and places.

Herein lay the dilemma of the Tory party, its fundamental contradiction. Its attitude was the attitude of opposition. It drew its strength from independently minded back-benchers, basically uncommitted to any group of leaders, although deeply sympathetic to the Tory attitude. Furthermore, no Tory leader succeeded in dominating all the groups who were not only sympathetic but also committed to the Tory cause. And here Professor Walcott's analysis of the Tory party becomes relevant and helpful. That its leadership was factionalized cannot be doubted. Marlborough loved power and Godolphin office; both were undertakers who, when out of favour or office, leaned to Toryism, but once in were eager to escape the xenophobic clutches of the country Tories.[35] Owing to the intransigence of the Tories, Marlborough became, in effect, a Whig and so did Godolphin, and it is interesting to note that Godolphin did his best to prevent the free operation of the spoils system in the interest either of the Whigs or Tories. Neither in power worked with the same single-mindedness of a Wharton or young Sunderland to extend the influence of their party colleagues; so long as their families were looked after, they were content. Similarly Rochester, Nottingham, and Leeds were as much courtier as Tory, willing to work at times with Harley, usually in opposition, but just as eager to leave him when the prospect of office loomed. Between Seymour, Harley, and Musgrave there were personal jealousies, usually submerged, but capable of causing disunity. Harley, indeed, never wanted to be the prisoner of the Tories. His dream, always, was of a middle party based on a thorough exploitation of patronage. He wished to see jobs going to men pliant enough to allow events to dictate policies. In many ways, he remained a Whig *manqué*. He tried to achieve the impossible: the system of Walpole with Tory materials. Also, he was hamstrung by the brilliant but destructive St John; the conflict between him and Harley became almost paranoic. But because the leadership of the Tory groups were often at loggerheads, it is absurd to deny that they were not bound by a party attitude and at times as capable of working in the common interest of their party as the Whigs. They did so from 1697 to 1702 and again from 1710 to 1715. Nor should the fact that coalition governments dominated politics from

35. Xenophobia was a very strong concomitant of Toryism. The Tory attitude to the Naturalization Act, passed by the Whigs but repealed by them, is indication enough of their attitude to foreigners. Also they bitterly attacked the Poor Palatines: Trevelyan, *Peace and the Protestant Succession*, 35–8. 'If you would discover a concealed Tory, Jacobite or Papist speak but of the Dutch, and you will find him out by his passionate railing' (Shaftesbury to Van Twedde, 17 January 1706): PRO, Shaftesbury MSS., quoted in Speck, op. cit., ii, 351. In George I's and George II's reigns the French replaced the Dutch as the Tories' *bête noire,* along with Hanover.

1689 to 1710 lead one into the fallacy that two parties did not exist. The Tories were more amorphous than the Whigs, more prone to division, more capable of splitting when tempted by office. The reason for this lies both in the nature of politics and the contradictions of Toryism. Men in politics in this period obeyed their monarch's command to serve. If offered an office they accepted it, and stayed until dismissed. They did not resign, or very, very rarely, and then, as with the Duke of Shrewsbury, usually on grounds of chronic illness. The convention was to obey the summons and stay. The force of this can be seen by the fact that when Sunderland was dismissed in 1710, nobody resigned with him; the suggestion that his Whig colleagues should resign in protest was regarded as outrageous.[36] And Walpole's action in 1717 in threatening to resign if Townshend was dismissed was regarded as a flagrant abuse of constitutional practice.[37] Hence, when summoned to office, individual Tories obeyed, even if it meant leaving colleagues in opposition. It was never difficult to split the Tories or even to draw off individual Whigs; once that is realized, it adds a different dimension to Professor Walcott's kaleidoscope of factional changes.

But the problem for the Tories went deeper than that. The image of a Tory was, as has been mentioned earlier, essentially oppositional, back-bench, concerned with liberties, purity of institutions, and economy rather than government. Yet, of course, all the young ambitious Tories, as well as the middle-aged and the cautious, wanted jobs and wanted power. It was a Tory, Peregrine Bertie, who said of his nephew that he could have no better lottery than the House of Commons to push his fortune in. It was a Tory, William Burslem, who exploited his position as land-tax valuer to play ducks and drakes with the electoral machinery in Staffordshire. It was a Tory who, in 1713, said that he hoped that every Whig in office would be eliminated in six months. After all, the Tories were not slow to work the spoils system, nor did they decide petitions about elections in any way differently from the Whigs; they decided them, when

36. Plumb, *Walpole*, i, 156 n. 2.
37. Ibid., ii, 239–40.

they could, on party lines.[38] Similarly, they were just as keen to acquire, to dominate, and to hold electoral property in the counties as any Whig. Nor were they above doing deals with the Whigs to protect their electoral property. In Herefordshire, Robert Harley and his family were doing just that. The active leaders of Tory groups – or factions – were out for office and were quite willing to work the system as they found it once they had achieved power. True, they could not deny their opposition principles entirely; they tolerated the exclusion of place-holders who might influence elections and secured a Land Qualification Bill, but it should also be remembered that St John pressed the latter in order to be able to quash a comprehensive Place Bill.[39] And the contradiction in their position is underlined by the fact that they could not in office always carry with them those back-benchers who had supported them in opposition. When, in 1712, they proposed a heavy excise on leather, they were hoist with their own petard. They lost it by forty, the back-benchers believing in their denunciation of excises even if they did not themselves.[40] Their great chance had come in 1710. In the previous two decades they had forged an acceptable Tory attitude, and the tactical situation was entirely in their favour – a country tired of war and taxes and irritated by the senseless impeachment of Sacheverell.[41] A sympathetic monarch and

38. Swift liked to think differently. He says of the Whigs on this matter, 'What shall we say to their prodigious skill in arithmetick, discovered so constantly in their decisions of elections; where they were able to make out by the rule of false, that three were more than three and twenty, and fifteen than fifty?' And so on. To which Macaulay has added the terse marginal comment, 'This was always the practice of the prevailing party. The Tories acted in just the same way after the election of 1710': Swift, *Works,* ed. Nichols, iii, 54 (my copy). A cursory glance at the *Journals of the House of Commons* is enough to show the justice of Macaulay's criticism.

39. Nor, of course, did they ever really try to make the Land Qualification Bill work. 'A bill', wrote Macaulay, 'of which the only effect has been to give a little easy work to the conveyancers at every election': marginal note, Swift, *Works,* ed. Nichols, iii. 174 (my copy).

40. *The Wentworth Papers,* ed. J. J. Cartwright, 1883, 189.

41. Sacheverell's trial demonstrated the immense advantage that the Tories enjoyed in regard to the religious sentiments of the political

Court was waiting to give them complete support, and the backing of the Court had grown in importance through the Union with Scotland, whose peers and commoners, sitting in the British Parliament, were *already* a prop to any ministry.[42] Yet in spite of quick and popular successes, they failed – not only because of the difficulties they had in securing a majority in the Lords, or because of the necessities bred by the increasing ill health of the Queen, but because of their own divisions. St John, always as acute in analysis as he was blundering in action, saw that the future would be achieved only by the total destruction of the Whig party, that the spoils system must be ruthlessly used down to the meanest local office, that single-party government in control of the executive and dominant in both Lords and Commons was the sole road to political stability.[43] Harley would not have it for both personal and political reasons. He loathed St John and all his life had been spent in manipulation, in playing on the emotions of ultra-Tories of the October Club type in order to use their intransigence to barter for office for himself and his followers. He had always seen his future in mixed ministries; even in 1710, he did his best to retain a few Whigs in his ministry. Although for a time he succeeded in keeping the Dukes of

---

nation. 'The Church in danger' was the cry to which the response was violent and uncritical. And here, too, there is an underlying continuity with some of the support given to Shaftesbury: fears of Popery and danger to Church swelled his supporters far more than an intellectual dedication to the principle of religious toleration. That many country gentlemen supported both Shaftesbury and Sacheverell is not so paradoxical as it seems; the fears were the same, the object had changed from Popery to Dissent. As with religion, so with government. They hated government, standing armies, and taxes, whether backed by the arbitrary intentions of the Stuarts or in the hands of the Whig aristocracy and financiers.

42. Riley, *The English Ministers and Scotland, 1707–27*, 157.

43. Plumb, *Walpole*, i, 193. '. . . my lord Bolingbroke farther added afterward that she [i.e. Queen Anne] would not leave a Whig in employ': Brabourne MSS., Knatchbull's Diary, 4 April 1714. Also 11 April 1714: 'Lord Bolingbroke swore . . . if there was one Whig in employment at the rising of this session he would give any one leave to spit in his face': ibid. See also A. N. Newman, 'Proceedings in the House of Commons, March–June 1714', *Bulletin of the Institute of Historical Research*, 1961, xxxiv, 211–17.

Newcastle and Somerset, he had failed to retain Robert Walpole, the leader of the younger Whigs in the Commons, a man whose sense of political realities and of parties was much more realistic than Harley's. In the last months before the Queen's death in 1714, he was again intriguing with the Whigs in the hope of ditching St John and getting a coalition government.[44] In a sense this is a reverse of what the Whigs had always attempted: once they had their foot in the door, they had constantly tried to force it open to let in more Whigs. Their aim had been to get as close to single-party government as they could; between 1689 and 1715 they had achieved this only for very brief periods for very simple, if constantly ignored, reasons. They were, except for very brief periods, a minority party from the Revolution to the death of Queen Anne.

Surveying these years, it is impossible to deny the ferocity of party strife, Whig versus Tory, in Parliament and in the constituencies. The impeachments – Somers, Portland, Wharton, Sacheverell, Marlborough, Walpole – were all party impeachments; the growing ruthlessness in the use of place; the keen struggles in county and borough elections; the acrid attacks in speeches and pamphlets: all these bespeak a world of politics totally different from that observed by Namier for the middle years of the eighteenth century. The needs of the State forced temporary coalitions, but they never lasted; they merely took party strife into the Departments of State and the Cabinet. Concepts of property, the pull of patriotism, an inbred sense of service owed to the Crown could, and did, confuse party issues and weaken party feeling at the centre. But party division was real and it created instability; indeed, it was the true reflection of it.

The problem of government, however, went deeper than party. Could either party, Whig or Tory, ever secure continuing majorities in the Commons? The Tory party had demonstrated time and time again the power of the back-benchers and their intense dislike both of methods of government and of the way in which they felt the ancient constitution was being violated, to say nothing of the fears that they felt for the Church. Every

44. Plumb, *Walpole,* i, 192.

ministry from 1689 onwards had run into difficulties in the Commons and failed to manage it for more than a session or two. And behind this intransigence of the Commons towards the executive, there was a century of tradition. Although in 1714 the materials for oligarchy everywhere abounded, it seemed as if no party could use them and that political instability, which had been such a marked feature of English life since the Revolution, would continue. Within a decade all was changed: aided both by events, and by the tidal sweep of history, a politician of genius, Robert Walpole, was able to create what had eluded kings and ministers since the days of Elizabeth I – a government and a policy acceptable to the Court, to the Commons, and to the majority of the political establishment in the nation at large. Indeed, he made the world so safe for Whigs that they stayed in power for a hundred years.

# CHAPTER SIX

# THE TRIUMPH OF THE VENETIAN OLIGARCHY

ALTHOUGH by 1714 the materials everywhere abounded by which a well-organized party, backed by the Crown, and its men of business, might bring about political stability, the prospect of such an achievement still seemed remote. In the interval between Queen Anne's death and the arrival of George I, only one thing was clear – the pendulum of Court favour had temporarily swung sharply towards the Whigs. But so had it done to the Tories in 1702. The Whigs had had their chances before, in 1695 and in 1708, yet nothing permanent had been achieved. Certainly Bolingbroke had blundered. His tentative approaches to the Pretender could be exploited against him, but James II's Sunderland had survived an infinitely worse situation in 1689, to emerge as one of the more powerful advisers of William III. Moreover, the House of Commons was still overwhelmingly Tory; indeed, as cannot be stressed too often, the Whigs had scarcely ever achieved a majority since the Revolution. Furthermore, the Tories possessed great strength in the House of Lords. So the outlook for Toryism was far from black. And this was the view of contemporaries.[1] No one expected an outright Whig ministry; nor did George I appoint one. The Earl of Nottingham, no friend, it is true, of either Bolingbroke or Oxford, was appointed Lord President of the Council, and although he carried no Tory of importance with him, others were offered places – Sir Thomas Hanmer the Chancellorship of the Exchequer, and Bromley the Treasurership of the Chamber, a Court office of considerable influence. Indeed, Bothmar had advised George I to fill offices 'without regard to whether a man is a Whig or Tory', so long as the leaders of Queen Anne's last ministry

1. Plumb, *Walpole,* i, 197.

were excluded.[2] Both Hanmer and Bromley refused, expecting
to have better opportunities in the immediate future. In the
autumn of 1714 the Tory situation was difficult and dangerous
but far from desperate. That the Whigs would impeach Oxford
and Bolingbroke was common knowledge, but in the past the
Tories had impeached Somers and Wharton without destroying
either them or the Whigs. Impeachments, as Sacheverell's had
shown, could boomerang. The need for the Tories whose
loyalty was not suspect – Hanmer, Bromley, Nottingham, and
the like – was to reorientate their public policy as soon as they
could and to hope for a Parliament well stocked with independent squires of Tory inclinations. A perceptive politician had
little difficulty in discerning the opportunities for a Tory revival:
the large, rapacious crowd of Hanoverians whom George I
had brought with him; the anxiety that was bound to arise that
British interests would be betrayed for the sake of Hanover; and
the fear of danger to the Church, a perennial fear which could be
exploited if the Whigs attempted to reverse Tory ecclesiastical
policy by introducing greater measures of toleration.[3] And
with the German ministers to intrigue with and against, how
soon would it be before Bernstorff and Bothmar opened negotiations with the Tories to balance the overweening demands of
the Whigs? Or the Whigs, divided among themselves, take on
the Tories as allies? After all, by 1717, Walpole and Townshend
had come to such a pass.

The difficult situation for the Tories was rendered more
critical, however, by the disastrous decision of Bolingbroke
to flee to the service of the Pretender in order to escape the
consequences of his impeachment. The enormity of this decision
cannot be too strongly stressed. His life can have been in no
danger; Parliamentary denunciation, a possible year or two in
the Tower, perhaps even a temporary sequestration of his
estates (which in any case he was bound to lose by his flight),
was the most he ought to have expected. If he feared for his life,

2. R. Pauli, 'Aktenstücke zur Thronbesteigung des Welfenhauses in
England', *Zeitschrift des Historischen Vereins für Niedersachsen*, Hannover,
1883, 66–7.
3. See Appendix I, p. 191.

it was sheer panic, and he did his party irreparable harm by making it far easier for Whig propaganda to label all Tories as Jacobites.

Doubtless Bolingbroke's nerve had been partly broken by the result of the election of 1715. Many a corporation promptly realized that the future – pickings and all – lay with the Whigs and acted accordingly. In some of the larger boroughs and counties the popular vote swung the same way; and, of course, the full weight of government patronage had been exercised on behalf of the Whig candidates. Its efficiency is well illustrated by what happened in Cornwall, where the number of Whigs rose from eight in the previous Parliament to thirty-two.[4] The Whigs were stronger than they had been in any Parliament since the days of Exclusion, and for the first time since the Revolution they enjoyed undisputed power.

With a majority in the Commons, and most of the Court offices in their pockets, the Whig leaders went about making the world safe for the Whigs. In 1714 Bolingbroke had threatened not to have a Whig in office within six months; in 1715 the Whigs were putting his threats into practice against his own party. The first purge was both complex and uneven in its incidence. It might have been expected that it would have been most thorough in the royal household. This was far from true. Some offices of the household, or course, changed. The Whig Lords dismissed in 1710–11 – Devonshire, Cholmondeley, Godolphin, St Albans, and Radnor – were reappointed to Court office. Except for two clerks, the entire Board of Green Cloth was swept away and replaced by sound Whigs. But not all officers were dismissed: two of Queen Anne's equerries, for example,

4. Lincoln Record Office, Worsley MSS., 'Liste Exact du Dernier Parlement et de Celuyci', fo. 38. This list, drawn up for the Court, gives the Whigs a majority of 152. It should be remembered, however, that in this majority there were a considerable number of country gentlemen of Whiggish inclination rather than of solid commitment to the Whig leaders, and therefore liable to be swayed very much by events. Also, many of them were new Members of untried loyalty as far as the Junto was concerned. After Cornwall, Wiltshire shows the largest Whig gain – from eleven to twenty-four. See below, Appendix II, pp. 192–4, for a list of swings by county.

William Breton and Guy Fielding, were promoted to be Grooms of the Bedchamber, and Fielding certainly had been a Tory.[5] Sir John Walter, the Tory M.P. for Oxford, who survived the initial purge in 1714, was kicked out in 1716 for continuing to speak against the government in the House of Commons. And here lies the key to the situation: known intransigent Tories were removed, particularly those with powerful electoral interests or pretensions to being within the leadership; out, too, went their immediate relatives – for example Lansdowne's brother, Bernard, lost his place as Carver – but some minor Tories were given time to adjust themselves to the future. If they did so, they stayed; if not, like Walter, out they went. Also, there was insufficient time to comb through all places great and small in the few months between the King's arrival in London and the election. And once arrived, the King proved less tractable about some offices than his Whig ministers expected. He disliked expulsion of minor servants from office for anything but incompetence. When the Duke of Argyll was dismissed from the Prince of Wales's service, the King was shown a list of Argyll's relations who had secured employment in the Prince's household, and 'he was pleased to declare, that such of them against whom the want of zeal or skill in their business could not be objected, should keep their place'.[6] Within a few years the purge had gone far deeper, in spite of the King's attitude; and the Tories who had survived only by forgetting their past rarely obtained promotion. Peter Wentworth, who pestered all and sundry and never lost an opportunity to put himself within the vision of the King or Prince and Princess, remained throughout the reign of George I what he had been in the reign of Anne, an equerry. On George I's death

5. 'Tis the wonder of all the world how Fielding made his interest': Peter Wentworth to his brother, Lord Strafford, in *The Wentworth Papers*, ed. Cartwright, 432. Wentworth, a Tory, was desperately hoping for a place for himself. The cynical might point out that the Fielding family shared the representation and costs of Castle Rising, Walpole's pocket borough in Norfolk. The Earl of Denbigh, the head of the family, took a very active Tory part in the Leicestershire election in 1715: Leicester Museum, Braye MSS., no. 2845.

6. W. Coxe, *Life and Administration of Sir Robert Walpole*, 1798, ii, 93.

he merely moved to the new Queen's household, still in the same post. For over twenty years his salary remained at £250 p.a., and it is no wonder that his son's greatest ambition was to avoid attendance at Court.[7] Others, such as John Trevanion, the Knight of the Shire for Cornwall, did their best to please by promptly voting Whig after a lifetime's service in the other lobby. This earned him neither place nor profit, even though he retained his title of Gentleman of the Privy Chamber which carried neither salary nor free diet. Disgruntled, he returned to his old habits and voted Tory in 1719. Others, having made their decision to change sides, bought their way into the Whig fold. James Brydges, who had ladled government money into his own pocket for over a decade, and could always trim his Toryism when threatened with the loss of office, decided, naturally enough, to thrive in the new Whig world as he had in the past. He bribed everyone he could, got first an earldom and then a dukedom for himself, offices for his dependants, and produced the votes when required. By 1715 he was on the same easy familiar terms with Walpole and Townshend as he had been with Bolingbroke and Oxford in 1714.[8] If others moved with less panache than Brydges, they followed his route. Within a few months of Queen Anne's death two of the leading Tory families of Northamptonshire had leaped on to the bandwagon: within a few weeks the Tory Lord Longueville was transmuted into the Whig Earl of Sussex; the Earl of Northampton, suppressing the powerful Tory sentiments that he had upheld throughout his life, set off for London to join the Whigs he hated, in order to retain the aristocratic perquisites that he could not resist. At the coronation of George I he performed, perhaps not inappropriately, as Lord Sewer. His lifelong friend, Sir Justinian Isham, the staunch Tory Knight of the Shire, viewed his actions with dismay.[9] As with many aristocratic Tories who leaped for

7. *The Wentworth Papers*, ed. Cartwright, *passim*.

8. For Brydges, see C. and M. Baker, *The Life and Circumstances of James Brydges, First Duke of Chandos*.

9. H. D. Turner, 'Five Studies of the Aristocracy, 1689–1714' (unpublished M.Litt. thesis, Camb. Univ. Lib., 1964), *sub* Northampton; also Forrester, *Northamptonshire County Elections and Electioneering, 1695–1832*, 37.

the bandwagon, in their eagerness they jumped too soon and were run over by it. Within a year, Northampton was back at Castle Ashby, stripped of his offices, his moral authority weakened by his antics. These defeats, as well as the successful conversions, helped to bring about the utter confusion and disintegration that overcame the leaders of the Tory party at this crisis in their fortunes.

It is necessary to stress this moral collapse, for this is usually saddled on Bolingbroke alone, but it ran very deep in the party. As Peter Wentworth had glumly noticed in 1710, 'the Tories are never noted to stick so fast to their friends as the others', and at no time is this so glaringly illustrated as in 1715.[10] Their disarray is highlighted not only by the treasonable defection of Bolingbroke on the one hand and the presence of Nottingham as Lord President on the other, but by the hysterical actions of local leaders such as Northampton or the quick, permanent treachery of such former Tory well-wishers as James Brydges or Sir Jacob Astley.[11]

The Whigs in the early days of the accession crisis neither drove their advantage too far, nor too fast. They rapidly removed the Tories from the majority of positions of power, whether at Court or in the administration. They took absolute charge of the Treasury down to the commissioners of all tax departments, leaving, of course, the professional civil servants – Lowndes, Scrope, and the like – who had always worked well with them. Also, for the first few months the Whigs, used as they were to the more confused political situation of Queen Anne's reign, did not appreciate the full extent of their power.[12] After

10. A fact also noted by Swift: see *Some Advice Humbly Offered to the Members of the October Club*, in *Works*, ed. Nichols, iii, 265.

11. Sir Jacob Astley, Bt, of Melton Constable, Norfolk, had been the Tory Knight of the Shire from 1685, apart from two defeats in 1690 and 1705. He defeated Walpole in the county election of 1710. He voted with the 'whimsical Tories' in 1713, and interpreting the signs of the times, turned his back on a lifetime's Toryism and linked his future in Norfolk and at Westminster with Walpole and Townshend. He was rewarded with a Commissionership of Trade in September 1714, and, of course, kept his seat in Norfolk. See Plumb, *Walpole*, ii, 210.

12. The deaths of many of their old leaders – Halifax, Somers, Wharton,

the election of 1715, the defection of Bolingbroke, and the fiasco of the Fifteen, they lost their doubts. Indeed, from before the election, the Treasury books and State papers give a clear indication of a growing policy of ruthlessness. The purges not only of the Justices of the Peace and the Deputy-Lieutenants but also of tax-collectors and minor office-holders became much more extensive. The pace intensified as soon as Robert Walpole became Chancellor of the Exchequer on 12 October 1715.[13] Before a week was out Walpole combed through the officers of the Treasury, obtained a Secretary's place for his brother, Horatio, and, among others, made an example of William Wecket. Wecket, who started life as a footman of Lord Radnor's grandfather, had used his Treasury influence in a highly personal fashion in the election for Bodmin and Cornwall in 1715. He had given his support in the county to John Trevanion, an erstwhile Tory who, as we have seen, was eager to change his coat, in opposition to Radnor's interest, which, oddly enough, was supported by Thomas Hoblyn, the son of a Tory M.P. for Bodmin and the Town Clerk in 1715. Wecket also opposed Radnor at Bodmin. Hoblyn was in debt to the government to the tune of £2,000; all he could raise was £1,000 and Wecket, through his attorney, put the screws on. Radnor complained to the Treasury. Trevanion was, of course, elected as he was almost bound to be for the county, but Radnor won at Bodmin. This was the type of situation that Walpole was always able to deal with sharply and effectively. He sacked Wecket from his post of office-keeper at the Treasury, which cost Wecket £348 p.a., and replaced him by his own entirely dependable

---

all in 1715 – must also have created suspicion and confusion among the Whig leaders.

13. 'He [Lord Lumley] was inquisitive if any officers either Custom House or Excise were not zealous for y⁰ Govt, that Mr Walpole had desired to be acquainted with them and he would take care to set these matters right' (Henry Liddell to William Cotesworth, October (?) 1715): E. Hughes, *North Country Life in the Eighteenth Century*, Oxford, 1952, 412. As far as purges were concerned, Walpole believed in a policy of thorough; as soon as he became Paymaster of Chelsea Hospital in 1714, he cleared the establishment of Tories and put in dependants: Plumb, *Walpole*, i, 205.

cousin, Thomas Mann. Wecket, however, was allowed to keep his office of messenger which was being discharged by a deputy, Thomas Lowther, a well-connected Whig whom Walpole did not wish to injure. This act of generosity cannot have brought Wecket more than a few pounds a year.[14] By such dexterous uses of the whip and the carrot, the Whig ministry were able to underline over and over again to all who wielded an ounce of political power where the future lay. Whigs, sound, dependable, committed, would obtain the posts of influence; to these would go the jobs of tax-gatherers, customs and excise officers, secretaries, doorkeepers, etc. Tories, it is true, might live down their past; quick advancement could not be expected even for those who suddenly became ardent for the Whig cause, but dismissal might be avoided.

The stiff-necked intransigents, however, received no mercy. Sir Justinian Isham humbled his pride, even if he would not change his principles, and asked Halifax, the head of the Montagus, one of his leading Whig opponents in Northamptonshire, to intervene on behalf of his son in the hope of saving his post in the Leather Office, which he had gained in the days of the Tory triumph of 1710. Naturally, Isham failed and the young Justinian was dismissed. He never held office again and took consolation in having his dedication to Tory rectitude carved on his tombstone.[15]

The appeal to the fundamental temptations that beset eighteenth-century politics – power and profit – corroded the Tories and brought about their disintegration more completely than the desertion of Bolingbroke or the impatience and misjudgements of their other leaders. Of course, it laid bare the fundamental contradictions, the basic immorality of their position in the last years of Queen Anne's reign, when they had wanted, and taken, every office they could lay their hands on, yet, at the same time, had posed as the defenders of political purity.

14. *Cal. Treas. Bks*, 1714–15, xxix, 297; *Cal. Treas. Papers*, 1714–19, 38–9. Radnor forecast the election of thirty Whigs for Cornwall; in fact thirty-two won their seats.

15. Forrester, *Northamptonshire County Elections and Electioneering, 1695–1832*, 38–9, 58 n. 1.

And the Tories too had very little confidence in their future. 1714 broke their will and they expected defeat, rejection, oblivion.[16] As each year passed, their position grew worse. Either they must face a world of haughty isolation, be content with positions of modest power among their neighbours, or capitulate to the Whig establishment. Within a decade dozens of families had gone over, genteel as well as noble. The Hedworths, the violent Tory squires of Durham, who persisted in their errors until the early 1720s, were doing Walpole's work in the election of 1727.[17] No one had bayed louder for Bolingbroke than Sir Edward Knatchbull, the leader of the Kentish Tories; by 1725 his principles had evaporated and new ones were sprouting; in 1728 he became the ministerial candidate for Lostwithiel.[18] Another ancient family felt it was back where it belonged. By then it was a well-trodden route – the Finches, the Foxes, the Winningtons, Chetwynds, and Legges had all made their peace and pocketed their perquisites. Of course, there was a hard core, iron in its pride, who lived and voted and died as their ancestors had done, detesting the government, voting with never-failing regularity, year in and year out, for Place Bills, frequent Parliaments, land qualification, and the like. The Ishams, the Cartwrights, the Caves, the Grosvenors, the Musgraves, etc., stayed true to Squire Western; but by 1725, in a mere decade, they were beginning to wear an archaic and rustic air.[19] The process, of course, varied as widely as the excuses made for defection. Often a change of generation provided a golden

16. 'The Grief of my soul is this, I see plainly that the Tory party is gone' (Drummond to Oxford, March 1715): Feiling, *A History of the Tory Party, 1640–1714,* 479.

17. Plumb, *Walpole,* ii, 179.

18. Ibid, ii, 177.

19. They remained a numerous, if dwindling, band, about 136 according to J. B. Owen, *The Rise of the Pelhams,* 1957, 66–7, in 1741. The majority of these were leaders of the minor gentry, often considerable and dominant landowners within their own counties, but linked with the squirearchy by marriage, tradition, and interest. By 1741, the great Tory aristocratic families of Queen Anne's reign had been absorbed into the Whig oligarchy. They could not face either provincial life or the loss of the perquisites and the power that seemed to them inherent in their nobility.

opportunity for a change of principles. Others moved with the measured stateliness that gratified themselves but deceived few, especially Walpole, whose sense of political realities in personal terms was unerring. They withdrew for a few years to the sidelines, avoided voting, never embarrassed the ministry and then, their peace made, began to apply for the fruits of their good behaviour.

Yet men ever need spiritual clothes in which to conceal their naked appetites, and also it would be quite wrong to think that cupidity alone corroded and corrupted the Tory party and reduced it to insignificance. Jacobitism played its part. No one understood the value of Jacobitism better than Walpole. The vast bulk of the Tory party, of course, never had been and never was to be Jacobite. This was the folly of Bolingbroke and a few extravagant men like him – Shippen, Ormonde, Forster, and the like – who derived a pitiful support from the broken-down gentry of the North, the depressed peasantry of the South-West who had been strong for Monmouth and now hoped for the Pretender, and, of course, the cantankerous clergy of Oxford and Cambridge. What strength Jacobitism had, came from the tribal ferocity of the Highlands. Even the bulk of the English Catholics were anti-Jacobite and few stirred or fought on the Pretender's behalf.[20] Yet between 1714 and 1724 the Jacobites raised a full-scale rebellion in Scotland and invaded England; in addition, there were further scares in 1717 and 1718, an abortive landing in 1719, and a plot was uncovered in 1723. In each of these a few Tories who had played a part in politics in Anne's reign could be shown to be involved. But the impact of this connexion, slight as it was, proved disastrous.[21] In the first flush of the Fifteen, the Whigs were able to get rid of sixty-eight J.P.s in Middlesex, mostly loyal Tories, and replace them by committed Whigs. Townshend and Walpole were soon in full cry after suspected Jacobites elsewhere, yet in some ways, and

20. Hughes, *North Country Life in the Eighteenth Century*, xvii.

21. The importance of Jacobitism, both as a reality and a bugbear, has been fully explored by my pupil, Mr Paul Fritz. Walpole, from 1714 onwards, used it whenever he could to smear his opponents and scare the public.

for a time, they and their colleagues were outmanoeuvred. Tories in the House of Lords and Tories in the House of Commons, realizing the danger of their being implicated in treason, leapt to their feet and protested loyalty; the Archbishop of Canterbury rallied the bishops and only Bristol, promptly dismissed and Whiggishly replaced, refused to sign a declaration abhorring the invasion. Such actions made it impossible for the time being to denounce the entire Tory party as Jacobite, much as Walpole would have liked to do so, and all that the Whig ministry could do was to insert a few smearing insinuations in the King's Speech for the session of 1716 which hinted darkly at 'the secret hopes of assistance' that were still sustaining the Jacobites.[22] Actually, the Tories rebounded with remarkable resilience: Nottingham for once moved wisely in his strong plea for leniency towards the convicted Scottish peers who had surrendered, expecting mercy, only to receive the sentence of death. George I did not conceal his desire to have all their heads off, but the majorities of the ministry narrowed so dangerously both in the Lords and the Commons and the alarm grew so great out of doors, that the ministry made a foolish compromise, beheading only two – Kenmuir and Derwentwater. As the last was very young, very rich, very inexperienced, and very handsome, the ministry's stock dropped low with the public, while the romantic escape of Nithsdale in his wife's clothes provoked further sympathy and provided excellent propaganda.[23] From the point of view of public esteem and popular support the Tories escaped from the consequences of the Fifteen far better than they might have expected. Also, with the purge of the Nottingham Tories from the administration for their persistent pleas for mercy of behalf of the Scottish lords, they were all united again; and in London, the popularity of the government, once the rebellion was over, had suffered badly. Even the situation in 1716 was not all that unfavourable to the Tories.

Nevertheless, Walpole realized the immense potential in a political situation that might permit him to smear his opponents with treason. Patriotism, almost xenophobic in its intensity, had

22. Michael, *The Beginnings of the Hanoverian Dynasty*, 204–5.
23. Ibid., 211–13; Plumb, *Walpole*, i, 218–21.

long been regarded by the Tories as one of their own sacred principles; it was an emotion, they half believed, that none could feel so intensely as themselves. Hence if Walpole could reveal, not once but time and time again, that leading Tories were involved in treason, he knew the effect would baffle many a country squire proud of his Englishry, and draw him to support the Crown. Walpole was not able to exploit this situation fully until he was back in power in 1720, but then he used it to the full. Throughout the South Sea crisis he hinted at Jacobite dangers, and the Atterbury Plot preoccupied him intensely; he himself played a great part in the constant examination of witnesses and the prisoners, as Layer's pathetic plea for mercy reveals.[24] And he exploited this plot so mercilessly that even his close colleagues felt that he was overdoing it; yet the results were so spectacular that his colleagues became even more frightened that he might overreach himself by arranging for another plot in 1724. Sure of the immense value of the scare that half the Tories were crypto-Jacobites, Walpole kept up the pressure. He bought the Postmaster-General of Brussels as a spy and intercepted all the Jacobite correspondence he could persuade Jaupain to lay his hands on. Spies, good, bad, and indifferent, found him a ready listener either at Chelsea or Arlington Street. His men, including the master spy John Mackay, roamed the Continent and by 1725 the Pretender's Court was thoroughly infiltrated.[25] A thoughtless visit on the Grand Tour by the son of a leading Tory was sure to be reported back to him at once and as assiduously exploited. As Sir Justinian Isham wrote to his son, 'the Prdr being now at Rome 'twill require a good deal of caution how you behave yourself in that respect, for this Court have their spies in all parts'.[26] And, of course, accusations of Jacobitism were extremely useful at elections. In the end Walpole's money proved well spent, even if it produced but

24. Plumb, *Walpole*, ii, 42–9.

25. The letters of Jacobite spies are scattered throughout Walpole's papers. The investigations of Mr Paul Fritz show that preoccupation with Jacobitism was even stronger than I thought.

26. Forrester, *Northamptonshire County Elections and Electioneering, 1695–1832*, 41.

little hard fact. Like McCarthyism in our own time, it generated public fear and sapped the will to oppose. Also, Walpole used Jacobitism to help maintain divisions within the Tory ranks in Parliament itself, continually harping on the 'honesty' of William Shippen who was an avowed Jacobite, and thereby insinuating that Sir William Wyndham's followers were secret Jacobites. It was in the critical years between 1720 and 1725 that Walpole was able to exploit this weapon most effectively, and it was these years that witnessed a considerable conversion to Whiggery.

Thus the Tory party was destroyed, destroyed by its incompetent leadership, by the cupidity of many of its supporters, by its own internal contradictions; weakened by its virtues and lashed by events, it proved no match for Walpole; feeble, divided, lost, it failed totally to exploit the opportunities that came its way at the time of the South Sea crisis. It failed to provide an effective barrier to Walpole's steady progress towards a single-party State. By 1725, Tories were outcasts, living on the frontiers of the political establishment; denigrated as political traitors, they were permitted little more than minor local office. By 1733, when the Excise crisis brought about an alternative Whig government in opposition, the two-party system was at an end, and Toryism as far as power politics at the centre was concerned had become quite irrelevant. The evolution of political stability had gone hand in hand not only with the diminution and close control of the electorate and a more thorough exploitation of patronage, but also with the evolution of single-party government and the proscription of a political opposition. Single-party government, combined with proscription of opposition, using proscription in its widest sense, that is ostracism from power, political or social, has, of course, helped to bring about political stability in other countries than England, such as Mexico or Russia, and maybe it will be as effective in the new states of Africa.

The destruction of the Tory party, however, was not enough to create political stability. The sympathy for Toryism was widespread – manifestations of it festoon the history of public opinion of these years – and a stable system of politics required a more solid basis than the neat exploitation of events or even the destruction of rivals. Furthermore, within three years of the accession of George I, the Whigs were as sharply divided as the Tories had ever been in the reign of Queen Anne; indeed, Walpole had moved into collaboration with the Tory back-benchers and was giving voice with all the natural warmth of his temperament to sentiments that Sir Edward Seymour or Sir Christopher Musgrave would have cheered in the days of his father. In 1717 it seemed as if the Whigs in majority would be as liable to factional divisions as the Tories before them, and that coalition of Whigs and Tories in opposition might lead to coalition of Whigs and Tories in power. In spite of the Fifteen and the disarray of the Tories, 1717 looked like a return to the political conditions of 1690 and 1706. It was. But it was to be the last manifestation of that type of political situation.[27]

Before Walpole, however, went into opposition, he had helped to make one structural change which, once accomplished, would have helped to stabilize politics whatever the outcome of the party strife between 1715 and 1725. From 1640, one of the most cherished tenets of those who had opposed the centralizing tendencies of the monarchy and worked to assure the supremacy of Parliament had been the belief in the efficacy of short Parliaments. There had been considerable support for annual Parliaments and Shaftesbury had favoured two years; but the compromise between executive and legislature had on several occasions settled on three, so that there was already in 1716 an aura of sanctity about the concept of triennial Parliaments when the Whig ministry decided to push through the Septennial Act.[28] The preamble bears all the marks of Walpole's style; commenting on the triennial clause of William III's Act,[29] it runs as follows: 'the said clause hath proved very grievous and burthensome, by occasioning much greater and more continued expen-

27. For the split in the Whig party and the policies pursued in opposition by Walpole and Townshend, see Plumb, *Walpole*, i, 243–92.

28. 1 Geo. I, stat. ii, c. 38. The preamble is quoted in E. N. Williams, *The Eighteenth Century Constitution*, Cambridge, 1960, 189.

29. 6 & 7 Will. & Mar., c.2, entitled 'An Act for the frequent meeting and calling of Parliaments'.

ses in order to elections of members to serve in parliament, and more violent and lasting heats and animosities among the subjects of this realm, than were ever known before the said clause was enacted [which was true enough]; and the said provision, if it should continue, may probably at this juncture, when a restless and popish faction are designing and endeavouring to renew the rebellion within this kingdom [which was dubious] and an invasion from abroad [which was a lie] be destructive to the peace and security of the government.' Presumably, as Walpole remorselessly lobbied the back-benchers, wining and dining them at Chelsea and arguing with them for hours as he walked them up and down his new terrace overlooking the Thames, he made the same pleas to their patriotism and their pockets. He was so ardent for this Bill that he caught a chill from the river mists and missed the debates.[30] So drastic a reversal of old Whig and new Tory policy was achieved with difficulty. The advantage both to the ministry and to owners of Parliamentary properties was very great: investment became more secure and a structure of power created for seven years was more likely to endure than one made for three. Costs, however, did not drop; they increased dramatically, and the next election, that of 1722, was one of the most expensive ever fought. Indeed, the Septennial Act intensified that drift towards oligarchical control of Parliamentary property, mentioned earlier. The effects of the Septennial Act were quickly appreciated and a renewed demand for annual or more frequent elections again became a part of the Tory, country, and radical programme, a stock-in-trade of opposition from Bolingbroke to the Chartists. Having been made dizzy by events, the Tories now had the carpet pulled from under their feet; and yet within a few months of this blow to their power in the constituencies, their hopes rose again.

There is no need here to discuss in detail the break-up of the Whig ministry.[31] It was due to differences about foreign affairs, rendered critical by deep divisions between ministers and worsened by the quarrel of the King with the Prince of Wales. After

30. Plumb, *Walpole*, i, 223.
31. Ibid., 224–42.

the split the ministry with a narrow majority clung to office for the next two years in spite of occasional defeats, their ecclesiastical policy and the Peerage Bill being the most important. If finally overturned, a reconstructed ministry with Tory participation seemed the most likely outcome and was actually canvassed in a mysterious memorandum which circulated in April 1720.[32] Yet when Walpole and Townshend were finally reconciled with Sunderland and Stanhope, no Tories came in with them. This is a fact of vital importance. There is no documentary evidence as to why Walpole was willing to jettison his erstwhile allies and commit himself to a further struggle at Court at a serious personal disadvantage with his enemies, but on tactical grounds his decision was admirably judged: a mixed ministry could only have given the German advisers of George I greater power and created further divisions and animosities in the Whig leadership.[33] Whatever the currents of economic, social, and political life, no matter how favourable events may be to one party, political stability usually rests on political decision – not one, but many – and this was the first decision, at least the first since 1711, that Walpole had taken that was likely to lead towards stability rather than to confusion. And it was made on terms that brought Walpole no personal political advantage. The reunited Whig ministry came just in time; without that reunion the uproar caused by the bursting of the South Sea Bubble must have sunk Sunderland and his colleagues and in these circumstances Walpole could never have formed a purely Whig ministry; his own following was at that time too small.

Again, his decision in 1720, in spite of immense unpopularity, to serve the Court, to fight inch by inch to save the major ministers from defeat and disgrace, was of exceptional importance for the future of English politics of the eighteenth century; indeed, it is not too far-fetched to say that they turned upon this decision. Nothing would have given Walpole more immediate power or greater popularity than to have taken over the leader-

32. Plumb, *Walpole*, i, 283–4.
33. Ibid., i, 223 ff. For new evidence see Beattie, 'The English Court in the Reign of George I' (unpublished Ph.D. thesis, Camb. Univ. Lib.), 364–8.

ship of the violent anti-government passions that were surging both within and without the House of Commons in 1720. The Bubble gave Walpole his opportunity to acquire personal power, to become the dominating Whig figure at Court, in the Commons and, just as importantly, in the executive. He seized it and, as so often, chance favoured him, as it must successful politicians; the deaths of Stanhope and Sunderland, the curious mortality of bishops in 1721–2, the willingness of Townshend to leave both domestic affairs and patronage to him, the impotence of his rivals, particularly Carteret, whose arrogance, combined with idleness, wrecked political gifts of the highest order: all of these things worked in Walpole's favour, made his task easier, and his decisions more effective. Yet the decisions had to be taken, and from 1720 onwards Walpole's policy – very obscure and tortuous from 1714 – becomes clear and the steps to achieve it are taken with increasing certainty.

He wanted to be what single-party government in its initial stages must have, a dominant leader possessing supreme power. He intended to control the House of Commons as well as the Court; to settle the problems of power himself, wherever they might occur, on terms that strengthened himself, the executive, and the Whigs. To achieve this he was willing to discard all those vestiges of old Whig principles that had clung to him during his early career. Not only would he have no truck whatsoever with Place Bills, Land Qualification Acts, and the like; he regarded the Septennial Bill not only as sacrosanct, but even favoured a Bill in 1721 that envisaged a return to Parliaments without any time-limit at all. More remarkable was his changed attitude to the problem of Dissent. His early career as well as his years in opposition between 1717 and 1720 taught him the strength of Anglican feeling in the Parliament that had rejected Stanhope's liberalizing policy.[34] Throughout his career he dexterously evaded all pressure from the Dissenters to change the *status quo*, and contented himself with minor palliatives.[35]

34. It should be remembered that the Sacheverell trial, of which Walpole was a manager, blighted his early career as well as his party's fortunes.

35. For Walpole's policy to the Dissenters, see Norman C. Hunt, *Sir Robert Walpole, Samuel Holden, and the Dissenting Deputies*, Dr Williams

His Church policy was scarcely distinguishable from Nottingham's. By 1717 he and Townshend had come to accept what was essentially a Tory foreign policy – friendship with France, and, if possible, Spain, and the avoidance of all situations likely to lead to military involvement in Europe. Both of these policies helped to sterilize pro-Tory inclinations among the independent country gentlemen sitting on the back-benches and lead them to support him without pay. It also enabled Walpole to diminish taxation, particularly the land tax; indeed, Walpole's financial policy was dominated by considerations of political stability. It was generous towards the Court, considerate of the country gentlemen and full of opportunity for the bankers, and grievous to none. And even if this bore little relation to the Whig policy of Anne's reign or William III's or even Charles II's for that matter, it was effective. After 1722 Walpole could rely on very considerable back-bench support, an achievement that had evaded the old Junto. Equally important and much less stressed was Walpole's handling of the Court. His methods were crude but immediately effective. Walpole quite simply bought it – hard cash for the King and titles for the mistresses. In return the German advisers retired to the sidelines and stayed there. By 1722, what power they had had in English affairs was gone.[36] Between the Court and the Commons lay a more complex field of political power, personalized in aristocrats, bishops, admirals, generals, bankers, lawyers, and local bigwigs, institutionalized in the Lords, the Church, the Army, Navy, City of London, Courts of Law, and the Deputy-Lieutenancies. The base of these

Lectures, No. 11, Oxford, 1957, and *Two Early Political Associations: The Quakers and the Dissenting Deputies in the Age of Sir R. Walpole*, Oxford, 1961.

36. The Duchess of Kendal always remained important to Townshend and Walpole because of her influence with George I; she was very helpful in the long intrigue against Carteret. She is 'the good duchess and ... fast friend to whom we have sworn an eternal and inviolable attachment'. See Coxe, *The Life and Administration of Sir Robert Walpole*, ii, 271, 294. She was handsomely paid in cash as well as titles. She was reputed to have a pension of £7,500 from the King; she certainly took £9,500 from the Duke of Chandos, and she held the patent from the copper coinage in Ireland which she sold to Wood. See Plumb, *Walpole*, ii, 67–8.

separate pyramids of power was often more easy to control than the apex. And it was at Court that the manipulation of power was at its most complex and not always attended with outstanding success.

Walpole needed, of course, to secure unanimity and a common loyalty among the major holders of office. This was never quite achieved. Realizing the danger of large Cabinets, he took the opportunity offered by the strong dislike George I had for his son to call them as seldom as possible. Indeed, contrary to common belief, Walpole did his best to destroy Cabinet government. Nothing is more fallacious than the still widely accepted view that George I's ignorance of English and his unwillingness to comprehend the English constitution led him to delegate power to Walpole and to withdraw from the Cabinet. Walpole as well as George I hated large Cabinets; like Sunderland's father before him, Walpole realized that they bred faction, not unity. He called them as infrequently as possible and worked through a small informal body composed of the chief officers of state, five in all apart from himself – the Chancellor, the Lord President, the Privy Seal, and the two Secretaries – a much easier body to keep harmonious. Walpole made as certain as he could that no politically dissident faction had a voice in its councils – hence his exclusion of Pulteney in 1724 and of Townshend in 1730. One of the factors that contributed to his difficulties between 1739 and 1742 was the revival, due to war, of more frequent and larger Cabinets and committees. Between 1722 and 1739, this tightly knit inner council contributed immensely to the stability at Court; but such stability was constantly threatened and indeed, in the decades that followed Walpole's fall, often lost.

The basic stability of politics, however, no longer rested on the Court. Essential though it was to possess the confidence of the King, domination of Parliament proved more important. When, at last, Walpole failed to do so, he went. By then, however, his system was so strong that it made little or no difference. The Whig aristocracy remained in power.

Once established in power, with the Tories broken and rivals eliminated, Walpole's system possessed two major aspects: control of the House of Lords and manipulation of the House of

Commons. This was done by the centralization of patronage and the solution of a number of secondary problems that had done much to disturb the political equilibrium in earlier generations – Scotland, Ireland, London, and by no means least the intransigence of the country interest. It is simpler to deal with minor matters first.

The government of Scotland and Ireland had presented difficult problems for centuries; in 1720, both were potentially dangerous territories, liable to rebel on behalf of the Stuarts. After the Revolution of 1689, the Scottish Parliament had seized a greater degree of independence than it had enjoyed for several reigns; its bid for greater economic and political independence had ended in the negotiations for the Union, of which the Whigs had been the strongest and most powerful advocates. But Union had created new problems of management. The pattern of political power in Scotland had to be adjusted to match and not clash with England's. Patronage had been extensively increased by the introduction of the English customs and excise system; although some of the major posts had gone to Englishmen, the host of minor offices created – land-waiters, surveyors, collectors, and the like – had been used to gratify the supporters of the Duke of Queensberry, who managed Scottish affairs for Godolphin. Godolphin himself had interfered little in its distribution. After his fall Harley, advised by John Scrope, had begun to use Scottish patronage far more dexterously and more effectively. It was probably on Scrope's advice that he had abolished the office of Secretary of State for Scottish Affairs. However, Harley's difficulties proved greater than he expected, owing to the loyalty of the Squadrone to the Whigs, and only by creating new fields of patronage, such as reviving the Chamberlainry, was he able to secure control over the representative Scottish peers and a majority of the Scottish M.P.s. The Scottish Secretaryship had to be revived.

After 1714, the situation in Scotland remained complex. The Fifteen and the subsequent alarms of 1719 made it essential that the bulk of the Scottish nobility should be kept steady for Hanover, and yet it was equally essential to prevent the build-up of an independent Scottish faction that could make its own terms by threats that might imperil the Crown. The problem, therefore, was to secure close management, preferably from London, and to retain the support of the major political influences in Scotland. Walpole did this quite simply, and probably in consultation with John Scrope, who was his closest adviser on all administrative matters of political importance. As the Duke of Roxburghe and his Squadrone faction, old Junto allies, had supported Sunderland and Stanhope in 1717, they were broken. Walpole abolished the Secretaryship of State for Scotland which had been revived by George I; in future the Duke of Newcastle undertook the Scottish business. Before this had been done, however, on the excuse of the malt-tax riots in Glasgow, Walpole had brought Scottish patronage firmly under the control of the British Treasury. In 1723 the shortcomings of the Scottish Customs – the evasions, the frauds, the smuggling, the loss of revenue – were paraded before Parliament. The upshot was the abolition of a separate Board of Customs Commissioners for Scotland. The Board of Customs for the United Kingdom contained two Scots only – both Campbells. Between 1723 and 1725 the customs service was purged with absolute thoroughness. It became no more efficient – smuggling, frauds, evasion, loss of revenue remained – but the jobs were now in the right hands. The right hands were largely the Campbells, led by the Duke of Argyll and his brother Islay, but, and this is important, they did not dispense the patronage, they asked for it. Also, as was Walpole's wont, although he broke the Dukes of Roxburghe and Montrose, he was willing to buy more complaisant men from the ranks of the Squadrone. He needed, of course, some counterpoise to Argyll. Although Scottish patronage had to pay, in future, sound political dividends in terms of politics at Westminster, it remained overwhelmingly in the hands of Scots. A few, but not many, Englishmen found niches for themselves in the Scottish establishment, but far fewer than the number of Scots who were preferred in England. This provided a system through which the needy political nation of Scotland, excluding, of course, most of the Highlands, could find both sustenance and power. At the same time, the Lowlands were being drawn increasingly into the economic system of England

and benefiting increasingly by it. The commercial expansion of the first half and the industrial expansion of the second half of the eighteenth century brought growing prosperity to the gentry and merchants of the Lowlands. The system of government and patronage that had been developed by Walpole was in no way inimical to their interests. Although ultimate power about persons rested in the hands of English politicians at Westminster, the persons appointed were Scots. Nor were the revenue systems ever made to work efficiently; in the interests of political stability they were left corrupt. The political nation in Scotland was given a direct path to power and affluence. Good behaviour was demanded; that was all. Hence patronage, created, extended, and controlled by the English for the use of the Scots, was one of the major reasons for the success of the Union[37] – in marked contrast to Ireland.

The problem of Ireland was contained by Walpole, but it was not solved as the problem of Scotland was solved; in consequence, the Anglo-Irish political establishment was never so contented as the Scottish. It remained restless and dissatisfied until, in the reign of George III, it became positively hostile. Technically, throughout this period, English control of Ireland was very complete. The Irish Parliament, which was never dissolved except by the demise of the monarch, was utterly servile. Irish Bills required the consent of the Privy Council in London. The Anglo-Irish lobby at Westminster, of whom the Earl of Egmont fancied himself as leader, proved to be quite impotent. As he moaned in his diary in 1731, 'We see how the welfare of that poor Kingdom lies in the breath of one Minister's nostrils.'[38] Battered by civil war, subjected to savage reprisals, and at the same time having its economy revolutionized not for its own benefit but for England's, Ireland was too weak to secure anything for itself. Ireland's chief weakness lay in this. It

37. For Scotland, see Riley, *The English Ministers and Scotland, 1707–27*, an excellent and penetrating study of patronage and politics; T. C. Smout, *Scottish Trade on the Eve of the Union*, Edinburgh & London, 1963; G. S. Pryde, *The Treaty of Union*, 1950; G. S. Holmes, 'The Hamilton Affair of 1711–12', *EHR*, 1962, lxxvii, 257–82.

38. HMC, Egmont's Diary, i, 174.

provided a field of patronage, but the Irish, as such, were of no significance at all at Westminster, and so could not claim it. For a time after the Revolution some Irish patronage, it is true, had been used to gratify those aristocratic Irish families who had supported William III, but even so a very large share had gone to Englishmen. After 1714 the danger of dissatisfaction that this might cause had disturbed Charles, Earl of Sunderland, who had adopted the policy of using Irish patronage for those Anglo-Irish families who had large political interests in Ireland; and indeed, his appointments did not neglect purely native Irishmen. Infuriated by the fiasco of Wood's Halfpence, Walpole reversed that policy. Henceforth, he deemed, patronage was to be dispensed in terms of Westminster's necessities;[39] Englishmen with Irish interests who sat in the English Parliament, such as Egmont, were able to wring a little patronage out of a reluctant Walpole, but it was very little. From Walpole's day onwards, the Irish administration, as with the Church in Ireland, wore an increasingly alien air. Had the Irish Parliament been abolished in 1714, and Irish patronage used as the Scottish was, there might have been a greater chance of securing ultimate stability in the relations between Ireland and England. As it was, too many Irish families of political stature remained outside the Irish establishment; with increasing prosperity in the eighteenth century the number of these families grew steadily, but positions of power and authority were all too difficult to come by. As a field of opportunity and profit opened for the Scots, the door closed on the Irish; a vocal leadership, aristocratic as well as middle-class, was created to voice Ireland's wrongs. Ireland, after all, was to become the most unstable feature in British politics for the next two hundred years. Some of the reasons for this go deeper than political history: the economic servitude, the religious intolerance, are obvious, but little remarked is the way in which Walpole, in order to gain immediate strength, blocked or rendered more difficult the legitimate aspirations of that part of the Irish political nation that in the early eighteenth century was not only by inclination, religion, and economic

39. Plumb, *Walpole*, ii, 103-4.

interest pro-British, but also the only part of that nation capable
of wielding effective political leadership.[40]

London had been the bugbear of the Stuarts, the rich and
powerful centre of their most intransigent opposition. Attacked
viciously by Charles II and James II, the City Corporation had, in
1689, recovered much of its old power, but even then there had
been considerable disappointment among the left-wing City
councillors that the old charters, renewed by James II just before
his flight, had not been followed by a more comprehensive
charter, liberalizing the constitution and putting greater power
into the hands of the common councillors and so circumscribing
the claims of the aldermen to veto their acts. Throughout the
wars the City had been neither obstreperous nor difficult. True,
it had been a prey to divisions: some had been hostile to the
Bank; the Recoinage scheme had outraged others; the strife
between the two East India Companies had been clothed in the
ferocity of party; religious difficulties had been violent enough;
and the capacity of the City to cock a snook at the government
had been boisterously demonstrated by Lord Mayor Sir
Samuel Garrard, who invited Sacheverell to preach. Although
Whigs had been very powerful in City offices from 1689 onwards, their position was far from unchallenged and the Tories
had become deeply entrenched in City politics. By 1723 the
situation was becoming increasingly difficult. The dislocations
caused by demobilization and peace to trade, the catastrophe of
the South Sea Bubble, which played snakes and ladders, but
mostly snakes, with many a small merchant's fortune, had
drawn many to the radical, 'country' aspects of Toryism. The
great parade that Walpole made of the Atterbury Plot, identify-
ing Jacobitism with Toryism, was as much to impress London as
the country gentlemen. Its effects did not prove very lasting
and the problem of London's government, the realization that

40. For the way in which this new middle class became steadily more
anti-British, see Maurice R. O'Connell, *Irish Politics and Social Conflict in the
Age of the American Revolution*, Philadelphia, 1965. Of course, not all Irishmen were denied patronage, but the number involved became very limited
after Wood's Halfpence. The nature and use of Irish patronage still
awaits detailed investigation.

it might become the focal point of an aggressive opposition and so threaten the stability of the régime, was very much in Townshend's as well as Walpole's mind from that date. They decided in 1725 to do as Charles II and James II had done – remodel the Corporation. True, the remodelling was not drastic, but the City Elections Act of 1725 rendered the City's government less democratic and gave the aldermanic bench far greater authority over the Corporation's formal acts. It was not very successful. Although Walpole's government had the support of the financiers and bankers, it failed to secure the adherence of the bulk of the trading merchants, great or small, and the craftsmen and journeymen had little use for it. In consequence, London became the seeding-ground of urban radicalism and remained the one factor in England important enough to create strain in the eighteenth-century political system. It was not until the late eighteenth century, when the population within its boundaries had dwindled to comparative insignificance, that the City Corporation as such became a firm prop of, rather than a political threat to, authority.[41]

In his handling of London, unlike Scotland and Ireland, Walpole secured not even a momentary success, and the political crises that he suffered arose partly from that fact. Yet they never seriously endangered his system. Whatever the clamour in 1733 or 1739–41, the Whig system was never in jeopardy. There was no sign of the revival of party, no violent division about policy in any constitutional sense, and certainly no wish to change a system of government that the political nation found curiously satisfactory, providing as it did status, power, and profit for many, and hope for more, of its leaders. By 1725, nodules of power, created very often by the needs of a modern State, had formed, which, in the hands of a statesman of genius, had been welded into formidable strength. Between 1689 and

41. For London, see A. J. Henderson, *London and the National Government, 1721–1742*, Duke University Press, 1945; Lucy N. Sutherland, 'The City of London in Eighteenth-Century Politics', in *Essays Presented to Sir Lewis Namier*, ed. Pares and Taylor. See also G. Rudé, *Wilkes and Liberty*, Oxford, 1962. There is a great need for studies of the relationship between the City of London and the national government for the reigns of Charles II, James II, William III, and Queen Anne.

1715 materials had been created – places and Parliamentary property were the most important – which at first intensified the divisions in the ruling class, giving them very concrete objects for which to fight. And yet the very nature of these materials also helped to corrode political principle. The desire to keep a Parliamentary borough for which a fortune had been spent, obviously made last ditches unattractive. So did place, not so much for the profit it brought, but for the status it confirmed. Men love the smell of power, which is one of the luxuries of place. Ardent Toryism or ardent Whiggery, for that matter, tended to wilt in its resplendent ambience. Nor should we regard this as over-cynical or peculiar to eighteenth-century life: many a Tory scientist, stern with disapproval of Labour policy, has found the invitation to serve on Labour government boards and committees irresistible. A sense of duty, fertilized by status and place, and heightened by the narcotic taste of power, can soothe the conscience and calm the rage of party. But until 1714, the moderates, the accommodators, the natural men of management, were still at a disadvantage. Political issues were still too profound; there was too much commitment. There was no certainty that the pattern of Whig oligarchy would establish itself before Walpole obtained power in 1722, although there were strong tidal forces moving English society in that direction. To establish itself thoroughly it required a long period of effective government by Walpole, and it also required him not only to take the right political decision on a number of specific issues but also to confirm the nature of power within the political system – to give not only individuals but classes of men their political identity in the pyramid of authority. And that pyramid, the conscious political establishment, built by Walpole with the materials that time and circumstance had created for him, lasted for centuries. Battered, sometimes badly cracked, frequently patched and extended, it remained almost to our own day.

Of course, what happened between 1670 and 1725 goes deeper than this, and both the Junto and Walpole influenced the development of this country in ways of which they were totally unaware. They separated Whiggery from radicalism, a separation of which Walpole's City Elections Act is the best ironic comment. Furthermore, the party fused the interests of aristocracy, high finance, and executive government, a process extended by Walpole to embrace the bulk of the landed gentry. By doing so he put the noblemen and gentlemen back at the heart of English political society. This was to be of tremendous importance for England's future development. The seventeenth century had witnessed the beginnings and partial success of a bourgeois revolution that came near to changing the institutions of government. In this, however, it never succeeded. The Revolution of 1688 and all that followed were retrogressive from the point of view of the emergence of the middle class into political power. Socially and economically they continued to thrive, but not politically. The power of the land and of commerce fused to create a paradise for gentlemen, for the aristocracy of birth; it thus became much easier for England to adopt an imperial authority, to rule alien peoples, and to train its ruling class for that purpose, rather than to adjust its institutions and its social system to the needs of an industrial society. And if the adamantine strength of much of England's structure of political power can be traced to the age of Walpole, so can many of the inherent contradictions in the nature of its social authority. Political and social stability, and one cannot exist without the other, came quickly to Britain, as they do to most countries that ever achieve them. But once established they acquire immense inertia: tradition, precedent, law, education, religion, all conspire to ensure them. It is a salutary thought that no stable society has ever yet altered the fundamentals of its social and political structure without revolution or overwhelming disaster in war; no matter how frequently the constitution may have been reformed, the true anatomy of power, which goes deeper than institutions, remains. What Sir Robert Walpole and the Whigs did was to make certain that political and social authority should devolve by inheritance; the methods have been purified, and tortuous by-ways evolved for talent, but birth still remains a broad highway to power. And power by inheritance must mean a world run by patronage; this must be so, for the political nation is always greater than the availability of place, and this was true even at the greatest extension of our Empire. It should also be remembered that patronage can, as it did in the nineteenth century, operate through seemingly disinterested boards as well as directly from patron to patronized; indeed, it is often forced to do so by the growth of the political nation. But patronage has been, and is, an essential feature of the British structure of power, no matter how varied the costume it may wear. In the eighteenth century it scarcely bothered to wear a fig-leaf. It was naked and quite unashamed. 'He thought', scribbled the Duke of Newcastle of himself, 'Neddy Townshend [and he always thought so] must have the Deanery [of Norwich] when thus pressed by all the Townshend and Walpole families.' Of course he must, and did.[42] Such sentiments have echoed down the centuries to our own time. It was patronage that cemented the political system, held it together, and made it an almost impregnable citadel, impervious to defeat, indifferent to social change. And yet there are historians who dismiss eighteenth-century patronage as little more than private charity.[43] This is absurd, and arises from considering the pecuniary rewards of place only. Place was power; patronage was power; and power is what men in politics are after. After 1715, power could not be achieved through party and so the rage of party gave way to the pursuit of place. This pursuit, of course, was never simple, never easy; it was full of pitfalls, full of the unexpected, created both by temperament and by events. It was conducted in a world of government, administration, and decision. To those who lived within it, and fought for the highest office, it must have seemed a precarious and fickle world; to us who can view it in relation to what went before and what came after, however, it possesses an almost monolithic stability, a political system more secure than England had ever known or was to know. And that was the work not only of those tidal factors that are discussed in the first chapter, but also of a man of uncommon judgement, political insight, and capacity for decision – Sir Robert Walpole.

42. N. Sykes, *Church and State in England in the Eighteenth Century*, Cambridge, 1934, 163–4.

43. Owen, *The Rise of the Pelhams,* 62. My one criticism of this valuable book is its underestimate of the effects of patronage and interest.

# APPENDIX I

Worsley MSS., 'Liste Exact du Dernier Parlement et de Celuyci', fos. 40–43.

At the end of his list, which gives M.P.s by constituency according to counties, listed alphabetically, the compiler explains his method – red for Tory, black for Whig, etc. – and then launches into this more general discussion of party and the corroding effects of place and influence. He sees as clearly as any contemporary that parties are a basic fact of political life but that the nature of government, with its rewards and punishments, acted at times as a spur and at others as a soporific in the context of party.

'... les Toris me paroissent tous reunis dans un seul corps [i.e. in 1715], ce pendant il est juste de mettre quelque difference entre ceux qui donnoint aveuglement dans les mesures du dernier ministere, & ceux qui de temps en temps s'y opposoient, outre cela comme cette liste est faite avant qu'il y ayt eu des debats dans la chambre on ne les peut marquer que par conjecture & selon la connoissance qu'on a de chaque personne, et pour parler naturellement les raisons pour quoy des Whigs votent avec de Torys & des Torys avec des Whigs venant souvent a changer, ils changent aussi de methode, par exemple dans un Parlement comme celuyci, Les Toris qui voteront quelque fois avec le Whigs le feront par un de ces deux raisons; 1re. Ils esperont de ne pas perdre entierement le fruit de leurs actions pandant le dernier Parlement. 2de. D'autres le feront pour conserver des emplois que le Roy leurs a laissés, ou dans l'esperance d'en obtenir, Les Whigs qui voteront avec les Toris, seront des gens mecontens de voir qu'ils n'ont rien ou peut-etre moins qu'ils ne croyent meritér, & qui pour cette raison prendront des pretextes populaires, pour s'opposer à la cour, Et ces raisons venant une fois à cesser leur conduitte changera en meme temps.

Car pour dire la verite, L'interest & la corruption sont venus a
un tel point dans cette nation que très peu de gens y agissent par
un principe pur & disinteressé, c n'est pas qu'il ny aye d'hon-
netes gens, mais on ne se trompera que rarement quand on
attribuera la conduitte d'un chacun a des raisons d'interest, et
presque toujours quand on s'imaginera qu'il y en a d'autres,
dans tous les partis il y a des Ministres d'Etat, ceux ci recom-
mandent & tachent d'avancer ceux qui s'attachent personelle-
ment a eux leurs parents & leurs dependants sans considerér
si ce sont toujours ceux qui sont les plus propres & les plus
capables, et ils feront toujours tort a ceux qui ne reconnoissent
pas leur Authorité quoyque d'alliours de meme parti. Il y a des
Membres de chaque Chambre de Parlement, ceux ci s'ils ne
sont pas employés, seront toujours d'une opinion differente de
celle dont ils auroient été s'ils avoient eu des charges, et quoy-
qu'en gros ils pourront suivre le meme parti dans des debats
qui seront de consequence pour la cour, ils nuiront en prenant
quelque pretexte populaire pour n'etre pas entierement de la
meme opinion, ou bien en s'absentant; Il y a outre cela le grand
nombre de ceux de differents especes qui ne sont point du parlement, & qui raisonnent ou ecrivent leurs sentiments selon
qu'ils obtiennont des douceurs pour eux pour leurs parents ou
leurs domistiques, dans leurs provinces leurs villes ou leurs
paroisses, Les pretentions de ceux ci sont assés modestes, ils ne
vont qu'à des emplois dans la milice, des justices à paix, & les
charges dependant de la Tresorie, la Douanne, la Marine &
c$^a$, & ils se croyent assés heureux & sont fort glorieux si par
ces moyens ils s'attirent du respect chés eux, Il y à aprés cela le
populace qui n'est pas la moins considerable, Car quand elle est
du coté de la cour elle n'a rien a craindre du reste, si elle sçait sen
servir, Au lieu que quand elle est contre, la cour n'est jamais en
seureté & il faut de bonnes tetes pour ne pas rencontrér souvent
de grandes difficultés. 'Cette race change souvent Il y à deux
cris qui ont prevalu bien des fois & tour a tour avec elle, Le
danger de la France & du Papisme, & le Danger de l'Eglise, le
Premier a toujours reussi dans des occasions ou la cour s'est si
entierement jettée entre les mains de celuy de Versailles que
chacun a ouvert les yeux, mais d'abord qu'on s'etoit un peu tiré

d'affaires par de bonnes mesures, Le Clergé qui est une autre espece à toujours resuscité celuy de l'eglise, & ceux a qu'il ils ne vouloient pas du bien ont en beau y allér, ils ont toujours declaré au peuple qu'ils vouloint la detruire; cest le point le plus delicat & plus dangereux, car ces gens ayant moyen au moins une fois la semaine d'assembler toute la nation & de leur precher ce qui bon leur semble, c'est ce qu'il y de plus a craindre, ce pendant Je crois qu'on peut aisément venir a bout de toute ce la, et si Prince peut trouver moyen de faire aimér sa personne, Le Clergé à beau précher.'

# APPENDIX II

Worsley MSS., 'Liste Exact du Dernier Parlement et de Celuyci', fos. 38–9.

It is quite clear from this list, giving the changes by county, that the major swings from Tory to Whig took place where the government possessed the greatest influence – Cornwall, Kent, Hampshire, Wales, Wiltshire. Although there was some swing in the highly populated counties, Middlesex for example, the Tories maintained their position in many counties, particularly in the Midlands and North-West. It is impossible, of course, to calculate from other sources how many votes were cast, nor is it very profitable to speculate, but from the nature of the constituencies that returned Tories, it is not improbable that they had a majority of votes cast in spite of the size of their defeat.

The Whigs, of course, strengthened their position during the next few months. This calculation was made before any election petitions were heard, and these were naturally decided in the majority of cases on party lines, i.e. Tories were turned out and Whigs declared elected.

| Nombre de Membres que chaque Comté envoye | Comtés | Dernier Parlement | | Parlement Present | |
|---|---|---|---|---|---|
| | | Torys | Whigs | Whigs | Torys |
| 4 | Bedfordshire | 3 | 1 | 3 | 1 |
| 9 | Berks | 9 | 0 | 2 | 7 |
| 14 | Bucks | 10 | 4 | 10 | 4 |
| 6 | Cambridgeshire | 4 | 2 | 1 | 5 |
| 4 | Cheshire | 4 | 0 | 1 | 3 |
| 44 | Cornwall | 36 | 8 | 32 | 12 |
| 81 | | 66 | 15 | 49 | 32 |

| Nombre de Membres que chaque Comté envoye | Comtés | Dernier Parlement | | Parlement Present | |
|---|---|---|---|---|---|
| | | Torys | Whigs | Whigs | Torys |
| 81 | Brought Over | 66 | 15 | 49 | 32 |
| 6 | Cumberland | 3 | 3 | 5 | 1 |
| 4 | Derbyshire | 4 | 0 | 2 | 2 |
| 26 | Devonshire | 17 | 9 | 16 | 10 |
| 20 | Dorsetshire | 10 | 10 | 12 | 8 |
| 4 | Durham | 3 | 1 | 1 | 3 |
| 8 | Essex | 6 | 2 | 5 | 3 |
| 8 | Gloucestershire | 5 | 3 | 5 | 3 |
| 8 | Herefordshire | 6 | 2 | 2 | 6 |
| 6 | Hertfordshire | 4 | 2 | 2 | 4 |
| 4 | Huntingdonshire | 0 | 4 | 4 | 0 |
| 10 | Kent | 9 | 1 | 9 | 1 |
| 14 | Lancashire | 10 | 4 | 5 | 9 |
| 4 | Leicestershire | 4 | 0 | 2 | 2 |
| 12 | Lincolnshire | 8 | 4 | 6 | 6 |
| 8 | Middlesex | 8 | 0 | 5 | 3 |
| 3 | Monmouthshire | 2 | 1 | 3 | 0 |
| 12 | Norfolk | 8 | 4 | 9 | 3 |
| 9 | Northamptonshire | 4 | 5 | 4 | 5 |
| 8 | Northumberland | 4 | 4 | 5 | 3 |
| 8 | Nottinghamshire | 8 | 0 | 5 | 3 |
| 9 | Oxford | 7 | 2 | 2 | 7 |
| 2 | Rutlandshire | 0 | 2 | 2 | 0 |
| 12 | Salop | 5 | 7 | 11 | 1 |
| 18 | Somersetshire | 15 | 3 | 6 | 12 |
| 26 | Southamptonshire | 19 | 7 | 15 | 11 |
| 10 | Staffordshire | 9 | 1 | 5 | 5 |
| 16 | Suffolk | 8 | 8 | 10 | 6 |
| 14 | Surrey | 3 | 11 | 12 | 2 |
| 20 | Sussex | 10 | 10 | 14 | 6 |
| 6 | Warwickshire | 6 | 0 | 2 | 4 |
| 396 | | 271 | 125 | 235 | 161 |

| Nombre de Membres que chaque Comté envoye | Comtés | Dernier Parlement | | Parlement Present | |
|---|---|---|---|---|---|
| | | Torys | Whigs | Whigs | Torys |
| 396 | Brought Over | 271 | 125 | 235 | 161 |
| 4 | Westmoreland | 2 | 2 | 2 | 2 |
| 34 | Wiltshire | 23 | 11 | 24 | 10 |
| 9 | Worcestershire | 7 | 2 | 5 | 4 |
| 30 | Yorkshire | 11 | 19 | 25 | 5 |
| 16 | Cinque Ports | 6 | 10 | 15 | 1 |
| 24 | Wales | 21 | 3 | 10 | 14 |
| 45 | Scotland | 14 | 31 | 39 | 6 |
| 558 | | 355 | 203 | 355 | 203 |

C'est quelque chose de remarquable qu selon cette liste il s'est trouvé dans le dernier Parlement a la premier election devant les petitions

> 203 Whigs & 355 Torys

et dans celuyci

> 203 Torys & 355 Whigs.

# INDEX

Abingdon, Montagu Bertie, 2nd Earl of, 88

Absolutism, political theory of, 28-9

Adams, Richard, Agent for James II, 67

Admiralty, 88, 108, 114, 124-5. *See also* Navy

Ailesbury, Thomas Bruce, 2nd Earl of, 70. *See also* Bruce

Aldborough (Yorkshire), 52 and n

Aldburgh (Suffolk), 100, 102 n

America, 17, 128

Amsterdam, 37

Andrewes, —, Agent for James II, 67

Anne, Queen of England, 114
  character of, 108, 111
  government of, 112
  and Scotland and Ireland, 36
  and the Tories, 17, 79
  wars of, 27, 106, 123, 133, 141, 151, 154

Argyll, John Campbell, 2nd Duke of, 164, 181. *See also* Islay

Arlington, Sir Henry Bennet, 1st Earl of, 45 n

Armed forces, and absolutism, 30. *See also* Army, Navy

Army, fear of a standing, 73, 126, 129, 138
  growth of, necessitates increased taxation, 122-4
  influence on the development of administration, 26, 32, 125-6
  as a source of patronage, 116, 125-7, 178

Army Bills, 126, 142

Army grandees (1650s), 49

Ashburton, 49 n

Assassination Plot, the, 32, 140

Association, the (1696), 131, 140

Astley, Sir Jacob, 1st Bt, M.P., 40 n, 166

Atterbury, Francis, Bishop of Rochester, 12 n, 172, 184

Attorneys, as financial agents, 21, 22 n

Auditors-General, 129

Backwell, Edward, 36

Baltic Sea, 19, 106, 125

Bank of England, 17, 120, 141, 152, 184

Barnard Castle, 52 n

Barnstaple, 68

Barrillon, Paul, French Ambassador, 67

Barsby, William, 33 n

Bass, Thomas, 19

Bath, John Granville, 1st Earl of, 71

Baxter, Richard, 21

Beaufort, Henry Somerset, 1st Duke of, 71

Beaumont, Sir George, 33 n

Beaumont, Thomas, 46 n

Bedford, 18

Bedfordshire, 81 n

Bell, Henry, Alderman of King's Lynn, 20 n

Bell, Robert, salt-tax collector, 123

Berkshire, 81 n

Bernstorff, Andreas Gottlieb, Baron von, Hanoverian Minister, 112-13, 162

Bertie family, 85, 95. *See also* Lindsey *and* Willoughby

Bertie, Peregrine, M.P., 58, 85-6, 95, 156

Bertie, Philip, M.P., 85, 97 n

Beverley, 64, 69

Bill of Rights (1688), 34, 72-3, 145 n

Birch, Col. John, M.P., 37

Bishop's Castle, 82

Black List (1700), 141

Blathwayt, William, M.P., Secretary at War, 24-6, 89 n, 126-7, 129, 131

Blofield, Henry, land-tax collector, 123, 142

Blois, Sir Charles, 1st Bt., M.P., 101-2n